A Public Health Approach to Bullying Prevention

American
Public Health
Association

APHA

PRESS

www.aphabookstore.org

Matthew G. Masiello, MD, MPH
Diana Schroeder, MSN, RN

WASHINGTON, D.C. ● 2014

American Public Health Association
800 I Street, NW
Washington, DC 20001-3710
www.apha.org

Georges C. Benjamin, MD, FACP, FACEP (Emeritus), Executive Director
Marilyn Krajicek, EdD, RN, FAAN, Publications Board Liaison
Jennifer Juras, PhD, Publications Board Liaison

Printed and bound in the United States of America
Production Editor: Teena Lucas
Typesetting: The Charlesworth Group
Cover Design: Alan Giarcanella
Printing and Binding: Victor Graphics, Baltimore, MD

Library of Congress Cataloging-in-Publication Data

A public health approach to bullying prevention / edited by Matthew G. Masiello, MD, MPH; Diana Schroeder, MSN, RN.
     pages cm
Includes bibliographical references and index.
ISBN 978-0-87553-041-3 (alk. paper)
1. Bullying in schools–Prevention. 2. Bullying–Prevention. I. Masiello, Matthew G., author, editor of compilation. II. Schroeder, Diana, author, editor of compilation. III. American Public Health Association, issuing body.
LB3013.3.P83 2013
371.7'82–dc23
                              2013021047

TABLE OF CONTENTS

Foreword

In the 30 years that I have been involved in youth violence prevention, I have seen a significant evolution in the thinking about and attention to the issue of bullying in this country. When I first started out in this work, discussion regarding bullying prevention was far from prominent and bullying was not seen by many as a serious risk factor for violence or other significant consequences. It was common for me to hear comments from teachers, even experienced ones, parents, clinicians, and others suggesting that bullying behavior was just part of normal social development and most kids would get over it.

Attention began to grow in the 1990s when it appeared that some episodes of violence in schools had at least an element of bullying as an instigating or contributing factor. It was around this time that some of the early articles about bullying and its short- and long-term consequences began to be published in American scientific journals and concern about this issue escalated. Research and prevention strategies from other countries were given increased attention because work in this area was far more advanced in places such as Sweden, where research psychologist Dan Olweus had been both studying the problem and developing comprehensive prevention strategies in schools for over 30 years. In fact, by the time attention had increased in the United States, a number of European countries were already replicating Olweus's work in schools, with growing success.

Over the last several decades, the research about bullying has expanded our understanding of the problem and the serious long-term consequences of bullying, being bullied, witnessing bullying, or combinations of these. Furthermore, risk and protective factors have been identified and programmatic efforts to address these factors have been developed. With this have come efforts to respond to bullying behavior as well as preventing it in the first place. From these efforts, it has become increasingly clear that the most effective ways of preventing bullying require broad, comprehensive approaches that start early, before the behaviors begin to appear. And there needs to be a focus not only on the behaviors of those at risk but also on the climate that supports healthy values of respect and tolerance, as well as on the reactions of bystanders to bullying behavior. In this context, various versions of Olweus's work have been implemented and studied along with other approaches both in schools and in communities.

As a result, there is a growing need for more information and translation of these efforts into materials usable by a wide base of groups, including educators, parents, and others who work with children and who want to promote and support healthy, prosocial development. This book is an important contribution to what is available for expanding the work in this field.

The first several chapters review what we know about bullying, its consequences, and why it is so important to address the issue with a proactive, public health approach. Then the book quickly moves to the practical elements of creating and building bullying prevention programs. Topics ranging from readiness, to capacity building, and ultimately to implementation and sustainability are presented in simple, understandable, and pragmatic terms. Lastly there is attention paid to how to bring this work to scale so that it is implemented not just in a school or two but in an entire community, however big it is. The authors are experienced in both the research and program evaluation as well as in actually doing the work itself at ground level. From these presentations, readers should gain valuable understanding of the issue of bullying—and more importantly, what they can do about it.

That is the ultimate goal of this work, to help others move to action and change using strategies that are evidence-based and comprehensive.

Howard Spivak, MD, PhD
Director, Division of Violence Prevention
Centers for Disease Control and Prevention, Atlanta, GA

Preface

In southwest Pennsylvania, as we were approaching our fifteenth year in community-based bullying prevention work, we were concerned that, as a nation, we were becoming reactionary and fragmented in our approach to the issue. As bullying events or bullying-like events were receiving more and more media attention, we felt that there was also a lack of how best to define and respond to the pervasiveness of school-based bullying. Our work in injury and violence prevention and other health promotion and disease prevention projects has allowed us to appreciate and benefit from the need to plan, monitor, and evaluate our work. We have learned that making a positive and sustainable cultural change in a school takes time, perseverance, and presence. The goal, ultimately, is to enable and empower the students, teachers, school administration, and parents to take on the work and responsibility of providing a safer and healthier environment for children.

With the leadership and funding from a regional foundation, we have been able to document success in establishing a private-public coalition to strategically develop a large-population, public health approach to bullying prevention. We felt that such an approach, to such a magnitude, has been lacking at the national level. Thus, we had reason to gather those professionals who have been working with us during this period of time, to offer a cohesive recommendation on how best to develop a coordinated public health approach to bullying prevention.

As compared to other countries where there has been a unified, national approach to bullying prevention, the United States has not responded in similar fashion. The realization that school-based bullying is a problem in our schools has come late in the conversation as compared to other countries. The research has lagged behind as well. On a positive note, recent executive and legislative support concerning the severity and extent of the problem has led to the beginnings of a national discussion regarding where we are now and where we need to go in the future. Hopefully, the direction is in large-population health promotion initiatives. Such an approach is crucial in light of the fact that bullying is now an extremely pervasive and costly societal issue, and unfortunately, to the majority of the severe acts of violence taking place in some of our schools.

We have clearly demonstrated in Pennsylvania that a public health approach to bullying prevention can be done efficiently and in a cost-effective manner. From a health, societal, and educational perspective, the coalition in Pennsylvania has been able to make that first and formative comment on the cost benefit of an internationally recognized evidence-based, bullying prevention program. We have accomplished this with knowledgeable and effective leadership, an appropriate level of funding, and collaborative partnerships focusing on the highest level of fidelity to implementation. This coalition of foundation executives, educators, public health professionals (including a pediatrician), and psychologists, who have all worked together over the years, are now ready to comment on the programmatic and financial benefits of prevention when done with a public health approach.

Matthew Masiello, MD, MPH
Director, Center for Health Promotion and Disease Prevention
Windber Research Institute, Windber, PA

Acknowledgements

With gratitude and appreciation I would like to thank the thousands of children, teachers, school administrators, and parents who have worked with us over the years. I would hope that all parties have learned and benefited from this unique and positive public health relationship. I am most grateful to Yvonne Cook, President of the Highmark Foundation, for preaching and practicing the benefit of a public health approach in addressing the health issues of children. Her leadership, thoughtfulness, and dedication to the health of communities have, and continue to be, remarkable.

When I made one of those rare but important professional decisions in life, I am glad it was to recognize the brilliance, patience, and professionalism of my co-editor, Diana Schroeder. From those early days we have been able to gather an extraordinary group of professionals dedicated to the effort of protecting our children. Consistent with our work motto of "collaborate until it hurts," and the spirit and fortitude of this small but dedicated group, are the words of Margaret Meade: "Never doubt that a small group of thoughtful committed citizens can change the world; indeed, it's the only thing that ever has." I would also like to thank those in health and education whom we encountered in this journey of bullying prevention but did not quite understand the benefit of a public health approach to preventing illness and injury. These challenges allowed us to persevere and work that much harder.

At the opposite end of that spectrum have been Tom Kurtz, Judge Dave Klementik, and Nick Jacobs, who saw the benefit in allowing us to do this work with the flexibility and support it required. From my early days of health promotion I thank my friend and colleague, Dr. Mike Hirsh. We successfully established that concept of a community-based coalition allowing a city to be and feel safer during and after our time there. As always, I continue to appreciate the guidance and support provided over the years by my public health mentors Professors Josef Reum and Richard Windsor of the George Washington School of Public Health and Health Services as well as to Professor Hanne Tonnesen, director of the WHO Collaborating Centre, Copenhagen, Denmark. Our colleagues at the University of Padua, Padua, Italy, and Spedali Civili, Brescia, Italy, have allowed us to think, practice, and collaborate globally in our bullying prevention efforts.

All of us working in the area of bullying prevention are indebted to Dan Olweus and his team of researchers at the University of Bergen. At key moments in our bullying prevention activity, the Pennsylvania chapter of the American Academy of Pediatrics was there to endorse and propagate our program and eventual statewide impact. With humble appreciation, I thank our contributing authors who have provided their incredible expertise, not only to this text but to the field of bullying prevention, here in the United States and globally. And of course, Teena Lucas, and the book editorial team at APHA deserve major kudos. They saw the need to get this public health message out to those who want to do something strategic and long term in addressing the physical and mental health issues related to bullying. It was our desire to present a message of hope in the design of our cover and they worked diligently to make that happen.

Finally, I thank my wife, Kathy, and children, Matt, Jason, and Kim, as well as Jim and Peg and all of those special friends who kept me energized when the challenges were there to stop or move ahead. The team keeps moving!

Matthew G. Masiello, MD, MPH, FAAP
Director, Center for Health Promotion and Disease Prevention
Windber Research Institute, Windber, PA
Pennsylvania Coordinator, International Network of Health Promoting
Hospitals and Health Systems

Fifteen years ago, the work that evolved to the writing of this book began as a conversation with a group of dedicated teachers and school nurses about the problems facing their schools. From those early discussions a plan unfolded that has become the defining work of my professional career. I have been blessed to move outside the traditional realm of "nursing" in hospitals to innovative and preventative strategies in schools and communities. Dr. Masiello has provided the avenue to expand my horizons, and his vision, insight, expertise, and support have brought all of us at the Center for Health

Promotion and Disease Prevention to a culminating effort of writing this book. From him we have learned the hallmarks of community engagement, effective prevention strategies, and the need to monitor and evaluate our outcomes. My colleagues and friends at CHPDP, including Shiryl, Allison, Karla, Charvonne, and Annalisa, have been the backbone of this statewide bullying prevention project, and we would not be in this place at this time without all of their dedication and hard work. The University of Pittsburgh at Johnstown has supported the research emphasis of this project, and the lessons learned about bullying prevention have been incorporated into teaching undergraduate students about effective public health interventions. Clemson University's Dr. Susan Limber and her Norwegian colleague, Dr. Dan Olweus, have changed the face of bullying prevention around the world, and we are grateful for their help and guidance on this project.

And finally, a big hug to my personal cheerleaders: my family and friends. My husband, Rick, has sustained me with his love and guidance, and my children have all worked on the project at some point in time over these years—often with jobs that no one else was willing to do or responding to an urgent, immediate need. Thank you to all who have impacted this journey from school-based bullying prevention to book!

Diana Schroeder, MSN, RN
Director, Bullying Prevention Initiatives
Center for Health Promotion and Disease Prevention
Windber Research Institute, Windber, PA

Introduction

Our children and our communities face complex and overlapping challenges: violence, a fragmented healthcare system, and schools struggling with measures to achieve academic excellence and financial stability. School-based bullying has been linked to all three. So how can we possibly respond to the pervasive social disorder that is bullying with any deliberate strategy?

The authors of this text have been asked to join forces to offer such a strategy, aimed at enhancing the safety and well-being of our children. This book brings together psychologists, a physician/public health researcher, educators, nurses, social workers, public health program experts, an economist, and a foundation program coordinator. They all have one thing in common—years of experience in addressing bullying/peer abuse, school climate, and coalition development. These are the key ingredients and information for educators, healthcare providers, legislators, media, foundations, and parents to tackle what we define as a public health approach to bullying prevention. This approach has been endorsed by professionals and organizations active in bullying prevention, but, to date, there has been a scarce amount of information describing exactly what that is or could be.

Our goal is not to focus on the same growing list of dismal data we hear every day on how our children (and adults) bully each other. We do not concentrate on the next best bullying prevention program, nor are we commenting solely on just one of the many concerning subplots of bullying, such as cyberbullying, the gay and lesbian connection to bullying, mental health issues, or even violence. Bullying is a multifactorial, complex health and social issue requiring a more comprehensive and sophisticated discussion and strategy than what we have been able to foster thus far as a national response.

In this book, we are attempting to paint a public health approach to bullying prevention in a comprehensive and deliberate manner. Formal public health strategies have been used to combat the early days of infectious disease epidemics, tobacco use, and motor vehicle injuries. When applied to bullying, it provides a scientific approach to community planning, the use of evidence-based programs, coalition development, and the ability to change the culture in a school and community to one that is positive and strong.

The chapters in this book could serve as individual resources to parents and professionals looking for advice on specific facets of school-based bullying. It is our hope and expectation, however, that readers use all the material contained in these chapters to develop a program that strategically makes that culture change in your school. It will not be easy, it will not happen in one year, but it will happen with a public health approach. It should and will enable and empower schools, parents, and school boards to take charge and realize that with the right approach and the appropriate knowledge, success can happen, as it did in many schools in southwest Pennsylvania. A foundation, two centers, and thousands of children, parents, and teachers made it happen in hundreds of Pennsylvanian schools.

Based on this Pennsylvania experience and the incredible professionals who supported that effort, we can now bring these bullying prevention experts together and, for the first time, talk about an approach that can work and have significant, positive social and financial benefits for everyone.

In the opening chapters, we define health, public health, bullying, and school climate, as well as the relationship they have to the physical and mental health of our children. We dig deeper into a public health strategy by commenting on the importance of an evidence-based program and on the need for that program to be implemented with the highest level of fidelity. Having a program in place is just one step; monitoring and evaluating it is another key step we discuss in the book. We talk about the importance of coalition development, having strong leadership, and the ability to work together toward the common goal of safer and healthier children learning in a progressive educational environment. This information supports the discussion in the chapters on the lesbian, gay, bisexual, transgender population; legislative issues; and the cost–benefit analysis of bullying prevention programs. Finally, we discuss how we can sustain the culture change to ensure a safer and healthier environment for our children.

A public health approach to bullying prevention will serve as that practical, sustainable, cost-efficient strategy to tackle bullying. More importantly, it may be our best approach to providing legitimate and sustainable hope to our children at a time when it is becoming increasingly more difficult to do so.

1

Public Health and Bullying Prevention

Matthew Masiello, MD, MPH, FAAP

Objectives

1. To understand the unique challenges that U.S. schools and communities encounter in addressing the complex issue of bullying and bullying prevention.
2. To understand the definitions of bullying, health, and public health in order to develop a public health approach to bullying prevention.
3. To understand basic concepts and tools used in a public health approach to bullying prevention.
4. To appreciate events, activities, and capacity-building recommendations in sustaining bullying prevention initiatives.

CHALLENGES PRESENTED BY VIOLENCE AND BULLYING

For decades, school-based bullying has been identified as a pervasive, stressful, and potentially violent issue affecting the lives of thousands of children. "By the year 2000, every school in America will be free of drugs and violence and will offer a disciplined environment conducive to learning," so states a 1993 goal from the National Education Goals panel.[1] Though it is clearly an international issue, the bullying taking place in the United States is of particular concern as it has become directly related to the ever-growing epidemic of child and adolescent violence.[2] To create a greater degree of social angst, bullying has been intimately tied to several of the school-based shootings of recent years.[3–5]

The United States faces unique challenges in attempting to address school-based bullying. The media often seem to drive the discussion but tend to be more reactive, especially in cyberbullying reporting, rather than providing possible answers or strategies to address the issue in a calm and deliberate fashion.

To a significant degree, the U.S. approach to bullying prevention mirrors our approach to healthcare. We have a fragmented healthcare system of various programs that do not necessarily support or communicate with one another. Meanwhile, several countries have been able to address, on a national level, their bullying issues with large-population-based initiatives. So far, only one U.S. state—Pennsylvania—has been identified as taking that similar, broad, public health approach to bullying.[6]

From a research perspective, the United States has been late in dealing with the issue of bullying prevention.[6] And there is a continued reliance on evaluation methods historically designed for clinical programs, which can potentially hinder the use of acceptable prevention programs. Adding to the list of challenges is the status of the educational system itself. It becomes increasingly difficult to address the important issues of bullying, childhood obesity, and childhood mental health while nationally we still grapple with school funding, curriculum development, teacher performance, charter schools, and more.[7] Though bullying prevention legislation is now present in most U.S. states, most policies lack eager buy-in from the on-site educators and school administrators, who often see such legislation as misdirected and more unfunded mandates. The legislation is more often punitive rather than providing the positive school climate that is the recommended public health approach to change.[8] A common public health goal for all involved is to enable and empower students and teachers to improve their school climate in a positive, long-term manner.

Many countries have adopted bullying as a human rights issue. Unfortunately, the U.S commitment to child human rights is met with some level of skepticism at the international level. A glowing misstep in our ability to affirm a strong U.S. approach to child human rights is that the United States has not ratified the United Nations Convention on the Rights of Children, one of two UN member countries who have not done so.[9] Our history of capital punishment for youthful offenders, as well as our inability to address school-based corporal punishment, further sets us apart on the human rights issue.[10,11] Although the United States has identified human rights as a civil rights issue, we have not yet been able to advance this agenda as fully as other countries have been able to do.[12]

Bullying has been identified as the most common form of violence in our schools and society in general.[13] It affects the mental and physical health of the children involved, and when it becomes violent, it can lead to dire and long-lasting consequences.[14] Bullying has been associated with violent crime and deadly school shootings.[5,15] America is unlike any other industrialized country when it comes to the issue of violence, particularly in youth. We far surpass these other countries in homicide and suicide-related deaths in our child and adolescent populations.[16] Unfortunately, the media and health peer review literature have made us clearly aware that violent acts of aggression, including the use of a firearm, may be associated with prior bullying events. In addition, children who perpetrate bullying behavior go through life with a greater likelihood of participating in criminal behavior.[17] All of this amounts to the possibility of lives lost, a stress on our mental health services, and an overall increased cost to society. More will be discussed in the text regarding the relationship between suicide and bullying. If not causal in nature, we at least know that there is an association between the two. Thus, attention to maximizing mental health resources for schools should also include bullying prevention initiatives.

DEFINITIONS

Defining bullying and its related characteristics remains a challenge for both educators and the media.[18] Oftentimes, the media will identify an event as bullying when—quite possibly—it does not fit the definition. This event goes viral with a continued focus on an event rather than the issues, with cause and solution being an afterthought. For generations, and even now, bullying has been considered to be a primarily physical act of harassment or abuse. But the definition grows with the realization that bullying can be psychological as well. Over the past several years, cyberbullying has challenged the definition of bullying even further.

Defining Bullying

Professor Dan Olweus, a long-time international expert on the subject of bullying, offers the following definition: "A person is bullied when he or she is exposed repeatedly and over time, to negative actions on the part of one or more other persons, and he or she has difficulty defending himself or herself."[19] There is general consensus that most bullying is not intentionally provoked, but is associated with some type of proactive social, physical, or psychological aggression. Fundamental to these characteristics are three basic criteria to the definition of bullying:

1. Intentionality.
2. Repetitiveness.
3. Imbalance of power.

There are several key points of discussion regarding these three criteria: Is the intentionality real or perceived from the perspective of the target, and to the school official or parent; and does it make a difference? The issue of repetitiveness may be less up to the victim for interpretation than to the school that is attempting to respond to the latest local or state legislation on the issue. We also need to be comfortable and clear in how we define imbalance of power as it relates to a bullying event or events. Many adults still interpret it as a physical threat by the bully to the victim. There should now be a greater understanding that peer pressure, popularity, and social status would also serve as reasons why one individual exhibits or is presumed to have power or sway over another.[6]

The issue of cyberbullying continues to gain attention. As there is a physicality to bullying or marginalization that takes place in the psychological realm of bullying, so too do the tools of social media add to the national dilemma of school-based cyberbullying. Most consider the viral nature of the technologic event to be clearly repetitive as well as mean and stressful. For cyberbullying, imbalance of power lies within the technological advancement of the bully as well as the desire to aggressively marginalize an individual by a peer or peers.[6]

Defining Health

Prevention has not necessarily served as a principal component, resource, tool, or practice in our U.S-based healthcare system.[16] *Health* to many Americans exists after one leaves the physician's office or hospital with the next best drug or plan to use the next best and expensive piece of technology. In the United States, health is more medical care than health promotion or disease prevention.[16] Until the individual, health insurers, healthcare providers, and legislators are able to appreciate the health and cost benefits of disease prevention and health promotion initiatives, significant social issues such as bullying, gun violence, and childhood obesity will remain difficult to address. American exceptionalism, as it relates to U.S. healthcare, has been both challenged and debated in the media and even during our last presidential election.

"Health is Everywhere!" is a phrase used by Ilona Kickbush, a noted international public health scholar, in her attempt to identify how to possibly facilitate and identify greater national health resources and opportunities for people.[20] It is important for those involved in prevention to appreciate how others define health. Many countries have been able to grasp and understand the World Health Organization (WHO) definition of health, which is "a state of complete physical, mental and social well-being and not merely the absence of disease and infirmity."[21]

Though some U.S. agencies and health systems have attempted to define that more expansive, holistic approach to health, the United States has not matched similar international efforts, especially in schools and communities.[22,23]

Defining Public Health

A public health approach to bullying is not a new concept. It has been recommended by U.S. public health scholars as well as the WHO.[24] But what exactly does that mean? In 1988, the Institute of Medicine defined public health as "what we, as a society, do collectively to assure the conditions in which people can be healthy."[25] Prior to this definition, Charles-Edward A. Winslow, public health leader in the 1920s, had offered a more expansive definition. According to Winslow, public health is[26]

the science and art of preventing disease, prolonging life and promoting physical health and efficiency through organized community efforts for the sanitation of the environment, the control of community infections, the education of the individual in principles of hygiene, the organization of medical and nursing services for the early diagnosis and preventive treatment of disease, and the development of the social machinery which will ensure to every individual in the community a standard of living adequate for the maintenance of health.

Unlike the field of medicine, public health activities are synonymous with large population events or programs. This requires a multidisciplinary team of professionals working together to improve the health of the group, school, or community. This team may include physicians and nurses as well as epidemiologists, educators, lawyers, sociologists, economists, psychologists, and others, often led by an individual with advanced training in public health.[27] Many of these community-based public health specialists have focused their education and training in the area of health promotion, disease prevention, and maternal and child health.

The Center for Disease Control (CDC) and the WHO have fostered a public health approach in their attempt to address the epidemic of violence. To a significant degree, the same principles and rationale hold for bullying prevention. The recommendations for a public health approach to violence reside in three points:[28–30]

1. Define clearly the problem by using available local, school, or state health surveys. In addition, make every effort to define the "who," "what," "when," "where," "why," and "how" associated with the issue at hand.
2. Determine the risk and protective factors involved. In other words, what are the direct and associated causes of the issue you are wishing to correct or improve?
3. Implement the program with the highest level of fidelity, and always evaluate what you are doing throughout the initiative. We often stress the importance of evaluating a school-based program from how we want to present our final outcomes. Our outcomes have less meaning if the implementation of the program was not done with the highest level of fidelity. The planning process should also be monitored and evaluated, prior to actual implementation.

THE EVIDENCE-BASED PROGRAM (EBP)

What exactly is an evidence-based program (EBP)? Which evidence-based program best fits the particular issue to be resolved or enhanced, and which EBP can be efficiently applied to a specific site or location and in a cost-effective manner? An EBP usually implies that it has been around for a while and evaluated in a professional manner using accepted tools, designs, and processes to determine its efficacy and value to a specific audience on a specific issue.

The challenge, based to a significant degree on tradition, is how to evaluate these large-population evidence-based health promotion initiatives. The gold standard in evaluating health promotion initiatives is the randomized control trial (RCT). It was developed in the 1950s primarily to evaluate clinical programs or initiatives. As the popularity and success of school- and community-based initiatives has grown, so has the need to evaluate these programs. Thus, the most likely tool to use was the RCT. However, over the last decade there has been exploration of more practical, less costly evaluation processes.[31,32] Why should this be an issue for teachers, schools, and communities? For one, significant social issues must be addressed. As we try to identify funding for RCTs or attempt to design an RCT to evaluate an initiative, time marches on and concerning social issues are not addressed. Educators, the population being impacted by these programs (as well as students through their teachers), need to voice their concerns and opinions on why there is often a delay from conception of a health promotion program to implementation of the program in our schools and communities.

The PRECEDE-PROCEED Model (PPM) serves as an example of how to apply more insight and information to what is a public health approach to a prevention initiative.[33] Or, in other words how to strategically plan a community-based initiative. From a public health perspective, the best planning tool is one that offers a framework or serves as a guide to organizing and developing the initiative. The PPM consists of nine steps. Over the years, the steps have been modified depending on the specific problem, where the stakeholders (educators, health professionals, foundations, etc.) were in dealing with that problem, and what resources were available to address the issue. The nine steps are:

1. Social assessment.
2. Epidemiological assessment.
3. Behavioral and environmental assessment.
4. Educational and ecological assessment.
5. Administrative and policy assessment.
6. Implementation.
7. Process evaluation.

8. Impact evaluation.
9. Outcome evaluation.

PRECEDE stands for **P**redisposing, **R**einforcing, and **E**nabling **C**onstructs in **E**ducational/environmental **D**iagnosis and **E**valuation. Steps one through four pertain to the PRECEDE component of the model. PROCEED, identified by steps five through nine, stands for **P**olicy, **R**egulatory, and **O**rganizational Constructs in **E**ducational and **E**nvironmental **D**evelopment.

Examples for each of these nine steps follow. Bullying will serve as the issue being addressed. Keep in mind that those questions of "who," "when," "what," "where," "how," and "why," can be used to plan and organize the strategy of addressing bullying or any other problem. These same questions can be used in organizing the common objectives used in developing a health promotion initiative. The four commonly used types of objectives are programmatic, educational, behavioral, and health. Depending on the issue and the desired level of response, each respective step of the PPM may require a different level of attention. It is a guide. The following is an in-depth look at how to apply the PPM to your school-based initiative:

Step 1: Social Diagnosis (concentrate on questions and answers describing the bullying)

- How important is the issue of bullying to the students, parents, teachers, school administration, school board, legislators?
- What is being done now, and what would the stakeholders like to do?
- Who are the leaders, stakeholders, and the population involved?
- What is the numerator (impacted population) and denominator (total population) of the students involved?
- When is the program to take place, and for how long?

Step 2: Epidemiological Survey

- What school, state, national, or local at-risk data are available?
- What data can or should be obtained to determine the extent of bullying in the school?
- Who, again, serves as the numerator and denominator of the population involved?
- Based on the data and the literature, to what degree do you want to impact bullying? A 20 percent reduction in bullying? 40 percent?

Step 3: Behavioral and Environmental Diagnosis

- What goals are appropriate? For example: based on the available literature and comments from our colleagues, we would like to aim for a 30 percent greater involvement by bystanders witnessing a bullying situation and a 70 percent greater awareness by teachers to bullying activities in playground, on the bus, in the cafeteria.
- How are we changing the environment in our school to garner a collective awareness of the task at hand? To further convey an attempt to a positive and deliberate culture change, schools have opted to develop eye catching signage in the school to highlight issues such as respect, help others, and no bullying here.
- What is the availability of the school counselor?
- What individuals or groups are available to talk about bullying prevention initiatives, school climate, respect, empathy, and compassion?

Step 4: Educational and Ecological Diagnosis

- Identify an evidence-based program to implement and evaluate.
- Identify a coalition of stakeholders with specific responsibilities.
- Who is the leader or champion of the initiative?

Step 5: Administrative and Policy Assessment

- What is the capacity of the school or system to proceed?
- What are the personnel, equipment, space, and financial resources available for the entire effort, including evaluation?

Step 6: Implementation

- What is being implemented? Who is doing the implementation? Does anyone need to be trained and monitored in the implementation of the evidence-based initiative?
- How long is the implementation?

Step 7: Process Evaluation

- Are the planning meetings taking place at the agreed upon dates and times? Are you documenting what is discussed and planned? Are timelines being developed?
- Is the program being implemented with maximum fidelity?

- Are you interacting with the identified population of students and teachers as originally planned?
- What is the budget at any given time, and who is responsible for it?

Step 8: Impact Evaluation

- Are you meeting your outcome goals as outlined in previous steps?
- Have you identified any obstacles, challenges, or opportunities that may impact your goals and objectives?

Step 9: Outcome Evaluation

- What does the evaluation of the program tell us? Have we been successful? (Keep in mind that unsatisfactory results can be informative as well.) Lack of evaluation may result in never knowing exactly what the extent of the problem is or the issues associated with the problem. Insufficient evaluation could also lead to a false sense of accomplishment and a possible misuse of funding.

Case Discussion: The Highmark Healthy High Five Initiative

In 2006, the Highmark Foundation, located in Western Pennsylvania, launched the Highmark Healthy High Five initiative (HHH5). It was a five-year, $100 million initiative focusing on five critical child health issues: nutrition, physical activity, grieving, self-esteem, and bullying. The Foundation has a long history of providing support and funding for community and regional health promotion and wellness, as well as disease and injury prevention programmatic activities. The HHH5 was an unprecedented public health effort by a charitable, nonprofit organization.

The Highmark Foundation identified two key partners. The Center for Safe Schools, led by Lynn Cromley, was established in 1988, and serves as a statewide resource on school safety and youth violence. The Center provides training and technical assistance to Pennsylvania schools and youth organizations. In 2001, the Center received funding from the Pennsylvania Commission on Crime and Delinquency (PCCD) and the Pennsylvania Department of Education to establish the Pennsylvania Statewide Bullying Prevention Network.

The second key partner was the Center for Health Promotion and Disease Prevention at the Windber Research Institute in Windber, Pennsylvania. From

1998 to the present, this public health group has introduced numerous school and community health surveys to the region, as well as evidence-based childhood obesity and other prevention programs to the 13 school districts of Cambria County, Pennsylvania. From 2000 to 2004, with the guidance and support of the Center, 18 of 52 schools in the county participated in the state's first implementation and evaluation of the Olweus Bullying Prevention Program (OBPP). This countywide project was significant for two reasons. First, the planning and implementation began before the school shooting at Columbine High School. In the media aftermath of Columbine, local and national media outlets made inquiries into this Pennsylvania initiative. The second important aspect of this project was that it yielded data from student and teacher surveys taken before and after the program was introduced to the school population.

These two partners were assigned the task of organizing a bullying prevention initiative for the schools of southwest Pennsylvania, using the longstanding and evidence-based Olweus Bullying Prevention Program. For U.S. bullying prevention, this was the beginning of a landmark public health initiative. Significant funding was made available. The leader, Highmark Foundation, was identified, along with well-versed educational and public health experts, both having a long track record in the area of bullying prevention. In addition, an internationally recognized bullying prevention program was identified as the foundation to the effort.

An extremely important factor was the support received from the top. In this case, it was the educational leader. Dr. Gerald Zahorchak served as secretary of education for the Commonwealth of Pennsylvania from 2006 to 2010. This was during a time when schools were under increased pressure to more effectively address school-based bullying. Dr. Zahorchak had established a special panel of educators, legal, public health, and school climate experts to respond to the nationwide demand for a safer school climate for all of our children, especially at a time when the media were reacting to isolated bullying events. Health promotion and wellness plans and strategies were imbedded into both the discussion and final report.

In 2007, with the leadership and team in place, the Highmark Foundation gathered Pennsylvania educators, health professionals, parents, community workers and agencies to a Bullying Prevention Summit in Hershey, Pennsylvania. The gathering has been identified as the largest assembly in the United States to address the singular issue of school-based bullying as a public health crisis. Professor Sue Limber of Clemson University joined the Pennsylvania bullying prevention initiative as a contractual partner in the five-year initiative. Supplementing Professor Limber's expertise, Dr. Olweus was present for expert panel discussions, ongoing advice and support. By 2012, 210,000 children, 400 schools, and 17,000 teachers were affected by this five-year initiative.[34–36]

From the beginning of the program, coalition meetings were held on a regular basis to review key deliverables. Data were gathered and analyzed. In addition to the actual bullying prevention program, an extensive continuing educational program was developed for teachers, administrators and parents. Various educational resources were developed and tested. A website was also developed, both as an educational tool and as a means to communicate with parents and teachers. At the five-year mark, various tool kits, reports, and peer review articles had been developed. Of note was the development of a report commenting on the cost–benefit analysis of a large-population-based bullying prevention initiative. At the international level, though cost analysis of bullying prevention programs was being eagerly requested, it was not yet available until this Pennsylvania project.[37]

As we review this case you can appreciate the reliance the group had on the PRECEDE-PROCEED Model. The issue was identified; key meetings took place before the actual implementation of the evidence-based program; implementation was monitored and took place with the highest level of fidelity; data were gathered and analyzed and submitted for public review. No other U.S.-based nonprofit organization has taken on such significant social responsibility as the Highmark Foundation has done under the guidance and leadership of Yvonne Cook, the president of the community-oriented organization.[34]

A Testimonial to the Success of HHH5

In addition to key support from a foundation and a state secretary of education, it was important to receive buy-in from the school leadership. The following testimonial expresses the opinion of one school superintendent. The HALT! program was the overall bullying prevention initiative implemented by the Center for Health Promotion and Disease Prevention.

I am writing in support of the HALT! program of the Highmark Healthy High 5 bullying prevention initiative (HHH5). The Woodland Hills School District supports fully this effort. The HALT! has a mission of paramount importance: preventing and reducing delinquent behavior and victimization in our schools, and to promote public safety by encouraging accountability for acts of delinquency. This approach can serve as a model of excellence in our nation. Our local problem, far too common in other urban centers as well, reflects a national problem. In short, African Americans are challenged with juvenile delinquency and interfacing with the penal system more often at younger ages than Anglo Saxon Americans. This well-documented, disproportionate burden is unacceptable. The approach taken by the HALT! program represents our best hope for closing the gap.

The Woodland Hills School District's past was plagued with several challenges around racial climate and disruptive behavior. The racial climate in the schools during the 2007–2008 school year, particularly in the high school, was, frankly, appalling. African-American students in the high school believed that no one cared about them and that they were being treated differently than white students—which they were. Thus, they tended to act out. There was no "connection" and little positive communication between the administration and the African-American students in secondary schools. Administrators tended to interact with African-American students in a contentious manner that further exacerbated self-behavioral problems. These students believed that administrators were treating them unfairly.

By the spring of 2008, the district reached a serious leadership crisis. The administrative teams in the secondary schools were unable to productively handle serious student disruptions that had significant racial overtones. Because of student–student and student–teacher assaults, the print and electronic media and local police officials were subjecting the district to public derision. There were over 60 teacher "assaults" in the high school with two teachers seriously injured. Since the start of school Fall 2008 to Spring 2009, of the 4,400 students served by the Woodland Hills School District, there were 639 administrative detentions, 333 expulsions, 487 in-school suspensions, and 947 out-of-school suspensions. For the 2010–2011 school year, to date, there have been zero expulsions—a stellar accomplishment, reflecting improvement in overall behavior.

The 2008–2009 numbers have shown marked improvement with major changes in administrative practices employed by the District. We are proud of the positive impact the HALT! program has had on our district and community. The HALT! is an example of an initiative that has strong implications for cultural changes and change in policy at the local, regional and national levels. Our district offers the additional guidance, tools, and expertise that the HALT! needs in order to reach its goals. We commit to in-kind services of consultation around best practices and resources that will enhance the programming to be offered by the HALT!.

On behalf of the Woodland Hills School District, I emphatically support the HALT! program. I would be happy to answer questions or provide additional information anytime, anywhere, and on my own time and expense.

Sincerely,

Walter M. Calinger, PhD

Former Superintendent, Woodland Hills School District

Pittsburgh, Pennsylvania

CAPACITY BUILDING: IMPLEMENTING AN EBP

After definitions and characteristics of bullying are understood, and implementation of an evidence-based bulling prevention initiative has proven to be successful, what's next? How does a school sustain the culture change that has taken place? How does the school administrator and bullying-prevention school champion keep it all going so as not to succumb to defeat two, three, or five years after a successful bullying-prevention initiative? Certainly, maintaining that public health approach as described throughout this chapter would be key, along with all the important information made available in the subsequent chapters. There are also tools and strategies to support bullying prevention initiatives in the context of the larger issue of student health. The Coordinated School Health (CSH) initiative is one example of how to support and sustain a bullying-prevention initiative, as well as how to provide the tools and resources to assist a school working toward addressing the many concerning school-based health issues. There are eight components to the CSH, ranging from health and physical education curriculum to recommendations on counseling, psychological, and social services. These latter recommendations have a heightened level of importance as we attempt to address the school safety issues highlighted most recently by the Sandy Hook tragedy, in Newtown, Connecticut, in which 26 people were killed by an armed young man with mental health issues. The School Health Index is an associated tool, available to provide assessment and planning strategies for schools.[38]

If an innovative and progressive school administrator is eager to venture beyond U.S. recommendations on guiding a school to better and more sustainable health, the World Health Organization Health Promoting School initiative is another option. The initiative began in the 1990s, resulting in a set of guidelines:

1. School health policies.
2. The school's physical environment.
3. The school's social environment.
4. School/community relationships.
5. The development of personal health skills.
6. School health services.

A key benefit of this international initiative is that it nicely defines what a health-promoting school is, as well as offers a set of principles and strategies to becoming a health-promoting school.[39]

EXCITING NEWS

Now that you have been introduced to both the challenges and opportunities in how best to develop a school-based health promotion initiative, allow me to comment on several exciting activities supporting prevention programs in general and bullying prevention specifically. Across the country, there is a growing trend to introduce undergraduate public health curriculums into our colleges and universities. This will give our future teachers, politicians, lawyers, and others the opportunity to add a health and social mission to their future interests and professional activities. There is also a growing discussion on how best to evaluate large-population-based health-promotion initiatives so as not to rely, completely, on study designs not applicable to community-based, public health projects. A new approach to evaluation will allow for a more readily available use of very acceptable evidence-based programs to large population of citizens in desperate need of support.

"*Clinical health promotion*" comments on the synergy between clinical medicine and outcomes and the benefit of directed health promotion strategies to a clinical setting. Through the World Health Organization-supported Health Promoting Hospital initiative, clinical health promotion strategies have been developed and coalitions identified to comment on the benefit of embedding the public health practice of health promotion into our current clinical practices.[40] One example of such an initiative is taking place in Brescia, Italy. In partnership with a U.S.-based public health team, a clinical health promotion database has been developed to improve the health of pediatric asthma patients by concentrating on the typical clinical issues of this patient population, as well as issues related to obesity, nutrition, exercise, and bullying behaviors.[41,42]

And finally, the availability of a Pennsylvania report commenting on the cost–benefit analysis of an evidence-based bullying prevention initiative should provide some national momentum in appreciating the importance and cost savings of well-designed and implemented health promotion initiatives.

CONCLUSION

In summary, there is a science to addressing the issue of school-based bullying. The ultimate success in bullying prevention is the need to appreciate how bullying is defined and the related characteristics of the bullying environment. Those involved should also be aware of the challenges that confront them in organizing and implementing an evidence-based approach to bullying prevention. Funding, coalition development, and time are real and obvious challenges. How we interpret and define health here in the United States can be a challenge to health promotion champions as we attempt to move forward with a public health approach to improving the physical and mental health of a child.

In order to have an orderly and sustained approach to bullying prevention, it is important to have some awareness of what exactly is a public health approach to bullying prevention. There are tools and planning strategies to support the effort. A multidisciplinary team effort will allow for maximum planning potential, implementation with the highest level of fidelity, and the ability to appropriately and adequately comment on the desired and actual impact of the initiative. Lastly, the ability to sustain a program using existing national and international strategies will allow for a strong capacity-building process. The subsequent chapters in this text will allow for more information and guidance on how to maximize a public health approach to bullying prevention. The authors will also demonstrate to the reader that, with the appropriate use and monitoring of an evidence-based program, the potential road to better physical and mental health is achievable—and with cost savings to schools, healthcare payers, and society in general.

FREQUENTLY ASKED QUESTIONS

1. What are the challenges to addressing the issue of school-based bullying?

There are challenges to addressing school-based bullying. Our national healthcare system does not necessarily support health promotion and disease prevention to the degree that it should. Our educational system is also experiencing challenges, especially in the area of curriculum development, teacher excellence issues and, of course, funding. This places other health-related programs on the back burner of importance. What health promotion initiatives are developed via new policy regulations often remain unfunded mandates. The relatively slow process of how we evaluate and disseminate health promotion programs also prevents us from implementing large-population-based initiatives. We are a more violent society as compared to other industrialized countries. Our legislators need to realize that bullying prevention programs, a more organized and expansive mental health system, along with some deliberate attempt to address firearm-related violence may serve as a reasonable, meaningful political agenda. Finally, a more honest and significant approach to child human rights in the United States may allow for a more comprehensive and progressive discussion regarding youth violence.

2. Why is the World Health Organizations' definition of health important in our attempt to address school-based bullying?

The World Health Organization (WHO) definition of health is "a state of complete physical, mental and social well-being and not merely the absence of disease and infirmity." A general acceptance of this definition by our healthcare systems and legislators would place greater emphasis on health promotion and disease prevention, allowing for a more optimal approach in how we provide health to our citizens.

3. How can a public health approach help in addressing school-based bullying?

A public health approach implies that there is a planning and implementation process supporting the use of an evidence-based program and the monitoring and evaluation of that program. A public health approach also supports the need to identify a working coalition of stakeholders. It is the best approach for addressing population-based health issues.

4. Why is bullying such a significant public health issue?

It is significantly stressful to the children and adults involved. We now know that bullying can have a significant impact on the physical and mental health of the children involved. A significant number of children who bully become involved in criminal activities as adults, creating a financial cost to society in general.

5. What is the definition of bullying?

The commonly used definition of bullying is: "A person is bullied when he or she is exposed repeatedly and over time, to negative actions on the part of one or more other persons, and he or she has difficulty defending him or herself." There is general consensus that most bullying is not intentionally provoked, but is associated with some type of proactive social, physical, or psychological aggression. It is also important to realize that there are three fundamental characteristics or criteria to the definition of bullying:

1. Intentionality
2. Repetitiveness
3. Imbalance of power.

6. What is an evidence-based program (EBP)?

An EBP usually implies that it has been around for a while and has been evaluated in a professional manner using accepted evaluations tools, designs, and processes to determine the efficacy and value of the program to a specific audience, and regarding a specific issue.

7. What should we be asking when we are attempting to initiate and develop a school-based bullying prevention program?

For any well-organized prevention program it is important to ask "who," "when," "what," "where," "how," and "why" to appropriately plan, organize, and implement any public health initiative. These same questions can be used in developing and defining the commonly used objectives of a health promotion programmatic goal, and they are: "programmatic," "educational," "behavioral," and "health."

8. What health promotion tools are available to support the planning, implementation, monitoring, evaluation, and sustainability of a school-based bullying prevention initiative?

The best "tool" is often the teacher, administrator, guidance counselor, or school nurse who wishes to champion a school-based bullying prevention initiative. Realizing the importance of a public health approach should prompt the school to seek out an individual trained in public health or, possibly, a school of public health that may be in the area. These individuals or institutions can lead the school to specific health promotion tools used in enhancing the "health" climate in the school. The Coordinated School Health initiative and the PRECEDE-PROCEED Model are examples of processes or tools that a school can use in any health promotion planning.

9. Who can you call on when seeking advice on how to address school-based bullying from a public health perspective?

Certainly start with the school administration and ask what the school is doing regarding a formal, organized approach to bullying. The local pediatricians or family medicine physicians may be of assistance. More likely, it will take some investigation on how best to facilitate a larger, more efficient approach to bullying prevention in the school. Suggestions of where one can start:

- Institute on Family and Neighborhood Life, Clemson University, Clemson, SC (Contact: Professor Susan Limber).
- Clinic for Health Problems Related to Bullying, Children's National Medical Center, Washington, DC.
- Bullying Prevention Initiatives, Center for Health Promotion and Disease Prevention, Windber Research Institute, Windber, PA (Contact: Shiryl Barto) stopbullying.gov www.bullyingpreventioninstitute.org.

10. What can we hope for in our attempt to address bullying a national level?

Our latest attempt to instill health promotion and disease prevention into our health care reform agenda is an extremely positive step. We also are introducing formal public health curriculums into our undergraduate college and university courses, which would allow professionals to appreciate and describe the larger issues of health regardless of the work force college graduates eventually migrate into. And, lastly, there seems to be some momentum in the United States in developing a "clinical health promotion" approach to health care.

REFERENCES

1. Goal Seven, National Educational Goals Report 1995.

2. Batsche GM, Knoff HM. Bullies and their victims: Understanding a pervasive problem in the schools. *Sch Psych Rev.* 1994; 23:165–175.

3. Leary MR, Kowalski RM, Smith L, Phillips S. Teasing, rejection, and violence: Case studies of the school shootings. *Aggressive Behavior.* 2003; 29(3):202–214.

4. Anderson M, Kaufman J, Simon TR, et al. School-associated violent deaths in the United States, 1994–1999. *JAMA: J Am Med Assoc.* 2001; 286(21):2695–2702.

5. Vossekuil B, Fein R, Reddy M, Borum R, Modzeleski W. *The Final Report and Findings of the Safe School Initiative: Implications for the prevention of school attacks in the United States.* Washington, DC: United States Secret Service and the United States Department of Education; 2002.

6. Olweus D. School Bullying: Development and some important challenges. *Ann Rev Clin Psychol.* Jan. 3, 2013.

7. Ravitch D. *The Death and Life of the Great American School System: How Testing and Choice Are Undermining Education.* New York, NY: Basic Books; 2011.

8. Hu W. Bullying law puts New Jersey schools on spot. *The New York Times.* Aug. 30, 2011.

9. UN Commission on Human Rights, Convention on the Rights of the Child, March 7, 1990, E/CN.4/RES/1990/74, available at: http://www.refworld.org/docid/3b00f03d30.html. Accessed April 19, 2013.

10. Gershoff ET, Bitensky SH. The case against corporal punishment of children: Converging evidence from social science research and international human rights law and implications for US public policy. *Psychol, Public Policy, and Law.* 2007; 13(4):231.

11. Masiello M, Kurtz J. Child protection must also focus on human rights. *The Tribune-Democrat.* 2012; Editorial.

12. Stein N. Bullying or sexual harassment—The missing discourse of rights in an era of zero tolerance. *Arizona Law Rev.* 2003; 45:783–799.

13. Cohn A, Canter A. Bullying: Facts for schools and parents. *Nat Assoc Sch Psychol.* 2003.

14. Nansel TR, Overpeck M, Pilla R, Ruan J, Morton M, Scheidt P. Bullying behaviors among us youth: Prevalence and association with psychosocial adjustment. *JAMA: J Am Med Assoc.* 2001; 285(16):2094–2100.

15. Luukkonen AH, Riala K, Hakko H, Räsänen P. Bullying behaviour and criminality: A population-based follow-up study of adolescent psychiatric inpatients in Northern Finland. *Forensic Sci Int.* 2011; 207(1):106–110.

16. *U.S. Health in International Perspective: Shorter Lives, Poorer Health*. National Research Council and Institute of Medicine; 2013.

17. Olweus D. Understanding and researching bullying: Some critical issues. In: Jimerson SR, Swearer SM, Espelage DL, eds. *Handbook of Bullying in Schools: An International Perspective*. New York: Routledge; 2010:x, 614 p.

18. Boulton MJ. Teachers' views on bullying: Definitions, attitudes and ability to cope. *Br J Edu Psychol*. 2011; 67(2):223–233.

19. Hazelden Foundation. What Is Bullying? 2007. Available at http://www.bluesprings-schools.net/gen/blue_springs_generated_bin/documents/basic_module/OlweusFactS_What_Is_Bullying.pdf.

20. Masiello M. Health is everywhere. *Western Pennsylvania Healthcare News*. 2008.

21. Constitution of the World Health Organization. 1946. *Bull World Health Organ*. 2002; 80:983–984.

22. Masiello M. A health promoting hospital: A strategy in the re-design of the U.S. health care system. *Commonwealth—A J Polit Sci*. 2008; 14(1):125–137.

23. Weber D. American Exceptionalism. *Hosp Health Netw*. 2007.

24. Srabstein J, Joshi P, Due P, et al. Prevention of public health risks linked to bullying: A need for a whole community approach. *Int J Adolesc Med Health*. Apr–Jun 2008; 20(2):185–199.

25. Committee for the Study of the Future of Public Health Division of Health Care Services. *The Future of Public Health*. The National Academies Press; 1988.

26. Noland VJ, Troxler C, Torrens Salemi AM. School health is public health. *Florida Public Health Rev*. 2004; 1:24–29.

27. American Public Health Association. What Is Public Health? Our Commitment to Safe, Healthy Communities. Available at http://www.apha.org/NR/rdonlyres/C57478B8-8682-4347-8DDF-A1E24E82B919/0/what_is_PH_May1_Final.pdf.

28. Center for Disease Control and Prevention. The Public Health Approach to Violence Prevention. 2008. Available at http://www.cdc.gov/violenceprevention/overview/publichealthapproach.html.

29. Organization WH. Definition and Typology of Violence. 2013. Available at http://www.who.int/violenceprevention/approach/definition/en/.

30. World Health Organization. The Public Health Approach. 2013.

31. Brownson RC, Baker EA, Leet TL, Gillespie KN. *Evidence-Based Public Health*. New York: Oxford University Press, Inc.; 2003.

32. Victora CG, Habicht JP, Bryce J. Evidence-based public health: Moving beyond randomized trials. *Am Public Health*. Mar 2004; 94(3):400–405.

33. Glanz K, Rimer BK, Viswanath K. *Health Behavior and Health Education: Theory, Research, and Practice*. 4th ed. San Francisco, CA: Jossey-Bass; 2008.

34. Schroeder BA, Messina A, Holliday C, Barto S, Schroeder D, Masiello M. The role of a health care foundation in a statewide bullying prevention initiative. *Acad Health Care Mgmt J*. 2012; 8(1):33–40.

35. Masiello M, Schroeder D, Barto S, et al. *Bullying Prevention: A Statewide Collaborative That Works*. Pittsburgh, PA: Highmark Foundation; 2009.

36. Masiello M, Schroeder D, Barto S, et al. *Bullying Prevention: The Impact on Pennsylvania School Children*. Pittsburgh, PA: Highmark Foundation; 2011.

37. Highmark Foundation. *The Cost Benefit of Bullying Prevention: A First-Time Analysis of Savings*. Pittsburgh, PA: Highmark Foundation; 2012.

38. Centers for Disease Control and Prevention. Coordinated School Health. 2012(09/06/12).

39. World Health Organization. Global School Health Initiative. 2013.

40. Tonnesen H. The global financial crisis increases the need for clinical health promotion. *Clin Health Promotion*. 2012; 2(1):3–4.

41. Guarnaccia S, Lombardi A, Gaffurini A, et al. Application and implementation of the GINIA asthma guidelines by specialist and primary care physicians: A longitudinal follow-up study on 264 children. *Prim Care Resp*. 2007; 16(6):357–363.

42. Masiello M, Guarnaccia S, Hollis C. An international clinical and public health collaboration. International Conference on Health Promoting Hospitals & Health Services; 2011; Turku, Finland.

2

Effective Bullying Prevention Efforts and School Climate Reform

Jonathan Cohen, PhD*

Objectives

1. To understand current research-based school climate policy and improvement practices.
2. To understand how school climate reform represents a data-driven strategy that supports students, parents or guardians, educators, and potentially community members learning and working to protect and support students feeling safe, supported, and engaged—the foundation for learning and positive youth development.
3. To understand school climate improvement models, implementation strategies, and related tools, and how they support effective bullying prevention efforts in particular and supportive, responsible, engaging, and democratically informed school communities in general.

There is growing awareness that mean, cruel, and bullying[i] behaviors are a public health crisis: They undermine students' healthy development and

---

*Jonathan Cohen is President of the National School Climate Center, and some of the services referred to in this chapter are for a fee.

[i]The question of how to define "bullying" is a complex one. There are practical problems associated with the traditional definition that is grounded in the notion that the bullying is (i) "an intentional act" carried out by a person or group who is (ii) more powerful than the target and necessarily a (iii) "repeated act." Educators often have great difficulty ascertaining "intent" and/or power differentials. In addition, it has never made sense to me that one act of "bullying" does not count if it is not repeated. Although I will use the term *bullying* throughout this chapter, kindly note that this is shorthand for "mean, cruel, and/or bullying behaviors."

capacity to learn.[1] In fact, it has significant and adverse effects on the bully and the witnesses as well as the target of those behaviors.[2-7] Yet, there is limited research about what effective bullying prevention efforts really look like.[8-11]

The U.S. Department of Education and the Department of Health and Human Services suggested in 2012 that effective bullying prevention efforts are characterized by six dimensions and processes:[12]

1. Getting started (e.g., assessing past school prevention and intervention efforts around student behavior).
2. Assessing bullying in your school.
3. Engaging parents and youth.
4. Creating policies and rules.
5. Building a safe environment.
6. Educating students and school staff.

These guidelines are important for several reasons. As detailed in this chapter, they provide information and suggestions about what we now understand to be research-based practices that work. And, guidelines— potentially—provide a road map and/or set of benchmarks that are grounded in meaningful goals and strategies that school leaders can use to actualize these goals.

The six dimensions outlined above begin to helpfully provide guidelines about research-based practices that work. However, I would suggest that they are too general and do not represent a road map that supports an effective implementation process for school leaders. In addition, I suggest that these guidelines do not recognize important research about effective school improvement efforts, such as the essential role of the principal's leadership[13] and the necessity of "igniting" students' and adults' intrinsic motivation to be a co-learner and co-leader in the process of preventing bullying and promoting a safe, respectful, and socially responsibility climate for students and educators.[14,15]

Our center—the National School Climate Center—works with building, district, and state educational leaders across the country who have raised questions about these guidelines: What are the best assessment tools to use, and how can and should we use these data to mobilize the whole community to learn and work together?

It is easy to say, "Engage students and parents or guardians," but—concretely and realistically—how do we do this? What are examples of policies and rules that are aligned with research and provide helpful guidelines, examples, and forums where teachers can learn from each other? Given how busy and focused educators are on reading, math, and science scores, how do we create a safe, respectful, and civil climate for learning in our classrooms and schools? What are the range of ways that we can promote meaningful student and adult learning, given how focused we are on test scores? And finally, how do we ensure that this bully/risk prevention effort will not be another "flavor of the month": A top-down initiative that most of the school community never buys into and eventually fades? This chapter is a response to these kinds of questions.

In this chapter, I suggest that school climate reform is a viable, data-driven school improvement strategy that promotes safer, more supportive, and civil schools. School climate reform provides a model and an implementation strategy that is aligned with the U.S. Department of Education's bullying prevention guidelines, and it addresses the questions previously noted. It is a strategy that is also aligned with the Centers for Disease Control and Prevention[16,17] guidelines for bullying prevention and school connectedness enhancing interventions. It also represents a school improvement strategy that recognizes the essential role of the principal in this and any effective school reform effort,[13,18] as well as the essential requirement that *everyone* in the school community feel engaged and intrinsically motivated to be co-learners and co-leaders in effective school improvement efforts.[14,15] Finally, school climate reform is also focused on health and mental health promotion as well as risk prevention.[19]

In short, this chapter will outline how school climate reform *is* an effective and sustainable bullying prevention effort that helps to prevent bullying behaviors as well as promoting a community of *Upstanders*—students and adults that think and act in socially responsible ways. First, I will briefly outline past and current school climate policy and improvement practices and trends. Then I will critique and add to the federal bullying prevention guidelines, detailing how school climate reform represents a data-driven strategy that supports students, parents/guardians, educators, and potentially community members learning and working to protect and support students feeling safe, supported, and engaged.

SCHOOL CLIMATE POLICY AND IMPROVEMENT PRACTICES— PAST AND CURRENT TRENDS

Educators and researchers have been studying school climate for over a century.[20] Over the last 60 years, there has been a growing tradition of empirically studying school climate, culture, and supportive learning environments[ii] (e.g., Anderson 1982[21]; Carter 2011[22]; Cohen et al., 2009[19]; Comer 2005[23]; Deal and Peterson 2009[24]; Freiberg 1999[25]). There is not one universally agreed-on definition of *school climate*. The majority of researchers have used the term to refer to people's subjective experience of school life.[19] Beginning with Perry,[20] practitioners and researchers have used a range of terms to describe the "atmosphere," "feelings," "tone," "setting," or "milieu," of the school.[25]

Virtually all school climate scholars and researchers think about school climate via group trends. In other words, the unit of analysis is not the individual, but groups and the school as a whole. Individual perceptions form the foundation for school climate assessment, but we are not focused on what one given person thinks and feels. Rather, the focus is on what groups of students and/or parents and/or school personnel think and feel about school life.

The National School Climate Council (www.schoolclimate.org/about/council.php) is a group of practice and policy leaders committed to narrowing the gap between school climate research on the one hand and school climate policy, practice, and teacher education on the other. The Council developed the following consensually created definition of *school climate* as well as a *positive, sustainable school climate* that recognizes current research and practice:

> School climate refers to the quality and character of school life. School climate is based on patterns of people's experience of school life and reflects norms, goals, values, interpersonal relationships, teaching, learning, leadership practices, and organizational structures.

[ii]These terms—*school climate, school culture, supportive learning environments,* and *conditions for learning*—have often been used interchangeably. There are some who suggest that it is helpful to differentiate these terms. Here I am a "lumper" and will use these terms interchangeably. For a detailed discussion of these issues, see Cohen 2012.[20a]

A sustainable, positive school climate fosters youth development and learning necessary for a productive, contributing and satisfying life in a democratic society. This climate includes norms, values and expectations that support people feeling socially, emotionally and physically safe. People are engaged and respected. Students, families and educators work together to develop, live and contribute to a shared school vision. Educators model and nurture an attitude that emphasizes the benefits and satisfaction from learning. Each person contributes to the operations of the school and the care of the physical environment (p. 5).[26]

Over the last three decades, educators and researchers have worked to identify specific elements that make up school climate. Although there is not one list that summarizes these elements, virtually all researchers suggest that there are four major areas that are essential to pay attention to: *Safety* (e.g., rules and norms; physical safety; social—emotional safety); *relationships* (e.g., respect for diversity; social support—adults; social support—students; school connectedness and engagement; leadership); *teaching and learning* (e.g., social, emotional, ethical, and civic learning[iii]; support for learning; professional relationships); and the *institutional environment* (e.g., physical surrounding). The National School Climate Council suggests that

school climate improvement is an intentional, strategic, collaborative, transparent, and coordinated effort to strengthen school learning environments. Democratically informed decision-making constitutes an essential foundation for the school climate improvement process. . . . The Council defines an effective school climate improvement process as one that engages all stakeholders in the following six essential practices:

1. The decision-making process is collaborative, democratic, and involves all stakeholders (e.g., school personnel, students, families, community members) with varied roles and perspectives (e.g., teacher, nurse, social worker, administrator as well as nontraditional student leaders and disempowered parents).

2. Psychometrically sound quantitative and qualitative data are used to drive action planning, intervention practices, and program implementation to continuously improve dimensions of school climate. Data are

---

[iii]I use the term *social, emotional, and civic learning* to recognize two overlapping educational traditions: character education and social emotional learning. As I have detailed elsewhere (Cohen 2006[71]), although there are some important differences between these two traditions, I suggest that there are more similarities and it is useful to be a "lumper" here.

collected regularly to evaluate progress and continue to inform the improvement process.

3. Improvement goals are tailored to the unique needs of the students and broader school community. These goals are integrated into overall school reform efforts, thereby leveraging school strengths while facilitating the sustainability of the improvement process.

4. Capacity building among school personnel promotes adult learning in teams and/or professional learning communities to promote collective efficacy and staff skills in providing whole child education.

5. Curriculum, instruction, student supports, and interventions are evidence-based and grounded in cognitive, social, and ecological theories of youth development. Interventions include strength- and risk-based practices and programs that together represent a comprehensive continuum of approaches to promote positive learning environments and address individual student barriers to learning.

6. The improvement process strengthens (a) policies and procedures related to learning environments, and (b) operational infrastructure to facilitate data collection, effective planning, implementation, evaluation, and sustainability.[27]

This definition of the school climate improvement process reflects a series of overlapping systemic or schoolwide processes that promote safe, supportive, engaging, and flourishing schools: (1) transparent, democratically informed *leadership*[13,18,28,29]; (2) *engaging* the students, parents, and ideally community members as well as school personnel to be co-learners and co-leaders in the improvement efforts (school–home–community partnerships)[30–32]; (3) *measurement practices* that recognize the social, emotional and civic dimensions of learning and school life[29,33]; (4) improvement *goals are tailored* to the unique needs of the students and school community[34,35]; (5) *adult learning* and professional learning communities that supports capacity building[36–40]; and (6) prosocial education.[41,42]

There has been a growing body of empirical as well as ethnographic research that shows that positive school climate is associated with and/or predictive of increased student achievement and school connectedness, decreased high school dropout rates, enhanced risk prevention/health promotion efforts, and increased teacher retention rates.[16,19,25,43] These findings have contributed to the Centers for Disease Control and

Prevention's 2009 recommendation of school climate improvement as one essential improvement strategy that supports students' feelings and school connectedness. The Institute for Educational Sciences and the What Works Clearinghouse suggests that there is "moderate" support for school climate improvement efforts as a dropout prevention strategy.[44]

The U.S. Department of Education and the U.S. Department of Health and Human Services fund the National Center on Safe Supportive Learning Environments (NCSSLE), whose mission is to provide "information and technical assistance to states, districts, schools, institutions of higher education, communities, and other federal grantees programs on how to improve conditions for learning."[45] To that end, the NCSSLE offers the Safe and Supportive Schools (S3) grant program that supports state education departments in (1) developing statewide school climate measurement systems and (2) studying the school climate improvement process with small groups of low-performing high schools.[45] In addition, more than 20 national organizations have endorsed *National School Climate Standards*.[46] The National School Climate Council developed *National School Climate Standards* in 2009. This framework comprises five standards (and 16 indicators and 30 related subindicators) that support local school communities. The standards address three essential questions that provide the foundation for the whole "village" coming to together to create an even safer, more supportive and engaging school:

1. What kind of school do we want ours to be?
2. Given this vision, what are the policies, rules, and supports we need to actualize this vision?
3. What are the practices (instructional and schoolwide) that we need to support this vision and policy?

There are two overlapping dimensions that shape school climate–related practice: Assessment and school improvement efforts. Those two factors support two foundational goals: Understanding the school's strengths and needs and mobilizing students, parents, school personnel and community members to use that information to work together to support positive youth development and student learning. As we have detailed elsewhere, a small but growing number of scientifically sound school climate surveys recognize student, parent or guardian, school personnel, and even community voices and evaluate safety as well as relationships, engagement, and a number of related social, emotional and civic aspects of learning and school life.[19,46] And, there are a growing number of evidence-based school climate improvement models and implementation strategies.[46]

Historically, we have often thought of bullying as an individual act. Building on the groundbreaking work of Slaby et al.[47] and Twemlow and colleagues,[48,49] we suggest that bullying is *always* a social process. There is almost never a bully and a victim without a witness. Students and adults alike make a decision, conscious or not, to be either a passive bystander who aids the bully or an *Upstander:* A person who thinks and acts in socially responsible ways to help the target of bullying. By definition, then, school climate is always—more or less—colored and shaped by *everyone* in the school community.

Our understanding and a growing body of research shows that effective bullying prevention efforts include a focus on promoting a culture of Upstanders. In other words, effective bullying prevention efforts—like school climate reform efforts—necessarily include mobilizing *everyone* in the community to learn about and understand the school's strengths and needs and supporting students and adults to protect targets of bullying and promote of culture of safety, respect, support, engagement, and social responsibility.

BULLYING PREVENTION AND PRO-UPSTANDER GOALS

The U.S. Department of Education, as well as other research-based bullying prevention frameworks[9,10,48,51] suggest that effective efforts need to be characterized by the following processes and goals:

- *Assessments* that provide helpful information about past prevention efforts and current needs, as well as schoolwide evaluations of current bully–victim–witness behavior.
- *Principal leadership* that supports comprehensive and sustained risk prevention, health promotion, and social, emotional and civic educational efforts.
- A *whole-village approach* in which everyone in the school community is a motivated co-learner about current bully–victim–witness behavior and a co-leader in improvement efforts.
- *Policies and rules* that are research-based and helpfully prevent bullying behaviors and support the norms of respectful and socially responsible school communities.

- *Practices* that prevent bully–victim–witness behavior as well promote social, emotional, civic, and intellectual learning and safe, supportive, respectful, and engaging schools.

EXAMINATION OF BULLYING PREVENTION GUIDELINES

At the beginning of this chapter, we noted that the in 2012 U.S. Department of Education and the Department of Health and Human Services characterize effective bullying prevention efforts through six dimensions: (1) getting started; (2) assessment; (3) engaging parents and youth; (4) creating policies and rules; (5) building a safe environment; and (6) educating students and school staff.[12] Let's examine those more closely.

Getting Started

Getting started or the process of planning and preparing for an effective bully prevention and school climate improvement process is often overlooked or given short shift by school leaders.

Our Center suggests that all schools are "ready" to embark on school climate improvement efforts in general and with regard to bullying prevention efforts in particular. But, all schools—like all people—evidence a unique array of strengths, weaknesses, and needs. Understanding how we, as a school, are prepared or less than prepared to carry out school improvement efforts is the first step. Many schools, for example, include educators who do not trust one another, teaching and learning in a culture of blame. Confirming a truth that James Comer[23] has talked about for three decades in a series of unusually sophisticated experimental and ethnographic school improvement studies, Byrk and his colleagues have recently shown—experientially and ethnographically—that "trust is the glue" that is the essential foundation for a successful school improvement effort.[52,53] School climate improvement readiness assessments (e.g., National School Climate Center 2011) can rapidly help school leadership teams understand where they are when it comes to the educator culture—how much blame and distrust is there, as opposed to a more trusting and collaborative environment? Understanding and addressing any potential obstacles provide a foundation for successful bullying prevention and pro-Upstander efforts, as well as any and all other attempts to improve school climate.

Evaluating readiness also supports schools leaders understanding how to best engage as many students, parents/guardians, school personnel and even community members in being co-learners and co-leaders in the bully prevention/improvement process as well as the other essential tasks and challenges that shape an effective planning process: creating representative leadership teams; building support and foster "buy in"; promoting an 'educator culture' of trust and collaborative problem solving; ensuring your team/school has adequate resources to support the process; celebrating success and building on past efforts; and, reflecting and learning from this process of planning and preparation.

Readiness assessments are the first of a series of assessments that support effective bullying prevention and school climate improvement efforts.

Assessment

The U.S. Department of Education suggests that "assessing school prevention and intervention efforts around student behavior, including substance use and violence and building on past risk prevention and health promotion efforts" is an important first step in effective bullying prevention efforts.

This guideline does not provide information or recommendations about the nature of the assessment or how to best use the data as a "flashlight" rather than a "hammer."[iv] In fact, there is a range of ways that schools can assess prevention/intervention efforts: Narrowly (e.g., focused on bullying alone) or broadly (e.g., the expectations, beliefs, norms, relational patterns, teaching, learning, leadership practices, and more that color and shape the climate for safety and learning). Schools can use focus groups, surveys, semistructured interviews, disciplinary reports, walk-throughs, and more to assess bullying.

We suggest that there are three forms of assessment that school leaders should consider and utilize:

1. Readiness assessments—as noted above—that help school leaders answer these questions: Where are we now with regard to our current risk prevention and health promotion efforts? What are next steps to

---

[iv]During the course of writing this chapter, the U.S. Department of Education has added some helpful details to these guidelines (e.g., about what an assessment can do and some ideas about how to implement an assessment).

consider that will support effective and sustained risk prevention and health promotion efforts?

2. Comprehensive school climate surveys that recognize student, parent or guardian and school personnel and, optimally, community voice. The surveys should also provide more detailed information about the quality and character of school life.

3. More detailed bully–victim–witness evaluations.

The National School Climate Council[46] and our Center suggest that comprehensive school climate survey evaluations is the most important "next step" in the assessment process, for two reasons. First, it provides a scientifically sound understanding about how students, parents, school personnel, and even community members perceive and rate safety, as well as how supported and engaged students are in learning and school life. One of the big problems with many past bullying prevention efforts is that we have focused too narrowly on the bully in ways that are short-term, fragmented, or punitive. How supported and engaged students feel actually colors and shapes bully-victim-witness phenomena. Second, school climate evaluations can be used as an engagement strategy—a way of recognizing everyone's voice in the community and using this as a springboard for collaborative learning and work.

The single most common school climate finding that our Center and others (e.g., Quaglia Institute for Student Aspirations) has discovered is that the adults believe that safety is a "mild" to "moderately severe" issue, but students consistently report that is it is a "severe" problem.[54] In addition to being surprising, this kind of discrepancy provides the opportunity and need to dig deeper and understand what it means. Typically, we recommend that students become participatory: Learning from peers as well as staff about "hot spots" and why so many people act as bystanders rather than Upstanders.

Assessing Bullying

The Centers for Disease Control and Prevention has recently released a compendium of bully–victim–witness assessment tools.[55] Although this compendium was developed first and foremost for researchers, there may also be focused measures here that can support a meaningful assessment process. Our Center's experience is that more focused assessments of bully–victim–witness behavior are most helpfully carried out after comprehensive school climate evaluations.

In any case, for school-based assessment processes to be useful, it is essential that the "captain of the ship"—the principal—direct this process and actively supports data being used as a "flashlight" rather than a "hammer."

Consider the goal of *principal leadership:* The U.S. Department of Education's suggestions do not focus on this foundational aspect of school improvement. It has been established that as fundamentally important as classroom leaders are in fostering student learning, principal leadership provides an essential foundation for whole school improvement.[13,18] We have repeatedly seen bullying prevention efforts fail because the principal does not really support a comprehensive, long-term effort. On one level, this is understandable, given how much principals are focused on raising reading, math, and science scores. But, it is also tragic. As important as linguistic, mathematical, and scientific learning are, students and educators need to feel safe. And, we know that feeling safe, supported, and engaged promotes students' healthy development, which is the foundation for learning.

Engaging Parents and Youth

The U.S. Department of Education appreciates this foundational goal and process when it states that we need to "Engage parents and youth: mobilizing everyone in the community to work together to send a unified message against bullying and then launching an awareness campaign to make the objectives known to the school, parents, and community members."[12]

We suggest that this guideline does not go far enough on several counts. First, as part of mobilizing the whole village, we suggest that in addition to parents and youth, we also need to engage school personnel and ideally community members as well. Second, this federal guideline does not suggest *how* we can "engage" members of the school community to be co-learners and co-leaders in a bullying prevention/pro-Upstander effort. Fullan[14] and Mourshed et al.[15] have recently underscored that this engagement needs to include a process that "ignites" everyone in the community to become intrinsically motivated to learn and help. There is a robust body of educational, sociological, and socioeconomic research that supports the notion that student learning and positive youth development are positively shaped not only by effective school–family partnerships (e.g., Henderson, Mapp, Johnson, and

Davies 2007; Patrikakou, Weissberg, Redding, and Walberg 2005)[56-58] but also by the social networks and norms of the larger community and collaborative school–community partnerships.[59-62] But how do we form these partnerships when school leaders are so busy and are forced to focus so much on the current metrics that drive public education?

Synthesizing research and best practices from a range of overlapping fields, our Center has developed a school climate improvement model that is defined by a series of tasks and challenges that—optimally—shape the improvement process.[19,50] A foundational task and challenge during the *planning and preparation* phase of the school climate improvement process is developing a shared vision of what kind of school we want ours to be. In fact, this is an essential task for any and all school improvement efforts. This process encourages as many as possible in the school community—students and adults—to consider together what we most want for our children and students.

In our work with schools and districts, we have repeatedly seen that when the principal asks fellow educators, parents or guardians, and students what their vision is for an ideal school, their answers are shockingly (but perhaps not surprisingly) similar across geographic regions and socioeconomic strata. People want children to learn to learn, to be able to discover their "healthy passions," to be a good friend and mate, to get a job, and to be a responsible member of the community. In any case, developing this understanding of our "shared vision" provides an opportunity to then conduct a gap analysis: Where are we now, and where do we want to go? To the extent that the principal authentically cares what students and adults want the school to be, this is a meaningful engagement strategy that concretely begins to mobilize the "whole village" to support children's healthy development over time.

The U.S. Department of Education's guidelines suggest that the school safety committee is one "mechanism" or group that can help bring the community together to prevent bullying. We agree. However, current safety committees almost always focus—more or less exclusively—on physical safety. In our work with the Ohio Department of Education (www.schoolclimate.org/programs/safeCivilSchools.php) and elsewhere,[51] we have suggested that school safety committees need to develop social crisis preparedness programs that complement existing physical crisis preparedness programs. Social crisis preparedness programs can and need to focus on social dangers, like bully–victim–witness behavior. Students and adults need to understand the social dangers and need to struggle with the following question: What can we most helpfully do when we witness bully–victim behavior?[v] We will detail how we are now working with students as well as educators to support their taking a leadership role in K–12 schools, transforming the school from a culture of bystanders to a culture of Upstanders.

Creating Policies and Rules

The U.S. Department of Education suggests that "creating policies and rules (e.g., creating a mission statement, code of conduct, schoolwide rules, and a bullying reporting system that promote a climate where bullying is not acceptable) is another essential aspect of effective bullying prevention efforts."[12] We know that research optimally shapes policies, which, in turn, dictates practice. Unfortunately, there is still a surprising gap between research regarding school safety on the one hand and policy and practice efforts on the other.[46,63]

There are a growing number of state-level bullying prevention as well as school climate policies and laws (for a recent review, see Piscatelli and Lee 2011).[63] And, growing out of President Barack Obama's *Federal Bully Prevention Partnership*, the federal government is now in the process of developing a bully prevention law. Today, too many of our bullying prevention laws focus on two issues: Identifying the bully and punishing the bully. These are examples of unhelpful bullying prevention policies that are not aligned with research. We know that punitive responses to bullying do not help, they hinder.[64,65]

As discussed earlier in the chapter, the National School Climate Council[67] has developed five school climate standards (and 16 indicators and sub-indicators) that support each school community addressing three essential

---

[v]An important recent *Youth Voice Project* (http://www.youthvoiceproject.com/) reveals that students report, for example, that when they directly confront the bully, it often makes matters worse. This is aligned with our clinical and educational findings in schools that have not addressed bully–victim–bystander behavior systemically. We are now beginning to study whether this is true in schools that have mounted the comprehensive school climate improvement efforts being outlined here. Our preliminary sense is that in these schools, when students confront bullying in direct ways, it often is helpful!

questions: What kind of school do we want ours to be? Given this vision, what are the policies and rules that we need to support this vision? And, given this vision and policies, what are the practices that we need to support it? We recommend that states and districts consider adapting or adopting these standards that provide benchmarks for safe, supportive, engaging schools as well as effective teaching and learning (for a series of critiques and discussions about these standards, see www.schoolclimate.org/climate/standards.php).

The federal guidelines appreciate how we can and need to use mission statements, rules, and codes of conduct to support effective bullying prevention efforts. There are two important aspects of this common sense statement that are worth unpacking. First, teachers and staff need to care about rules, policies, and practices. Too often rules, policies, and practices are unilaterally decided in a central office (e.g., by the superintendent) and passed down in ways that, inadvertently, undermine buy-in and the process of supporting the development of a shared vision and intrinsic motivated to work together. Second, administrators can take steps to facilitate this. We appreciate the recently revised and expanded federal guidelines that underscore that we need to include parents and students as well as staff in the development of these rules and policies.

There are many ways of conceptualizing educational practice. One way of thinking about the nature of educational practices is that there are two essential and somewhat overlapping processes that shape it in schools: (1) teaching and learning and (2) systemic or schoolwide practices. Schoolwide or systematic approaches, for example, include codes of conduct, schoolwide rules, and reporting systems.

The federal bullying prevention guidelines recognize and focus on both "educating," or teaching and learning with students (e.g.,"*Educate about bullying*': Training school staff and students to prevent and address bullying can help sustain bullying prevention efforts over time"), and systemic interventions (e.g., "'*Build a safe environment*': A safe and supportive school climate can help prevent bullying") designed to promote a safe environment.[12]

If we consider the definitions of school climate and the school climate improvement process, there are a range of practices that shape teaching and learning as well as systemic interventions that will build safe environments. We now examine the environment and the education of students and staff in relation to preventing bullying.

Building a Safe Environment

The federal guidelines suggest that we need to establish "a safe and supportive school climate." And that we need to establish "a culture of inclusion and respect that welcomes all students and reward students when they show thoughtfulness and respect for peers, adults, and the school."[12]

There is no one schoolwide intervention that will actualize the goals noted here. The federal guidelines include four specific—and helpful—suggestions: (1) consider how PBIS can support this effort; (2) monitor hot spots; (3) enlist the help of *all* school staff; and (4) set a tone of respect in the classroom.

There are wide ranges of systemic practices that support safe, respectful, and socially responsible school climates. Synthesizing research and best practices from a number of overlapping fields (school reform in general and character education, social emotional learning, community schools, service learning, risk prevention, and health and mental health promotion efforts in particular), we have suggested a series of tasks and challenges that shape an effective school climate improvement process designed to promote safe, supportive, engaging, helpfully challenging, and joyful schools.[19,50,67]

For example, if we really care that all students become linguistically fluent, it is well known that language learning and teaching need to intentionally and helpfully color and shape all aspects of school life: From what we measure (recognize and track) to norms that support language learning to meaningful partnerships between educators and parents. Naturally, the same holds true if we care about building safe school environments. We need to measure safety and the social, emotional, and civic dimensions of student learning and school life; institutionalize; and repeatedly engage in practices that support these goals.

Educating Students and School Staff

The federal guidelines focus on three aspects of learning and teaching. First are activities to teach students about bullying. This is certainly an important goal. And, we appreciate that these guidelines are not only focused on a bullying prevention curriculum alone. In fact, there are a range of ways that classroom leaders can further this process: Through preexisting curriculum that has been developed and shown to be helpful, infusing these bullying prevention-related learning objectives, assessments, and activities into existing lessons (as well as advisory activities and morning meetings).

The second aspect of teaching and learning about bullying that the federal guidelines focus on is evidence-based programs and curriculum. There is a range of "approved" evidence-based curriculum (e.g., U.S. Department of Health and Human, 2012 as well as Blueprints, Collaborative for Academic, Social and Emotional Learning (CASEL), Find Youth Info, Guide to Community Prevention Services, National Dropout Prevention Center, National Registry of Evidence-based Programs and Practices, Office of Juvenile Justice and Delinquency Prevention, Model Programs Guide, Promising Practices Network for Children, Families and Communities and the What Works Clearinghouse). However, as important as evidence-based curriculum is, there is clearly only one possible facet of an effective bullying prevention effort. There is a range of ways that classroom leaders can intentionally and helpfully use existing lesson plans as a springboard to intentionally infuse bullying prevention/pro-Upstander "lessons."[68–70]

The Safe and Supportive Learning Technical Assistance Center (http://safesupportivelearning.ed.gov/) that supports the U.S. Department of Education's Safe and Drug Free School Division has recently developed professional development materials for bus drivers (http://safesupportiveschools.ed.gov/index.php?id=1481) as well as classroom teachers (http://safesupportiveschools.ed.gov/index.php?id=1480) to cultivate meaningful relationships with students while creating a positive climate on the bus and in the classroom.

Too often in the past—and today—school-based bullying prevention efforts begin and end with a series of lesson plans. This will always be inadequate. In fact, there are several other essential aspects that shape curriculum and the process of teaching and learning: Adult learning and what kind of "living example" the teacher (or parent) is; classroom management; and the utilization of a range of other strategies (e.g., cooperative learning, conflict resolution and mediation-related learning, service learning, and moral dilemma discussions) that can promote social emotional and civic competencies and enhance protective factors.[71]

There are also ways that we can helpfully support students being teachers and leaders as well as learners in this area. As noted throughout, an essential aspect of effective bullying prevention—and school climate improvement—is that *everyone* in the community is more or less involved. Our Center for example, has developed tool kits for middle and high school students to be

Upstander leaders, helping to raise awareness about bully–victim–witness behavior and transforming schools from a culture of bystanders to a culture of Upstanders (www.schoolclimate.org/bullybust/upstander).

Teaching and learning are shaped by our goals and the climate within which we teach. There is a growing body of research that underscores the fundamental importance and power of educators being intentional, systematic, and helpful social, emotional civic, and intellectual teachers.[71–73] Prosocial education not only promotes protective factors but also promotes a climate of caring and social responsibility that provides an essential foundation for effective bullying prevention efforts. When educators, for example, promote the following processes, they not only support innovation[74] but also student engagement in meaningful and potentially fun ways. These processes encourage more collaboration as opposed to focusing on individual achievement; support trial and error learning rather than—inadvertently—a risk-avoidance enterprise; and increase focus on creating (acquiring knowledge and developing skills). The federal teaching and learning related guideline is focused on staff training on bullying prevention. We suggest that this needs to include learning not only about effective bullying prevention efforts but also about how we can promote a community of Upstanders. The federal guidelines do not explicitly appreciate or underscore the essential importance of educators and parents—as well as students—being ongoing and vital adult learners. We have discovered, for example, that when educators and parents are "living examples" of being an Upstander, it is more powerful than anything the adult says or tells the student. And many adults are vulnerable to acting as bullies themselves! Historically, this has been a taboo topic in K–12 education: How often educators (and the same can said for parents and guardians) can act in mean, cruel, and/or bullying ways with kids. Typically, adults act in this manner when an interpersonal moment triggers frustration, anxiety, and/or pain and there is an "automatic pilot" response. We are all human. And, we are all vulnerable to these moments. We suggest that this underscores the essential importance of educators and parents being ongoing social, emotional, and civic learners, as well as teachers!

IMPLEMENTING BULLYING PREVENTION EFFORTS

Ttofi and Farrington's review of bullying prevention efforts underscore the essential importance of *how* we implement those efforts.[76] The federal guidelines do not shed light on this critical issue. We suggest that the following systemic processes support research-based implementation efforts that will be sustainable: Recognizing student, parent or guardian, school personnel and community voice in the (1) planning, (2) evaluation, (3) understanding evaluation findings and action planning, (4) implementation, and (5) reevaluation/beginning the cycle anew process. Parents and guardians and students, for example, need to be actively involved with understanding core values and developing norms and rules that grow out of this shared vision. In an overlapping manner, Farrington and Ttofi's work underscores the importance of school–home and, we would add, school–home–community partnerships.

Another fundamentally important aspect of school life is the nature of parent–educator–mental health professional partnerships. Students who chronically "fall into" the role of bully and/or victim may be troubled: This chronic behavior may signal underlying problems. Curiously, the federal guidelines do not touch on this goal: That parents, educators, and school counselors can and need to support one another in recognizing children who may be troubled and helpfully addressing their needs and/or the needs of their family.

To the extent that school climate assessment data are used as a flashlight (rather than a hammer), we are saying—institutionally—that the social, emotional, civic, ethical, as well as intellectual aspects of student learning and school life matter! This is a powerful systemic intervention. School climate improvement efforts, by definition, seek to engage *everyone* in the process. So, codes of conduct can and should be co-created by students as well as adults rather than being handed down from a central office in ways that typically resulted in a signed but *dead* document—a contract that is sent to students and their parents and read quickly (if at all), signed and too often, forgotten. On the other hand, to the extent that students and their parents are "pushed" to review, reflect, and co-author codes of conduct, this typically becomes a *living* document that is lived! (We suggest that educators also create codes of conduct for themselves in the same way.)

The recently revised federal bullying prevention guidelines include a new section: *Working in the Community*. We appreciate this addition and the information and tool kits that are included (www.stopbullying.gov/prevention/in-the-community/index.html). In conversations with building and district leaders across America, we have learned that most educational leaders deeply appreciate the importance of school-community partnerships. However, they typically also describe two challenges: Lack of time and a lack of understanding about how to foster these partnerships in effective ways. School leaders can use school climate evaluations that recognize the voice of community members, leaders, and student leadership/service learning efforts to engage, learn, and work with community members.[46] The Center on School, Family and Community Partnerships (http://www.csos.jhu.edu/p2000/center.htm) and the Coalition for Community Schools (http://www.communityschools.org/) and others have helpful research-based guidelines that support these essential partnerships.

CONCLUSION

In summary, mean, cruel, and bullying behaviors are epidemic today. Although this behavior has been normative throughout much of human history, there is a growing awareness that these behaviors are not just "kids being kids." Rather, mean, cruel, and bullying behaviors undermine a K–12 student's ability to learn and develop in healthy ways.

Past bullying prevention efforts have tended to be fragmented, focused on the bully and/or protecting the target, punitive and/or exclusively focused on a bullying prevention curriculum. Not surprisingly, past and current bullying prevention efforts tend to be less rather than more helpful.[11]

School leaders (e.g., principals, superintendents, and school board leaders) are concerned about how to build on their current safe and supportive school efforts and develop even more effective bullying prevention efforts. This chapter focused on the six federal bullying prevention guidelines. In essence, these are a useful "first step" that summarizes research-based findings about bullying prevention efforts. However, they do not integrate essential research findings about school improvement in general and how we can and need to mobilize the "whole village" to learn—socially, emotionally, and civically as well as intellectually— and work together to prevent bullying.

I have outlined how school climate reform is an effective bullying prevention and pro-Upstander effort: It is a data-driven improvement strategy that recognizes the social, emotional, and civic aspects of learning and school life; it recognizes student, parent and guardian, school staff, and even community voice in ways that support the whole-village learning and working together to not only prevent bullying but also promote socially responsible— Upstander—behavior as well as safe, supportive, engaging, and joyful schools.

FREQUENTLY ASKED QUESTIONS

1. Are there guidelines that can help school leaders to select a school climate survey?

Yes. There are two sets of guidelines as well as three independent reviews of existing school climate surveys.

The U.S. Department of Education suggests that school climate surveys be (1) reliable and valid, (2) recognize student, parent, and school personnel voice, (3) can be completed in under 20 minutes, and (4) assess various aspects of safety, engagement, and the environment. The National School Council (www.schoolclimate.org/about/council.php) recommendations are aligned with these guidelines but suggest the following three additional recommendations: (1) school climate surveys should assess teaching and learning as well as safety, relationships (engagement), and the environment; (2) recognize the "voice" of community members as well as students, parents/guardians and school personnel, and also very importantly; (3) be yoked to resources, road maps, and tools that practically support school leaders understanding what they need to consider *before* school climate assessment as well as how to use these findings *after* an assessment to—practically—foster improvement goals.

There are currently three independent reviews of school climate surveys[77-79] that support school leaders identifying reliable and valid measures. Some of these are aligned with the guidelines already noted (e.g., that student, parent, and school personnel voice are recognized) and some are not.

2. Are there guidelines and/or educational programs that support the kind of principal leadership you just described?

Yes. On the one hand, the national associations for principals (National Association of Elementary School Principals and the National Association of Secondary School Principals) have a wonderful range of ongoing professional development opportunities. And, recently the *Educational Leadership Coalition on School Climate* (which is now comprised of the Center for Character and Citizenship, University of Missouri–St. Louis; Character

Education Partnership; *Making Caring Common Initiative*, Harvard Graduate School of Education; National Dropout Prevention Center/Network; and the National School Climate Center) have developed a National School Climate Leadership Certificate Program (http://www.schoolclimate.org/programs/certification.php). This program is designed to further three goals:

1. To support and recognize the development of socially, emotionally, and civically skilled school leaders who understand and use the theory, research, and practice of school climate reform and evidence-based character education, socioemotional learning, risk prevention, and health/mental health promotion efforts.

2. To grow and support a network of school climate improvement leaders who appreciate and focus on adult learning and mobilizing the whole school community to support the "whole child" and advance social, emotional, and civic learning, academic achievement, and positive youth development.

3. To assist State Departments of Education to develop professional resources they can use to strengthen their school climate efforts, by helping to train, support, and recognize certified school climate leaders in their states.

3. It is easy to say, "Mobilize the whole village," but this is challenging to do for many reasons. What suggestions do you have that will support this goal?

It is very true that engaging and mobilizing students, parents/guardians, fellow educators and other school personnel, not to mention community members, is challenging! As already noted, our Center—in partnership with educational, mental health, family, student, and community leaders—developed a *School Climate Implementation Road Map* (http://www.schoolclimate.org/climate/roadmap.php). This *Road Map* is both text-based and web-based and includes detailed guidelines and tools (rubrics and protocols) designed to support school leaders doing just this.

NSCC has also developed a social forum within the *School Climate Resource Center* (http://scrc.schoolclimate.org/) designed to support educators learning from one another about just these kinds of challenges.

There are also many case studies that describe how principals as well as district leaders have done this, too (e.g., Hal Kwalwasser's recent 2012 *Renewal: Remaking America's Schools for the Twenty-First Century*).

4. Where can I learn about current state-level school climate policies and bullying prevention laws?

The National School Climate Center tracks and reports this information here: www.schoolclimate.org/climate/database.php.

The U.S. Department of Education also developed a listing of bullying prevention laws, as of 2010: http://www.stopbullying.gov/laws/index.html.

5. Are there district-level guidelines that support building and district as well as school board leaders learning more about school climate reform and models of helpful rules, supports, and policies?

The National School Climate Center, in partnership with a growing group of collaborators (e.g., State Departments of Education, the federally funded Equity Assistance Centers, State Safety Centers, Character Education Partnership, Special Olympics, ACLU, and others), are focused on *district-* and *school-level school climate policies,* so that those responsible for accountability and results as well as those responsible for day-to-day practice will have the support necessary to successfully integrate and sustain a school climate that leads to effective student development, achievement, and success. You can learn about these resources here as well, as information and guidelines about *the National School Climate Standards* (http://www.schoolclimate.org/climate/standards.php) and a *School Climate Guide for District Policymakers and Educational Leaders*: www.schoolclimate.org/climate/policy/distractguide.php.

6. Where can I learn about evidence-based prosocial (character education and social emotional learning) instructional programs?

Several centers have conducted reviews of prosocial curriculum. The Character Education Partnership (CEP) has published *What works in character education: A report for policy makers and opinion leaders.*[73] CEP also "harvests" and shares a growing array of instructional and other character education informed best practices from its famed *School of Character* program (http://www.character.org/schools-of-character/). The Collaborative for

Academic, Social and Emotional Learning (CASEL) includes very helpful guides to effective social emotional learning programs (http://casel.org/guide/).

In addition, the Institute for Educational Sciences publishes a "what works clearinghouse" that includes a range of independent evaluations for a wide range of educational efforts, including instructional programs: http://ies.ed.gov/ncee/wwc/.

7. Are there ways that classroom leaders can intentionally infuse social, emotional, and civic learning objectives, assessments, and activities into existing lesson plans and/or advisory activities?

Yes. A growing number of educators are using a backward design model of curriculum development to do just this. In the *School Climate Resource Center* (http://scrc.schoolclimate.org/) we have developed resources, guidelines, examples, and PowerPoints to support educators forming study groups (or working individually) to understand, practice, and share efforts to infuse prosocial education goals and activities into existing curriculum.

8. Are there forums where educational, parent/family, school boards, and others can learn from each other about effective bullying prevention and school climate reform efforts?

There are a number of forums. ASCD's *Edge* (http://ascdedge.ascd.org/), http://ascdedge.ascd.org/) and the National School Climate Resource Center's Connect (http://scrc.schoolclimate.org/connect) are two of many.

9. Is school climate reform really new? In many ways it seems like a combination of "what works" in school improvement efforts.

School climate reform is certainly *not* new. Educators have been thinking about and focused on school climate or the systematic as well as instructional aspects of school life for over 100 years. In addition, it is true that school climate reform efforts have increasingly learned from a variety of educational "what works" research efforts. In fact, one of the reasons school climate reform is increasingly highlighted is that there is such compelling empirical evidence that the following practices profoundly shape student development and learning as well as how safe and supportive the school is: (1) transparent, democratically informed *leadership*; (2) *engaging* students, parents, and (ideally) community members as well as school personnel to be co-learners and co-leaders in the improvement efforts (school–home–community partnerships); (3) *measurement practices* that recognize the social, emotional, and civic dimensions of learning and school life; (4) improvement *goals tailored* to the unique needs of the students and school community; (5) *adult learning* and professional learning communities that support capacity building; and (6) intentional and helpful prosocial learning and teaching.

Another terribly important educational research finding that supports school climate reform efforts is the growing realization that one of the most common challenges to any and all improvement efforts is fragmentation. Typically, principals and classroom leaders are involved in an array of improvement efforts. And too often, the "left hand" doesn't know what the "right hand" is doing. Coordinating improvement efforts is important! School climate reform efforts—whether they focus on promoting even safer and more supportive schools or literacy—are grounded in explicit processes and goals that support students, parents/guardians, school personnel, and, if possible, community members learning and working together.

10. How can school climate assessment and improvement contribute to school accountability?

School climate assessment—by definition—recognizes the social, emotional, and civic aspects of student learning and school life. Given how profoundly important these aspects of learning and school life are for both school and life success, school climate assessment and accountability systems will support educational leaders understanding even more how we are ensuring that our country will really NOT leave children behind.

It is also terribly important to consider—in general—to what extent accountability systems are used as a "hammer" or a "flashlight." Unfortunately, current accountability systems are often used punitively (like a hammer) and without appreciating the context and history of the school.

11. In what ways can state Departments of Education incorporate school climate into the education reform efforts?

There are two ways that state Departments of Education are incorporating school climate reform efforts into their goals and recommendations: Practice efforts and policy reform. On the one hand, in addition to the eleven states that were awarded federal Safe and Supportive School grants, a growing number of states are developing school climate surveys and supporting school climate improvement efforts.[80] On the other hand, a growing number of state Departments of Education as well as districts are considering adopting or adapting the National School Climate Standards. For example, the Connecticut and Georgia Departments of Education are both incorporating school climate assessment into their accountability systems and are considering adopting School Climate Standards (www.schoolclimate.org/climate/standards.php).

REFERENCES

1. Nansel TR, Overpeck M, Pilla RS, et al. Bullying behaviors among US youth: prevalence and association with psychosocial adjustment. *JAMA: Am Med Assoc.* Apr 25 2001; 285(16):2094–2100.

2. Arseneault L, Bowes L, Shakoor S. Bullying victimization in youths and mental health problems: 'Much ado about nothing'? *Psychol Med.* Vol 40. 2010:717–729.

3. Esbensen FAC, Carson DC. Consequences of being bullied: Results from a longitudinal assessment of bullying victimization in a multisite sample of American Students. *Youth Society.* 2009; 41(2):209–233.

4. Hawker DS, Boulton MJ. Twenty years' research on peer victimization and psychosocial maladjustment: a meta-analytic review of cross-sectional studies. *J Child Psychol Psychiatry, Allied Disciplines.* May 2000; 41(4):441–455.

5. Kim MJ, Catalano RF, Haggerty KP, Abbott RD. Bullying at elementary school and problem behaviour in young adulthood: a study of bullying, violence and substance use from age 11 to age 21. *Crim Behav Mental Health: CBMH.* April 2011; 21(2): 136–144.

6. Nishina A, Juvonen J, Witkow MR. Sticks and stones may break my bones, but names will make me feel sick: The psychosocial, somatic, and scholastic consequences of peer harassment. *J Clin Child Adolescent Psychology: The Official Journal for the Society of Clinical Child and Adolesc Psychol, American Psychological Association, Division 53.* March 2005; 34(1):37–48.

7. Winsper C, Lereya T, Zanarini M, Wolke D. Involvement in bullying and suicide-related behavior at 11 years: a prospective birth cohort study. *Am Acad Child Adolesc Psychiatry*. March 2012; 51(3):271–282 e273.

8. Cohen J, Espelage D, Twemlow SW, B et al. Rethinking effective bully and violence prevention effects: Promoting healthy school climates, positive youth development, and preventing bully–victim–bystander behavior *(in review)*.

9. Farrington DP, Ttofi MM, Coid JW. Development of adolescence-limited, late-onset, and persistent offenders from age 8 to age 48. *Aggress Behav*. 2009; 35(19172660):150–163.

10. Swearer SM, Espelage DL, Napolitano SA. *Bullying Prevention and Intervention: Realistic Strategies for Schools*. New York: Guilford Press; 2009.

11. Twemlow SW, Sacco FC. *Why School Antibullying Programs Don't Work*. Lanham, MD: Jason Aronson; 2008.

12. U. S Department of Education & the Department of Health and Human Services. *Prevention at School*. 2012. Available at www.stopbullying.gov/prevention/at-school/index.html.

13. DeVita MC, Colvin RL, Darling-Hammond L, Haycoc K. *Education Leadership: A Bridge to School Reform*. The Wallace Foundation; 2007.

14. Fullan M. *Choosing the Wrong Drivers for Whole System Reform*. Centre for Strategic Education; 2011. Available at http://www.michaelfullan.com/media/13501655630.pdf.

15. Mourshed M, Chijioke C, Barber M. *How the World's Most Improved School Systems Kkeep Ggetting Better*. New York: McKinsey & Company; 2010.

16. Centers for Disease Control and Prevention. *School Connectedness: Strategies for Increasing Protective Factors among Yyouth*. 2009. Available at www.cdc.gov/healthyyouth/adolescenthealth/pdf/connectedness.pdf. Accessed January 30, 2012.

17. Center for Disease Control and Prevention. *Understanding Bullying*. 2011. Available at www.google.com/url?sa=t&rct=j&q=&esrc=s&source=web&cd=3&ved=0CDgQFjAC&url=http%3A%2F%2Fwww.cdc.gov%2FViolencePrevention%2Fpdf%2FBullying_Factsheet-a.pdf&ei=LBtvT8SWAoTo0QGIwJH2Bg&usg=AFQjCNFb2LhyGBYwTS3QbbWKU7HwU-SlmQ. Accessed January 30, 2012.

18. Leithwood K, Louis KS, Anderson S, Wahlstrom K. *Review of Research: How Leadership Influences Student Learning.* Center for Applied Research and Educational Improvement, University of Minnesota and the Ontario Institute for Studies in Education, University of Toronto; 2004.

19. Cohen J, McCabe M, Michelli N, & Pickeral T. School climate: Research, policy, teacher education and practice. *Teachers Coll Rec.* 2009; 111(1):180–213.

20. Perry AC. *The Management of a City School.* New York: The Macmillan Company; 1908.

20a. Cohen J. Measuring and improving school climate: A pro-social strategy that recognizes, educates and supports the whole child and the whole school community. In: Brown P, Corrigian MW, Higgens-D'Allessandro, editors. *The Handbook of Prosocial Education.* Roman & Littlefield; 2012.

21. Anderson C. The search for school climate: A reivew of the research. *Rev Educ Res.* 1982; 52(3):368–420.

22. Carter SC. *On Purpose: How Great School Cultures Form Strong Character.* Thousand Oaks, CA: Corwin Press; 2011.

23. Comer JP. *Leave No Child Behind: Preparing Today's Youth for Tomorrow's World.* New Haven, CT: Yale University Press; 2005.

24. Deal TE, Peterson KD. *Shaping School Culture: Pitfalls, Paradoxes, and Promises.* 2nd ed. San Francisco: Jossey-Bass; 2009.

25. Freiberg HJ. *School Climate: Measuring, Improving, and Sustaining Healthy Learning Environments.* London; Philadelphia: Falmer Press; 1999.

26. National School Climate Council. *School Climate.* http://www.schoolclimate.org/climate/. Accessed April 12, 2013.

27. National School Climate Center, The school climate improvement process: Essential elements. School Climate Brief 4; 2012. http://www.schoolclimate.org/climate/documents/policy/sc-brief-v4.pdf, p. 2.

28. Berkowitz MW. Leading schools of character. In: Blankstein AM, Houston PD, editors. *Leadership for Social Justice and Democracy in Our Schools: The Soul of Educational Leadership Series.* Vol 9. Thousand Oaks, CA: Corwin; 2011:93–121.

29. DuFour R, Eaker R. *Professional Learning Communities at Work: Best Practices for Enhancing Student Achievement.* Bloomington IN: National Educational Service; 1998.

30. Morton M, Montgomery P. Youth empowerment programs for improving self-efficacy and self-esteem of adolescents. *Campbell Syst Rev.* 2011; 5.

31. Pomerantz E, Moorman E, Litwack S. The how, whom, and why of parents' involvement in children's academic lives: More is not always better. *Rev Educ Res.* 2007; 77(3):373–410.

32. Sheldon S, Van Voorhis F. Partnership programs in U.S. schools: Their development and relationship to family involvement outcomes. *Sch Effectiveness Sch Improvement.* 2004; 15(2):125–148.

33. Cohen J, McCabe L, Michelli NM, Pickeral T. School climate: Research, policy, practice, and Teacher education. *Teach Coll Rec* 2009; 111(1):180–213.

34. Polanin JR, Espelage DL, Pigott TD. A meta-analysis of school-based bulling prevention programs' effects on bystander intervention behavior. *Sch Psychol Rev.* 2012; 41(1):47–65.

35. McCabe D, Trevino LK. Honor codes and other contextual influences on academic integrity: A replication and extension to modified honor code settings. *Res Higher Educ.* 2002; 43(3):357–378.

36. Davis S, Darling-Hammond L, LaPointe M, Meyerson D. *School Leadership Study: Developing Successful Principals.* Stanford, CA: Stanford University, Stanford Educational Leadership Institute; 2005.

37. Giles C, Hargreaves A. The sustainability of innovative schools as learning organizations and professional learning communities during standardized reform. *Educ Admin.* 2006; 4(1):124–156.

38. Hawley W, Valli L. The essentials of effective professional development. In: Darling-Hammond L, Sykes G, editors. *Teaching as the Learning Profession: Handbook of Policy and Practice.* San Francisco, CA: Jossey-Bass; 1999.

39. Stein MK, Smith MS, Silver E. The development of professional developers: Learning to assist teachers in new settings in new ways. *Harv Educ Rev.* 1999; 69(3):237–269.

40. Vescio V, Ross D, Adams A. A review of research on the impact of professional learning communities on teaching practice and student learning. *Teaching Teacher Educ.* 2008; 24(1):80–91.

41. Brown PM, Corrigan MW, Higgins-D'Alessandro A. *Handbook of Prosocial Education*. Lanham, MD: Rowman & Littlefield Publishers, Inc.; 2012.

42. Durlak JA, Weissberg RP, Dymnicki AB, et al. The impact of enhancing students' social and emotional learning: a meta-analysis of school-based universal interventions. *Child Dev.* Jan–Feb 2011; 82(1):405–432.

43. Thapa A, Cohen J, Higgins-D'Alessandro A, Guffey S. A review of school climate research. *Rev Educ Res.* In press.

44. Dynarski M, Clarke L, Cobb B, et al. *Dropout Prevention: A Practice Guide (NCEE 2008-4025)*. Washington, DC: National Center for Education Evaluation and Regional Assistance, Institute of Education Sciences, U.S. Department of Education; 2008.

45. National Center on Safe Supportive Learning Environments. Safe Supportive Learning. Available at safesupportiveschools.ed.gov/index.php?id=01. Accessed April 13, 2013.

46. National School Climate Council. *School Climate Improvement (SCI) Formative Self-Study Tool (verson 2.0)*. New York; 2011.

47. Slaby RG, Wilson-Brewer Re, Dash K. *Aggressors, Victims, and Bystanders: Thinking and Acting to Prevent Violence*. Newton, MA: Education Development Center; 1994.

48. Twemlow SW, Sacco FC. *Preventing Bullying and School Violence*. 1st ed. Washington, DC: American Psychiatric Pub.; 2012.

49. Twemlow SW, Fonagy P, Sacco FC, et al. Improving the social and intellectual climate in elementary schools by addressing bully-victim-bystander power struggles. In: Cohen J, editor. *Caring Classrooms/Intelligent Schools: The Social Emotional Education of Young Children*. New York: Teachers College Press; 2001:162–182.

50. Devine J, Cohen J. *Making Your School Safe: Strategies to Protect Children and Promote Learning*. New York: Teachers College Press; 2007.

51. Hord SM, Association for Supervision and Curriculum Development. *Taking Charge of Change*. Alexandria, VA: Association for Supervision and Curriculum Development; 1987.

52. Bryk A, Sebring P, Allensworth E, et al. *Organizing Schools for Improvement: Lessons from Chicago*. Chicago: University of Chicago Press; 2012.

53. Bryk AS, Schneider L. *Trust in Schools: A Core Resrouce for Improvement*. New York: Russell Sage Foundation Publications; 2002.

54. Quaglia Institute for Student Aspirations (2010). *My Voice National Student Report* (Grades 6–12). Available at: www.qisa.org/publications/reports.jsp. Accessed August 15, 2011.

55. M.E. H, K.C. B, AM. V. *Measuring Bullying Victimization, Perpetration, and Bystander Experiences: A Compendium of Assessment Tools*. Atlanta, GA: Centers for Disease Control and Prevention, National Center for Injury Prevention and Control; 2011.

56. Henderson AT. *Beyond the Bake Sale: The Essential Guide to Family–School Partnerships*. New York: The New Press; 2007.

57. Patrikakou EN, Anderson AR. *School–Family Partnerships for Children's Success*. New York: Teachers College Press; 2005.

58. Weissberg RP, Kumpfer KL, Seligman ME. Prevention that works for children and youth. An introduction. *The American Psychologist*. Jun–Jul 2003; 58(6–7):425–432.

59. Adelman HS, Taylor L. *The School Leader's Guide to Student Learning Supports: New Directions for Addressing Barriers to Learning*. Thousand Oaks, CA: Corwin Press; 2006.

60. Berg A, Melaville A, Blank MC. *Community and Family Engagement: Principals Share What Works*. Washington, DC: The Coalition for Community Schools, Institute for Educational Leadership; 2006.

61. Putnam R. Community-based social capital and educational performance. In: Viteritti DRJP, editor. *In Making Good Citizens: Education and Civil Society*. New Haven, CT: Yale University Press; 2001.

62. Renée M, McAlister S. *The Strengths and Challenges of Community Organizing as an Education Reform Strategy: What the Research Says.* Quincy, MA: Annenberg Institute for School Reform, Brown University; 2011.

63. Piscatelli J, Lee C. *State Policies on School Climate and Bully Prevention Efforts: Challenges and Opportunities for Deepening State Policy Support for Safe and Civil Schools (A School Climate Brief).* New York: National School Climate Center; 2011.

64. Ciolfi AA, Shin C, Harris J. *Educate Every Child: Promoting Positive Solutions to School Discipline in Virginia.* Charlottesville, VA: Legal Aid Justice Center; 2011.

65. American Psychological Association. *Bullying.* 2006. Available at http://www.apa.org/about/index.aspx.

66. National School Climate Council. *National School Climate Standards: Benchmarks to Promote Effective Teaching, Learning and Comprehensive School Improvement.* New York: Center for Social and Emotional Education; 2009.

67. Eyman W, Cohen J. *Breaking the Bully–Victim–Passive Bystander Tool Kit: Creating a Climate for Learning and Responsibility.* New York: National School Climate Center; 2009.

68. Cohen J. *Educating Minds and Hearts: Social Emotional Learning and the Passage into Adolescence.* New York: Teachers College Press; 1999.

69. Cohen JB, Janniger CK, Piela Z, et al. Dermatologic correlates of selected metabolic events. *J Med.* 1999; 30(17312668):149–156.

70. Elias MJ. Strategies to infuse social and emotional learning into academics. In: Zins J, Weissburg RW, Wang MC, and Walberg H, editors. *Building School Success on Social Emotional Learning: What Does the Research Say?* New York: Teachers College Press; 2004:113–134.

71. Cohen J. Social, emotional, ethical an academic education: Creating a climate for learning, participation in democracy and well-being. *Harv Educ Rev.* 2006; 76(2):201–237.

72. Zins J, Weissberg RW, Wang MC, Walberg H. *Building School Success on Social Emotional Learning: What Does the Research Say?* New York: Teachers College Press; 2004.

73. Berkowitz MW, Bier M. *What works in character education: A report for policy makers and opinion leaders.* 2005.

74. Wager T. *The Making of Young People Who Will Change the World.* New York: Scribner/Simon and Schuster; 2012.

76. Ttofi M, Farrington D. What works in preventing bullying: Effective elements of anti-bullying programmes. *J Aggression, Conflict Peace Res.* 2009; 1:13–24.

77. Clifford M, Menon R, Condon C. *Measuring School Climate for Gauging Principal Performance: A Review of the Validity and Reliability of Publicly Accessible Measures.* Washington, DC: American Institutes for Research; 2012.

78. Haggerty K, Elgin J, Woolley A. *Social-emotional Learning Assessment Measures for Middle School Youth.* Seattle: Social Development Research Group; 2011.

79. Gangi TA. *School Climate and Faculty Relationships: Choosing an Effective Assessment Measure.* 2010.

80. Webb JA. U.S. Department of Education Awards $38.8 Million in Safe and Supportive School Grants. October 5, 2010. Available at http://www.ed.gov/news/press-releases/us-department-education-awards-388-million-safe-and-supportive-school-grants. Accessed April 13, 2013.

3

Why Should We Care About Bullying? The Social and Mental Health Consequences of Bullying

Gianluca Gini, PhD

Objectives

1. To identify the social consequences for bullies and victims.
2. To recognize the factors that moderate/mediate the expression of these consequences.
3. To link social consequences of bullying to intervention (e.g., how can knowledge about consequences inform effective intervention?).

Several years ago, I met a middle-school teacher who was the warm and caring father of an eight-year-old daughter. We were talking about the issue of bullying and he shared his own experience with me. One day, he found the drawings of his daughter. He immediately noticed that they looked somewhat different from her usual drawings. There were a lot of people on the sheets. However, none of them had a face: they were all looking the other way. This looked quite strange to him. Some days later, he found another drawing, with the words: *At school I have no one. At school I do not exist.* These were written with an eight-year-old hand.

Every time I talk about the negative effects of peer bullying experiences on victimized kids, I cannot help thinking back to those words.

INTRODUCTION

Aggressive behavior during childhood and adolescence has been studied for several decades, is the most common reason for youth referrals to psychiatric services, and is predictive of later maladjustment. One of the most pervasive and harmful forms of aggression among peers is bullying. Compared to the long tradition of studies about aggressive behavior, however, bullying research is a relatively new area of focus.

Though the amount of studies on this topic has increased tremendously during the last two decades, it is startling to see to what extent popular assumptions and mass media's imagination on bullying still diverge from the empirical findings on prevalence, risk factors, and consequences of this phenomenon. Therefore, it is important that clinicians, school psychologists, teachers, educators, and all adults who work daily with children and parents better understand what bullying really is and recognize its negative consequences on children's and adolescents' lives to be more motivated to intervene promptly and efficaciously. To this end, this chapter briefly reviews the literature about the main psychosocial consequences of school bullying.

IS SCHOOL BULLYING A REAL PROBLEM?

Prevalence figures of bullying behavior appear to vary somewhat across countries. Olweus[1] assessed bullying in a sample of 130,000 Norwegian children aged 7 to 16 and found out that between 5% and 9% of students reported being bullied on a regular basis. Similarly, surveying more than 15,000 adolescents in the United States, Nansel and colleagues found that 8% bullied others and 9% were bullied by peers (once a week or more).[2] In the United Kingdom, Whitney and Smith reported that, among 2,623 students aged 8 to 11, 4% declared they had bullied others "once a week or more," while 10% reported being victimized[3]; in a survey of 4,700 pupils aged 11 to 16, 7% of students reported being involved either as bullies or as victims of repeated bullying.[4] In Italy, data from a representative sample of 4,386 11- to 15-year-old students showed a prevalence rate of 9% for bullying others (at least two or three times a month) and 6.7% for being bullied.[5] Between 3% and 4% of the sample reported both experiences (being bullied and bullying others). In a sample of more than 25,000 Australian students, reported that one in seven children experienced bullying at least once a week.[6]

Direct comparisons among countries are still limited. One of the largest cross-national study on prevalence of bullying has been published by Due and colleagues,[7] who compared prevalence rates from nationally representative samples of 11- to 15 year-olds in 28 Western countries participating in the Heath Behavior in School-Aged Children study—HBSC (surveying over 4,000 students per country on average). Overall, 18% of boys and 15% of girls reported being bullied. Recently, a total of 202,056 students from 40 countries participated in the 2005/06 HBSC survey.[8] Of these, 10.7% reported bullying others and 12.6% reported being bullied two or three times a month or more. A smaller percentage of students (3.6%) reported dual involvement (both bullying others and being bullied).

In sum, notwithstanding differences across studies, after more than 20 years of research it is now clear that victims of bullying are a substantial minority of the student population (between 5% to 20% of pupils), and bullies are a smaller minority (between 2% to 20%).

WHY DOES SCHOOL BULLYING MATTER?

In my experience working with teachers and parents, one of the most frequent questions about this phenomenon regards its relevance. Why should we be interested in the occurrence of bullying? Is it really a problem? The most simple answer is yes, because bullying is harmful. Although the effects of bullying are not fully known yet, a substantial body of evidence so far has documented the negative consequences of bullying on targets, perpetrators, bystanders, and, to some extent, the whole school community. However, there are few topics in which the clash between popular beliefs and scientific findings is as blatant as that regarding the consequences of bullying.

For a long time, being the victim of bullying has been considered an unpleasant yet normal experience, one that is frequently encountered by students when they enroll in the formal school system. However, far from being a conflictual interaction that teaches negotiation or helps people become tougher, bullying is neither inevitable nor beneficial; in contrast, it can be very harmful and is a significant risk factor for youths' behavioral adjustment and psychosocial well-being. Sometimes, the consequences can be dramatic: analyzing school shootings, the U.S. Secret Service discovered that 71% of the shooters had been victims of peer violence at school.[9] Most of the time, the consequences of involvement in bullying cover a wide range of psychosocial problems—both internalized and externalized ones.

Consequences of bullying can be divided into different categories: consequences for the physical health of children (see Chapter 5), social/behavioral consequences, and consequences for children's mental health and psychological well-being.

Social and Behavioral Consequences

Frequent bullying at school is a risk factor for a variety of concurrent and long-term problems at the behavioral and social level for all children involved, even though, compared to bullied children, the negative consequences for the bullies may not be immediately obvious because they often seem unscathed, at least during (early) adolescence. However, both being bullying and bullying others are associated with poor social and academic adjustment (including decreased appreciation of school, lower grade point averages (GPAs), and increased absenteeism and drop out), as well as greater risk of drug and alcohol abuse, carrying weapons to school, and involvement in fighting.

Moreover, particularly bullies are at increased risk for a variety of antisocial, violent, and criminal behavior. For example, Eron and colleagues showed that bullies identified by age 8 had about a one in four chance of having a criminal record by age 30 compared to other children, whose chance was 1 in 20.[10] Similarly, follow-up studies in Norway indicated that, of those originally identified as bullies in the sixth to the ninth grades, 70% were convicted of at least one crime by age 24.[11] Because antisocial and criminal acts begin early in adolescence and are extremely stable over time, bullying prevention may be considered a critical aspect of crime prevention at the societal level.

There are two main reasons for the fact that bullying predicts later offending. First, bullying and offending may both be symptoms of the same underlying theoretical construct, such as antisocial tendency, which persists over time and has different behavioral manifestations at different ages. If so, bullying would not predict offending after controlling for an earlier behavioral measure of antisocial tendency. The second possibility is that bullying actually increases the likelihood of later violent offending. This could occur, for example, if bullying was an earlier stage in a developmental sequence leading to offending, and if progress to each stage increased the probability of progressing to the next stage. A recent longitudinal study supports the latter hypothesis, by showing that bullying at age

14 predicted later life outcomes, especially violent convictions at age 15–20, self-reported violence at age 15–18, drug use at age 27–32, and an unsuccessful life at age 48.[12] Interestingly, these results held up after controlling for numerous childhood explanatory and behavioral risk factors. Overall, these findings suggest that bullying specifically predicts violent offending, and that interventions that decrease bullying would most likely be followed by decreases in violent offending, drug use, and unsuccessful lives.

Another area that is receiving increasing attention in recent years is the possible comorbidity of bullying and substance use starting from early adolescence. For example, a recent study was conducted on this topic with a representative sample of Italian middle and high school students (aged 13–15).[13] A significant association between different forms of bullying (including physical, verbal, relational, sexual, racist, and cyberbullying) and smoking and drinking consistently emerged. These findings clearly showed that all children involved (as either bullies, victims, or bully-victims) are at increased risk for both tobacco and alcohol use than their uninvolved peers. Similarly, a recent survey on about 78,000 adolescents living in Ohio showed that students who bully their classmates are more likely than other students to use cigarettes, alcohol, and marijuana at least once a month.[14] For example, marijuana use was reported by only 1.6% of middle school students not involved in bullying, compared with 11.4% of bullies and 6.1% of bully victims; in high school, marijuana use was reported by 13.3% of students not involved in bullying, compared with 31.7% of bullies and 29.2% of bully victims. Similar results were found for alcohol and cigarette use.

Percentages, however, tell only part of the story; the statistically higher-than-expected levels of substance use among bullies and bully victims suggest a relationship between experimenting with substances and engaging in bullying behavior. It appears that engaging in one deviant behavior increases the likelihood of engaging in another.

A possible explanation for the positive association between bullying and substance use may be related to bullies' desire to gain social status and to be perceived by peers as cool and attractive. During adolescence, smoking and drinking indeed contribute to the social image of the individual within the peer group and can be well used for this purpose. Moreover, adolescents within the same peer context tend to socialize each other's (anti)social attitudes and behavior and share problem behaviors, a phenomenon known as *homophily*.

The two commonly used explanations for homophily are selection and socialization. Selection effects refer to the tendency of young people to affiliate with peers who exhibit attitudes or behaviors similar to their own. Socialization effects, by contrast, refer to the process by which youths' behavior may be affected by their affiliation with other peers, so that similarity between members grows over time as a result of peer influence. There is consistent evidence that supports selection and socialization effects for a wide variety of behaviors, including delinquency, violence, antisocial behavior, risky sexual behavior, substance use, weight-related behaviors, and suicidal behavior. Interestingly, similar selection and/or socialization effects have been demonstrated for prosocial behaviors and health-promoting behaviors, such as charity work, altruism, or fitness exercises.

Finally, the associations between bullying and substance use fit with the *problem behavior syndrome*,[15] according to which adolescents involved in one problem behavior (e.g., antisocial behavior) are more likely to be involved in others (e.g., substance use) simultaneously. More in general, bullying may be linked to substance use via a developmental model of antisocial behavior. This model suggests that antisocial behavior, including substance use and use-related behavior, is a persistent display of behavior that begins in early childhood and evolves and further exacerbates in severity over time.[16] Therefore, bullying might be considered a marker by which school psychologists, school staff, and parents may be able to identify both current and potential adolescents involved in substance use and abuse, and other negative behavior as well. In a broader perspective, a higher prevalence of one type of problem behavior at the school/community level may be considered a sign for potential presence of other problem behaviors within the same population of adolescents.

Increasing awareness on the frequent co-occurrence of bullying and substance use may have important implications. Despite its potential risk for adolescents' health, substance use is often more difficult to detect for adults than other externalizing behavior. Consequently, our capacity to intervene promptly in such situations may be limited. Research results suggest students involved in bullying be considered a good target for selective prevention programs for current and potential smokers and drinkers starting from middle school (however, in such cases the risk for so-called *deviancy training* should always be seriously considered). In other words, involvement in bullying might represent a warning signal for the co-occurrence of other problem behavior meriting further investigation. Furthermore, in accordance with studies that demonstrate the importance of using adequate campaign in preventing substance use,[17] professionals working on substance use prevention should take into account the differences among groups of "vulnerable youths" (e.g., bullies, victims, and bully-victims) that may differ from each other and from their uninvolved peers on some relevant psychosocial characteristics. At the same time, from a broader perspective, working on bullying prevention and health promotion can contribute validly to tackling other problem behavior, such as substance abuse.

Mental Health Problems

Bullying during childhood and adolescence also has negative consequences in the psychological domain especially because of the relative stability over time of this traumatizing experience. Moreover, victimization often goes unreported and adults fail to intervene adequately.

Compared to nonvictimized peers, bullied children show many psychological problems, such as anxiety and stress, low self-esteem and self-worth, depressive symptoms, loneliness, and self-blame. Unfortunately, the majority of evidence supporting an association between experiences of being bullied and mental health problems is either concurrent or within a short timespan. This raises the possibility that symptoms of mental health problems are temporary and disappear when the bullying stops. A few studies, to date, have examined the long-term outcomes of being bullied in childhood and adolescence. Overall, these studies report that bullied children show adjustment problems also in late adolescence and in adulthood.

A recent meta-analysis has examined the prospective relations between peer victimization and psychological maladjustment in children, as indexed by internalizing problems[i] (i.e., depression, anxiety, withdrawal, and loneliness).[18] Importantly, only longitudinal studies that followed the same group of children over two or more points in time were included. This quantitative review showed that, after controlling for internalizing problems at baseline, peer victimization at

---

[i]The term *internalizing problems* mainly refers to emotional problems associated with negative life experiences and difficulties using adaptive coping strategies and regulating negative emotions. Internalizing problems may manifest as shy or withdrawn behavior, frequent worrying, self-denigrating comments, and low self-confidence. Internalizing problems, unless severe, may not be apparent to others and can include exaggerated feelings of guilt, negative beliefs such as believing one is a failure or perceiving that one is not loved, and experiencing other troubling emotions and thoughts.

time 1 was significantly associated with higher levels of internalizing problems at follow-up. However, the reverse path of internalizing problems leading to subsequent changes in peer victimization was also significant, thus suggesting that internalizing problems also maintain and solidify children's standing as a victim of peer harassment, as opposed to only being a consequence of peer victimization.

Along the same line, another meta-analysis focused on the link between peer victimization and later depression,[19] by summarizing the results from 29 longitudinal studies, and reported that victims of bullying are two times more likely to report depression later in life compared to noninvolved students, even after controlling for several potential confounders. This analysis has therefore confirmed that bullying victimization is a major childhood risk factor that uniquely contributes to later depression.

Important results on this issue can also come from genetically informed research based on monozygotic (MZ) twin pairs. Because MZ twins are genetically identical, variation in the outcome cannot result from genetic variation between the twins. In addition, because some environmental experiences shared by twins are necessarily constant within a pair, shared environmental factors cannot account for the differences in the outcome variable either. Findings from a cohort study of MZ twins indicated that the variation in the experience of being bullied was significantly associated with variation in children's internalizing problems at age 10.[20] Twins who had been bullied had more internalizing problems compared to their co-twins who had not been bullied, and this difference remained significant even after controlling for internalizing problems assessed when the twins were aged 5 years—that is, prior to being bullied. Therefore, this study provided strong support for a causal effect of peer victimization on children's internalizing problems.

Furthermore, both bullies and victims are at risk for psychiatric disorders. For example, in a review of empirical studies, Salmon et al. found that being bullied was frequently a factor influencing the referral of adolescents to psychiatric services[21]; moreover children victims of bullying show increased rates of psychotic symptoms later on.[22] Furthermore, studies have observed a dose–response relation between the frequency of bullying victimization and levels of psychotic symptoms.[23] These findings suggest that detrimental effects of bullying on individuals' mental health may extend to delusions and auditory and visual hallucinations. Repeated victimization may be also associated with clinically significant levels of posttraumatic stress symptomathology.[24,25]

Finally, being repeatedly bullied has been associated with an increased risk for suicidal ideation, suicidal attempts, and self-injurious behavior.[26] Suicidality, which is the third leading cause of mortality for adolescents,[27] has been found to be related to all bullying types, both in general populations of children and adolescents and in particularly at-risk groups, such as lesbian, gay, bisexual, and transgendered youths. Longitudinally, the victims' risk for suicidal ideation is exacerbated by parental internalizing disorders and feelings of rejection at home.[28] This suggests that family factors may interact in influencing victims' adjustment. In sum, not only does bullying interfere with normal developmental and educational processes but also places adolescents at an additional risk for suicidal thoughts and actions.[26] In this respect, we suggest the inclusion of screening and monitoring of suicidal signs and symptoms for students in anti-bullying programs as a strategy to prevent suicidality in the pupils with bullying experience. Symptoms include anxiety or depression, ongoing sadness, severe agitation, loss of interest in activities they used to enjoy, hopelessness, and persistent thoughts about the possibility of something bad happening. Finally, careful clinical evaluation for suicidality in children and adolescents with bullying experience should be a standard practice that is part of routine primary care visits.

CONCLUSIONS

The literature on the psychosocial adjustment of children and adolescents involved in bullying shows both similarities and differences between bullies and victims. For example, both groups of children are characterized by academic problems and poor emotional adjustment. However, while victims more often report internalizing problems, such as low self-esteem, withdrawal, depression, and anxiety, bullies usually show more externalizing problems, especially substance use, antisocial behavior, and violence. Potential negative consequences are also associated with bullying for students who do not fall into the "typical roles" of bullies and victims. When classmates who are bullies or victims are affected, then everyone's education suffers. Witnessing peer victimization within school is indeed associated with a low sense of safety at school, more negative perceptions of school climate and decreased school engagement. Bystanders are also at risk of an increase in daily feelings of anxiety and school aversion. Thus, even when students are seemingly not directly involved in bullying, they may be negatively impacted in ways that can impede the learning process. In general, schools with a high prevalence of bullying may have students who are less engaged, less able to concentrate during curricular activities, and more prone to school avoidance.

Despite the documented association between bullying and maladjustment, not all children are at the same risk for developing behavioral and mental health problems. Some children seem to be resilient against high-risk environment. To explain this adaptive success, protective factors have to be considered. According to the literature, among the many protective factors that can be identified, parental and school support play important protective roles in children and adolescent development and well-being. Supportive parent–child relationships, characterized by parental warmth, supervision, support, and involvement, are a widely cited factor shown to protect children from adverse life experiences and to reduce externalizing behavior. Similarly, attachment to school and sense of belonging are related to better health, to lower levels of problem behavior, and to higher participation in extracurricular activities. Furthermore, positive class-room management based on teacher support, empathy, and active listening tend to model socially competent behavior in the classroom, and school support may also compensate for a lack of parental support, possibly also protecting against the impacts of risk factors like peer victimization.

Finally, peer support is another important protective factor against both bullying victimization and negative psychosocial outcomes, whereas school-children who have none or few friends and report low levels of support and help from peers are at a heightened risk for repeated victimization. This indicates the need for including peer support systems into bullying prevention initiatives. These systems involve training peers to work toward preventing and intervening in bullying behavior in their schools. Typically, these programs implement different aspects of peer support, such as everyday support and befriending, and peer counseling or mentoring in one-to-one relationships.

FREQUENTLY ASKED QUESTIONS

1. How frequent is bullying?

Figures vary somewhat across countries and even schools. However, it is estimated that around 5% to 20% of students are victims of bullying, and about 2% to 20% are bullies.

2. What are the major consequences of bullying for children's health?

Children frequently involved in bullying can experience a variety of problems, including physical health, behavioral, and mental health problems.

3. What are the most important risks for children/adolescents who bully?

Compared to nonaggressive age-mates, bullies are at increased risk for substance abuse, as well as a variety of antisocial, violent, and criminal behavior.

4. Why is bullying related to substance use in adolescence?

A possible explanation for the positive association between bullying and substance use may be related to bullies' desire to gain social status and to be perceived by peers as cool and attractive. During adolescence, smoking and drinking contribute to the social image of the individual within the peer group and can be well used for this purpose. Moreover, adolescents within the same peer context tend to socialize each other's (anti)social attitudes and behavior and share problem behaviors.

5. What are the most common mental health problems for bullied children?

Compared to nonvictimized children, bullied children are more likely to develop anxiety and stress, low self-esteem and self-worth, depressive symptoms, loneliness, and self-blame.

6. How serious can be mental health consequences of bullying?

A minority of both bullies and victims are at risk for psychiatric disorders, including psychosis, delusions, and auditory and visual hallucinations. Repeated victimization can be also associated with clinically significant levels of posttraumatic stress symptomatology. Finally, being repeatedly bullied has been associated with an increased risk for suicidal ideation, suicidal attempts, and self-injurious behavior.

7. Does bullying have negative consequences for others, apart from bullies and victims?

Merely witnessing bullying within school can be associated with negative outcomes, such as low sense of safety at school, more negative perceptions of school climate, and decreased school engagement. Bystanders are also at risk for an increase in daily feelings of anxiety and school aversion. In general, schools with a high prevalence of bullying may have students who are less engaged, less able to concentrate during curricular activities, and more prone to school avoidance.

REFERENCES

1. Olweus D. Bully/victim problems among schoolchildren: Basic facts and effects of a school based intervention program. In D Pepler, K Rubin, editors. *The Development and Treatment of Childhood Aggression.* Hillsdale, NJ: Erlbaum; 1991:411–438.

2. Nansel TR, Overpeck M, Pilla RS, et al. Bullying behaviors among US youth: prevalence and association with psychosocial adjustment. *JAMA.* 2001; 285:2094–2100.

3. Whitney I, Smith PK. A survey of the nature and extent of bullying in junior/middle and secondary schools. *Edu Res.* 1993; 35:3–25.

4. Glower D, Gough G, Johnson M, Cartwright N. Bullying in 25 secondary schools: Incidence, impact and intervention. *Edu Res,* 2000; 42, 141–156.

5. Nation M, Vieno A, Perkins DD, Santinello M. Bullying in school and adolescent sense of empowerment: An analysis of relationships with parents, friends, and teachers. *J Community Appl Social Psychol.* 2008; 18:211–232.

6. Rigby K. *Bullying in Australian Schools—And What to Do About It.* London: Jessica Kingsley; 1997.

7. Due P, Holstein BE, Lynch J, et al. Bullying and symptoms among school-aged children: International comparative cross sectional study in 28 countries. *Eur J Public Health.* 2005; 15(2):128–132.

8. Currie C, Gabhainn SN, Godeau E, et al. (eds.). *Inequalities in young people's health: HBSC international report from the 2005/2006 Survey.* Health Policy for Children and Adolescents, No. 5. Copenhagen, WHO Regional Office for Europe; 2008.

9. Vossekuil B, Fein RA, Reddy M, et al. *The Final Report and Findings of the Safe School Initiative: Implications for the Prevention of School Attacks in the United States.* Washington, DC: U.S. Secret Service and U.S. Department of Education; 2002.

10. Eron LD, Huesmann LR, Dubow E, et al. Aggression and its correlates over 22 years. In D Crowell, I Evans, editors. *Childhood Aggression and Violence: Sources of Influence, Prevention, and Control.* New York: Plenum; 1987: 249–262.

11. Olweus D. Bully/victim problems at school: Facts and intervention. *Eur J Psychol Edu.* 1997; 12:495–510.

12. Farrington DP, Ttofi MM. Bullying as a predictor of offending, violence and later life outcomes. *Crim Behav Mental Health.* 2011; 21, 90–98.

13. Vieno A, Gini G, Santinello M. Different forms of bullying and their association to smoking and drinking behavior in Italian adolescents. *J Sch Health.* 2011; 81:389–395.

14. Radliff KM, Wheaton JE, Robinson K, Morris J. Illuminating the relationship between bullying and substance use among middle and high school youth. *Addict Behav.* 2012; 37:569–572.

15. Willoughby T, Chalmers H, Busseri M. Where is the syndrome? Where is the risk? Co-occurrence among multiple "problem" behaviors in adolescence. *J Consul Clin Psychol.* 2004; 72:1022–1037.

16. Moffit TE. Life-course-persistent and adolescent-limited antisocial behavior: A 10-year research review and a research agenda. In BB Lahey, TE Moffitt, A Caspi, editors. *Causes of Conduct Disorder and Juvenile Delinquency.* New York: Guilford Press; 2003: 50–55.

17. Crano WD, Siegel JT, Alvaro E, et al. Overcoming adolescents' resistance to anti-inhalant appeals. *Psychol Addict Behav.* 2007; 21:516–524.

18. Reijntjes AHA, Kamphuis JH, Prinzie P, Telch MJ. Peer victimization and internalizing problems in children: A meta-analysis of longitudinal studies. *Child Abuse Negl.* 2010; 34:244–252.

19. Ttofi MM, Farrington DP, Losel F, Loeber R. The predictive efficiency of school bullying versus later offending: A systematic/meta-analytic review of longitudinal studies. *Crim Behav Mental Health.* 2011; 21:80–89.

20. Arseneault L, Milne BJ, Taylor A, et al. Being bullied as an environmentally mediated contributing factor to children's internalizing problems. *Arch Pediatr Adolesc Med.* 2008; 162:145–150.

21. Salmon G, James A, Cassidy EL, Javaloyes MA. Bullying a review: Presentations to an adolescent psychiatric service and within a school for emotionally and behaviourally disturbed children. *Clin Child Psychol Psychiatry.* 2000; 5:563–579.

22. Schreier A, Wolke D, Thomas K, et al. Prospective study of peer victimization in childhood and psychotic symptoms in a nonclinical population at age 12 years. *Arch Gen Psychiatry.* 2009; 66(5):527–536.

23. Campbell MLC, Morrison, AP. The relationship between bullying, psychotic-like experiences and appraisals in 14- to 16-year-olds. *Behav Res Ther.* 2007; 45:1579–1591.

24. Mynard H, Joseph S, Alexander J. Peer victimization and posttraumatic stress in adolescents. *Personality Indiv Diff.* 2000; 29:815–821.

25. Storch EA, Esposito LE. Peer victimization and posttraumatic stress among children. *Child Study J.* 2003; 33:91–98.

26. Kim YS, Leventhal B. Bullying and suicide. A review. *Int J Adolesc Med Health.* 2008; 20:133–154.

27. Grunbaum J, Kann L, Kinchen S, et al. Youth risk behavior surveillance—United States, 2001. *MMWR Surveill Summ.* 2002; 51(4):1–62.

28. Herba CM, Ferdinand RF, Stijnen T, et al. Victimisation and suicide ideation in the trails study: Specific vulnerabilities of victims. *J Child Psychol Psychiatry.* (2008); 49, 867–876.

4

Practical Implications of Bullying for the School Administrator

James A. Bozigar, ACSW, LCSW

Objectives

1. To discuss the impact of various types of bullying on the mental health of youth.
2. To review the long-term mental health implications of bullying on youth.
3. To identify strategies that school officials can utilize to decrease the mental health impact of bullying in schools.
4. To identify the specific issues associated with students who are lesbian, gay, bisexual or transgendered (LGBT) and their risks of bullying and the sequelae that affect mental health.

MENTAL HEALTH ISSUES

This chapter examines the impact of bullying on students' mental health, and provides suggestions for minimizing them. Suicidal behavior connected to bullying is of particular concern and so the most recent information on this specific issue will be reviewed. At the end of this chapter, there is an appendix with a suggested format for interviewing students involved in bullying behaviors and recommendations on handling these situations.

Research on the connection between bullying and students' mental health is nascent but robust. In his initial work on bullying, Dr. Dan Olweus noted the presence of mental health issues for students involved in bullying behaviors not only as targets but also bullies, and those who occupy both roles.[1] Throughout the 1990s and 2000s, a steady stream of research has identified several mental health concerns connected to bullying. One variable this research identifies is the consistent connection between bullying and depression.[1-8] Bond et al.,[2] Olweus,[1] Nansel et al.,[3] Hazler et al.,[9] and a significant number of other researchers in the field have identified depression in the students involved in bullying behaviors. Current neurobiological research is identifying connections between stress and adverse impact on physical and mental health. The stress of being bullied seems to impact physiological functions, intensifying the production of certain stress hormones that may increase the risk of depression.[10-12]

National Institutes of Health research indicates that symptoms of depression affect 5–13% of youths.[13] Youths who are bullied experience depression at significantly higher rates than youths who are not involved in bullying. Various studies indicate that depression rates can be as high as 65% for youths who are targets of bullying.[14] In addition to depression, targets of bullying experience anxiety, somatic problems, low self-worth, feelings of loneliness, sleep disturbance, and suicidal ideation and behavior.[15] Seals and Young[16] in their research found that both targets and bullies experienced more depression than students who were not involved in bullying.[16] In a longitudinal study conducted over two years, Lyndal Bond[2] and her colleagues found that up to 30% of the 13- and 14-year-old students who were bullied had clinical symptoms of depression that were attributed to their history of victimization.[2] A longitudinal study of adolescents conducted by Rigby found that high levels of victimization predicated physical health problems for both genders and mental health problems for girls.[5]

Not only is being bullied connected to immediate unfavorable mental health outcomes for youth, but it is also identified as a significant factor in elevated psychiatric disorders in adults. Cope and colleagues[17] examined the impact of bullying behaviors on over 1,400 individuals over a 17-year period. These individuals were assessed both as youths and as young adults. This study concluded that youth targets of bullying had increased risk of anxiety disorders as adults and that those individuals who were targets/bullies were at increased risk for depression and panic disorder. Females in the study who were targets/bullies seemed at increased risk for agoraphobia as adults, and male targets/bullies appeared to be at increased risk for suicidality as adults. As adults, individuals in the study who only engaged in bullying behaviors as students were at risk for antisocial personality disorder.[17]

The type of bullying committed against a target has an impact on mental health. Both indirect bullying (e.g. exclusion, rumors, backbiting) and direct bullying (e.g. hitting, name-calling) negatively impact mental health, although indirect bullying seems to have more long-term effects.[18] The most common form of bullying is verbal abuse and name calling. Swearer's study of ninth- to eleventh-grade boy bullying showed that 48% of the boys were targets of bullying behaviors. Not all the boys were bullied in the same way: 26% of these boys were "gay-baited" (e.g. verbally assaulted with homophobic epithets), while the remaining 74% of the targeted boys were verbally bullied without homophobic remarks. The boys who were bullied because they were perceived as being gay experienced greater psychological distress, greater verbal abuse, and more physical bullying than those boys who were bullied for other reasons.[19] The issue of the mental health effects of bullying on lesbian, gay, bisexual, and transgendered youth (LGBT) will be covered in more depth later in this chapter.

In younger children, research shows a connection between being bullied and disruption of developmental achievements. Williams showed in her work that elementary schoolchildren who were bullied had recurrent sleep disturbances, increased episodes of bedwetting, a greater incidence of sad feelings, more headaches, and frequent gastrointestinal upsets. Her work showed a significant trend for greater risk of symptoms when the bullying intensifies.[4]

The question of the bullying being an antecedent to or consequence of mental health problems has been studied. One study concluded that depression and anxiety could be mental health symptoms of children who are targeted both before and after being bullied. However, it appears that physical health problems occur only after a child has been targeted.[20] Other studies show that when children are targeted, they are more likely to experience loneliness, have difficulty with friendships, and try to avoid going to school.[21] The evidence is clear that being bullied in school has a direct effect on negative mental health outcomes for students.

But victims are not the only ones who suffer mental health consequences from bullying—those engaging in the behavior face them as well. Depression affects those who do the bullying and those who are both targets and aggressors. Students who engage in bullying behavior are at increased risk for antisocial behaviors, conduct problems, dropping out of school, and depression.[3] Recent research indicates a connection between being a bully and suicidal ideation and suicidal behaviors.[22]

The students who seem to experience the most significant assault to their mental health are those who are both targets and bullies. These students seem to have more problems with depression, anxiety, loneliness, social relationships, aggressive behaviors, and suicidal thoughts and behaviors.[23]

Children who are targets and students who are both targets and bullies seem to have similar behavioral, mental health, and school adjustment problems. Both groups seem to suffer from depression and anxiety and adjustment disorders in the first years of schooling. These negative effects seem to be uniquely linked to the experience of being a target or a target/bully. These students' success in school appears to be at risk because of the bullying. Girls who are targets and targets/bullies have been shown to have externalizing problems such as conduct disorders and aggressive behaviors that are hurtful to others.[24]

Students who are targets and targets/bullies are also at long-term risk for other mental health problems such as depression and suicidal ideation and behavior.[25]

BYSTANDERS AND MENTAL HEALTH

There are few specific studies of the effects on students witnessing bullying. Juvonen et al. (2003)[26] reported that sixth-grade students they classified as "uninvolved" in bullying showed fewer problems with depression and anxiety compared to both targets and targets/bullies.[26] In a study of elementary-age bystanders, Glew et al. (2005)[27] found that these children felt connected to their school, safe, and less sad than students who experienced bullying.[27] The lack of studies on the effects of bullying on bystanders does not preclude the possibility that these students may experience co-victimization that has an adverse impact on their mental health.

LONG-TERM EFFECTS OF BULLYING

Olweus found that when boys between the ages of 12 and 16 were targeted for bullying three or more times a month, they had increased levels of depression when surveyed as young adults. The long-term impact on mental health was more significant. Independent of their social relationships, girls targeted in early adolescence developed more significant emotional problems as adults.[1] Olweus's longitudinal study of youth who engaged in bullying behaviors in school were four times as likely to have three or more convictions by the time they were 24 years old.[1]

When young people have poor social relationships and become the target of bullying, the possibility of emotional problems in adolescence increases. If the school does not address the bullying behaviors, or intervenes in tepid and halfhearted responses, it increases the prospect of serious mental health problems in adulthood.[2]

Several researchers have found that being a victim of violence such as bullying when young is associated with mental health problems in adulthood.[28,29] Other research indicates that some psychopathology in adults is rooted in negative childhood mental health.[3] Arseneault's[24,30] research on bullying among 5- to 7-year-olds indicates that some of the children who are targets of bullying may have behavioral or school adjustment disorders prior to their enrollment. Her data might mean that these mental health issues may evoke aggressive encounters or make the child more vulnerable to targeting by children who bully. Moreover, her work indicates that children who are targets or targets/bullies showed exacerbated behavioral and school adjustment problems at age seven even after preexisting problems were removed from consideration. She concludes that bullying behaviors play a significant and unique factor in symptoms of depression, anxiety, aggressive behaviors, and maladjustment in young, school-age children.[30]

CYBERBULLYING

Does cyberbullying cause mental health problems? The research in this area is embryonic. As Prensky[31] notes, "Students today are all 'native speakers' of the digital language of computers, video games and the Internet." He labels them, "Digital Natives," whereas adults are "Digital Immigrants." Living a digital existence, students are creating the future of what 24/7 communication is, including bullying through electronics.[31]

Cyberbullying is bullying that can be 24/7 and is more insidious and powerful than the bullying typically committed in the school environment.

With no physical barriers and an infinite number of bullies, targets, and bystanders, cyberbullying presents a minefield of potential trauma.

The studies that exist on the mental health impact of cyberbullying indicate that this form of bullying can do as much harm as other methods of bullying. According to the work of Kowalski and Limber,[32] about a quarter of the 3,767 middle school students they studied reported involvement in cyberbullying, including 4% as bullies, 11% as victims, and 7% as both. They conclude from their research that targets of cyberbullying experience emotional distress and adverse mental health outcomes similar to targets of other forms of bullying.[32]

Hinduja and Patchin[33] completed a study of almost 2,000 middle school students examining their experiences using the Internet and being cyberbullied on it. Approximately a third of the students reported being cyberbullied two or more times in the last month, and 22% of the students reported that they had engaged in bullying someone two or more times in the last month. Both the targets and the students doing the cyberbullying had considerably lower self-esteem when compared to those who had not been involved in cyberbullying.[33]

In another study completed by Hinduja and Patchin, the authors report that 29.4% of 384 students studied had been cyberbullied.[34] In a 2008 study of 1,378 students, the researchers found that 32% of the males and 36% of the females reported being cyberbullied. The study included consideration of the student's offline school behaviors that indicated these targeted students seemed to have more truancy, problems with cheating, being targeted in other ways, fighting, and substance abuse.[33] A Hinduja and Patchin 2010 study of a random sample of 2,000 middle school students who experienced cyberbullying or traditional bullying as either a target or an offender indicated that both groups had more suicidal ideation and behaviors than students who had not been bullied. The targets in this study were more likely to have suicidal thoughts and behaviors than the students doing the bullying.[35]

Ybarra[36] found that reports of cyberbullying were three times higher for students who reported major depressive symptoms compared to students who had none or mild depressive symptoms in his study of 1,501 students between the ages of 10 and 17. The study also indicted that males with major depressive symptoms were three times more likely to be targets than males with mild or no symptoms of depression. This finding did not seem to apply to the female students in the study. He concluded that students with depression who use the Internet regularly are significantly more likely to be cyberbullied.[36]

In 2010, the Annenberg Public Policy Center published research on cyberbullying of adolescents and young adults.[37] The 600 subjects, ages 14 to 20, were interviewed by phone. The interviews revealed that one out of seven, or 14%, had been cyberbullied. Of these individuals, their suicidal ideation over the last year was 27.4% compared to 7.5% for individuals who had not been cyberbullied. Females were twice as likely to be cyberbullied as males. Both males and females were at increased risk for depression and suicidal ideation. About 8% of the interviewees reported that they had cyberbullied others. These individuals were at increased risk for depression. This was true for all genders and ages in this study. The individuals who were both the target and perpetrator seemed to be at increased risk for depressive symptoms. The study concluded, "The higher rates of depressive symptoms are associated with higher rates of suicidal ideation."[37]

The scant research on cyberbullying and mental health documents the negative impact on students at all levels. As with other research on the effects of bullying on mental health, we see that all individuals suffer from this form of school violence.

BULLYING AND LESBIAN, GAY, BISEXUAL AND TRANSGENDERED YOUTH

In the United States, research indicates that between 5% and 6% of youth identify as LGBT. This means that approximately 2 million school-age youth are dealing with the issue of non-heterosexual orientation.[38] Additionally, nearly 1.6 million youth in public schools report that they are bullied because of either perceived or extant homosexuality.[38]

LGBT youth are at high risk for being targets of bullying behaviors. A 2009 survey shows that 84.6% of LGBT students reported being verbally harassed, 40.1% reported being physically harassed, 18.8% reported being physically assaulted at school in the past year, and 61.1% reported that they felt unsafe because of their sexual orientation.[39] According to a study by Human Rights Watch, the possibility of being assaulted in school is nearly three times as likely for LGBT students as those for a heterosexual peer. We know that being the target of bullying has a negative impact on mental health.[38]

How are LGBT students' mental health affected by bullying? There is a paucity of research in this area. Mustanski et al. (2010)[40] did a study of 16- to

20-year-old LGBT individuals. Each subject was given a structured psychiatric interview. (This was the first research study of LGBT youth to do this.) A third of the individuals met criteria for a DSM mental health disorder. About 10% met criteria for post-traumatic stress disorder, approximately 15% met criteria for major depression disorder, and 33% reported having attempted suicide. Of these, 6% made a suicide attempt in the last year.[40]

LGBT youth seem to be at higher risk for suicidal behavior. A number of studies show LGBT youths have a significantly higher chance of attempting or completing suicide than their straight peers. One study by Eisenberg and Neumark-Sztainer concluded that LGBT students in grades 9 and 12 were much more likely to have attempted suicide than their heterosexual peers. According to this study, 52.4% of students who were lesbians attempted suicide while their straight peers had an attempted suicide rate of 24.8%. The attempted suicide rate for gay males was 29% while their straight peers had an attempted suicide rate of 12.6%.[41]

Bullying has far-ranging impacts on LGBT youth. The National Youth Climate Survey reports that bullied LGBT youths' grade point average is almost half a grade lower than nonbullied peers. As with other youths, intensity of bullying seems to increase levels of depression and anxiety while diminishing feelings of self-worth. Students who were open about their orientation seemed to have higher levels of bullying, but they also seem to have better overall mental health.[41]

In most schools, LGBT students do not report bullying. According to the National Youth Climate Survey, over 60% never report bullying incidents to the school. The most common reason given was that they did not believe anything would be done to address the situation. When students informed school officials about the LGBT bullying, the school did nothing to stop the bullying a third of the time.[41]

Research shows that a strong school policy on bullying and having specific language about sexual orientation, gender identity, and gender expression deters LGBT bullying and may have a positive nominal impact on reducing the suicide rate for LGBT students and the overall youth suicide rate.[42]

A gay–straight alliance (an LGBT club) in school seems to create more positive experiences for LGBT students. In schools with this resource, students hear fewer homophobic remarks, experience less homophobic victimization, miss fewer days of school, and express more connection to the school community. LGBT supportive school staff has the same impact.[39]

In a school of 500 students, there may possibly be 25 to 30 LGBT students. These students are at risk for being bullied and having mental health problems. This reality should be considered when implementing a bullying prevention program.

BULLYING, DEPRESSION, AND SUICIDE: POSSIBLE CONNECTIONS

When a child dies by his own hand, it is an incomprehensible tragedy. Suicide leaves the survivors devastated; it defies logic and leaves overwhelmingly painful questions in its aftermath. The most fundamental question, "Why?" can only be answered by the person who can no longer respond. Examining the reasons a child has taken his own life may help to prevent future tragedies. Current research indicates that bullying is a factor in some youth suicides. This monograph presents current research on the relationship between bullying behaviors and suicide.

Youth suicide, at the rate of 4.16 per 100,000 people, is the third leading cause of death for youth ages 10 to 19 in the United States.[43] In 2001, Tim Field and Neil Marr[44] coined the term *bullycide* to describe suicide attributable to someone who was the target of bullying behaviors. Recently, the term has achieved prominence from highly publicized youth suicides and because of suicide contagion has a potential negative outcome among youth.

As this chapter makes clear, there is evidence indicating a link between bullying and adverse mental health for youths. Youth who are targets of bullying, students who engage in bullying behaviors, students who witness bullying behaviors, and especially students who are both targets and bullies show a propensity for adverse mental health outcomes.

There is a growing body of research examining the connections between bullying and suicide. These studies, in general, demonstrate a relationship between bully victimization, depression, and suicidal ideation and behaviors. In a cross-sectional analysis of the data from the National Longitudinal Study of Adolescent Health (2001), Russell and Joyner[45] determined that adolescent targets of bullying are more likely to express suicidal thoughts and actually attempt suicide.[45] Klomek and colleagues, in various studies between 1999 and 2010, have consistently found that students engaged in bullying have increased risks of suicidal ideation and behavior.[7,22,25,45–47]

Some studies show gender differences in risk for depression and suicidality. Females who engage in bullying behaviors, even infrequently, may be at risk for depression and suicidal ideation and behavior. Males who engage in frequent bullying behaviors seem to be at risk for suicidal ideation and behavior. Longitudinal studies indicate that girls in all categories can be at risk of more adverse psychological outcomes than boys.

As noted, a number of studies that examine bullying and sexual orientation consistently conclude that targets of bullying based on sexual orientation and perceived sexual orientation correlate with depression, suicidal ideation, and behaviors.

The studies on cyberbullying and suicide, while few, appear to indicate that electronic bullying can contribute to depressive symptoms and are associated with higher rates of suicidal ideation and behaviors.

The connection between being the target of bullying and suicidal ideation and behavior appears evident for youths who have a mental health diagnosis. However, the bullying behavior is not necessarily the lone factor for suicide in these cases. Whenever a youth suicide occurs there are many important variables that must be considered when determining the "reason." A single issue or event does not usually predicate suicidal ideation and behavior.

The students at most risk for depression and suicidal ideation and behaviors are the targets/bullies. The frequency of involvement in bullying is a significant risk factor for suicidal behaviors, whether the student is a target, a target/bully, or a bully.

The current studies of bullying and suicide indicate a correlation between these two kinds of violence. The research shows a complex connection between bullying behaviors and the risk of suicidal ideation and behaviors. Although there are creditable data from these studies, there are limitations on how we can interpret and apply this knowledge. Hinduja and Patchin's study provides limited information about students' experiences with bullying and suicidal ideation and behavior.[35] What is important is that the studies indicate a "correlation" between bullying behaviors and suicidal ideation and behaviors. Correlation does not imply a cause; therefore, the studies do not show that bullying behaviors cause a person to commit suicide. To fully understand this connection, more cross-sectional and longitudinal studies of bullying and suicide are needed.

In addition, the other numerous risk factors associated with adolescent suicide must be taken into consideration. Psychological autopsy studies confirm a substantial link between clinical depression and adolescent suicide. Up to 60% of adolescent suicide victims have a depressive disorder at the time of death. Studies of adolescent suicide attempters conclude that 40–80% meet the criteria for depression.[43]

The other risk factors linked to adolescent suicide are availability of firearms to the potential victim; individual psychopathology; alcohol and drug use; family psychopathology, family history of suicidality; sexual and physical abuse; frequent change in residences during childhood; contagion due to exposure to suicide in the community; ethnicity; and sexual orientation. The relationship between these risk factors and bullying requires further study and examination in order to establish causality.

Implementation in schools of a research-based bullying prevention program, such as the Olweus Bullying Prevention Program, is a major step leading to reductions in bullying behavior. Reducing bullying, in turn, may lead to improved mental health and reductions in youth violent behaviors. However, a bullying prevention program is not a suicide prevention program. Schools should consider an evidence-based program for youth suicide prevention as part of their preventative violence efforts.

WHAT CAN SCHOOLS DO?

Educators can play a major role in helping students' mental well-being by reducing bullying behaviors. However, the school's role in students' mental health is limited and should be defined by school district policy and procedures. These procedures should define the educators' limited role in student mental health concerns as identifying and referring students with possible problems. The procedures should spell out how the school will work with the students' parents or guardians on a referral. Some schools have student assistance program (SAP) committees that work with students with mental health and substance abuse problems. A SAP committee is a useful resource for schools.

School personnel should be aware of symptoms that indicate that a student is engaging in bullying behaviors or that a student is being targeted. Be aware of the symptoms of depression. Document your concerns about a student and refer to the appropriate professional in your building.

Educators have expertise on childhood development, normative peer behaviors, and evaluation of academic standards. Records of attendance, grades, behavior, appearance, and class participation are part of every student's school record. Student changes in any of these areas should alert an educator to the possible need for a referral to a mental health professional. School personnel should monitor any student who is involved in bullying.

Conducting classroom meetings that address bullying, building school community cohesion, improving social relationships, enhancing bystanders' response, conducting effective consistent interventions, and increasing parent involvement all contribute to improving the school climate and reducing bullying. Creating a school environment where students feel safe and respected and adults are seen as being caring and concerned leads to improvement in safety and reductions in peer violence.[1]

The most effective teaching tool educators have is their relationship with the student. To a large extent, the concern, empathy, respect, and application of justice in the school determines the responses of students to educators and the quality of their relationships.

CONCLUSIONS

The literature on the psychosocial adjustment of children and adolescents involved in bullying shows both similarities and differences between bullies and victims. For example, both groups of children are characterized by academic problems and poor emotional adjustment. In contrast, while victims more often report internal problems like low self-esteem, withdrawal, depression, and anxiety, bullies usually show more external issues, especially substance use, antisocial behavior, and violence. However, students who do not fall into the "typical roles" of bullies and victims also may face some negative consequences from bullying around them. When classmates who are bullies or victims are affected, then everyone's education suffers. Witnessing peer victimization within school is indeed associated with a low sense of safety at school, more negative perceptions of school climate and decreased school engagement. Bystanders are also at risk for an increase in daily feelings of anxiety and school aversion. Thus, even when students are seemingly not directly involved in bullying, they may be negatively affected in ways that can impede the learning process. In general, schools with a high prevalence of bullying may have students who are less engaged, less able to concentrate during curricular activities, and more prone to school avoidance.

Despite the documented association between bullying and maladjustment, not all children are at the same risk for developing behavioral and mental health problems. Some children seem to be resilient against a high-risk environment. To explain this adaptive success, protective factors have to be considered. According to the literature, among the many factors that can be identified, parental and school support play important protective roles in children and adolescent development and well-being. Supportive parent–child relationships, characterized by parental warmth, supervision, support, and involvement, are a widely cited factor shown to protect children from adverse life experiences and to reduce externalizing behavior. Similarly, attachment to school and sense of belonging are related to better health, to lower levels of problem behavior, and to higher participation in extracurricular activities. Furthermore, positive classroom management based on teacher support, empathy, and active listening tend to model socially competent behavior in the classroom, and school support may also compensate for a lack of parental support, possibly also protecting against the impacts of risk factors like peer victimization.

Finally, peer support is another important protective factor against both bullying victimization and negative psychosocial outcomes, as schoolchildren who have none or few friends and report low levels of support and help from peers are at a heightened risk for repeated victimization. This indicates the need for including peer support systems into bullying prevention initiatives. These systems involve training peers to work toward preventing and intervening in bullying behavior in their schools. Typically, these programs implement different aspects of peer support, such as everyday support and befriending, and peer counseling or mentoring in one-to-one relationships.

FREQUENTLY ASKED QUESTIONS

1. What is the current status of research on the impact of bullying behaviors on youths' mental health?

Current research on bullying behaviors and mental health in youth is nascent but robust. Dr. Dan Olweus's research beginning in the mid-1970s identified mental health issues for students involved in bullying behaviors not only for targets but also youth who engage in bullying behavior and those who are both a target and a bully.

2. What does research indicate is the most frequent mental health diagnosis associated with bullying behaviors in youth?

There appears to be a consistent connection between bullying behaviors and a diagnosis of depression in youth. Studies from the earliest research through the present indicate that youth targets, bullies, and especially those who are both the target and engage in bullying behaviors (provocative victims) are at risk for depression. The National Institutes of Health research suggests that 5–13% of youth may have symptoms of depression. Various studies have found that 30–65% of youth targets may be diagnosed with symptoms of depression.

3. In addition to the diagnosis of depression, what other mental health diagnoses and developmental problems seem to be associated with youth bullying behaviors?

The other mental health issues associated with bullying in youth are anxiety, somatic problems, low self-worth, feelings of loneliness, sleep disturbance, and suicidal ideation and behavior. In younger children bullying may cause increased episodes of bedwetting, a greater incidence of sad feelings, more headaches, and frequent gastrointestinal upsets.

4. How does the type of bullying impact mental health in youth?

The type of bullying committed against a target has an impact on mental health. Both indirect bullying (exclusion, rumors, backbiting) and direct bullying (hitting, name-calling) negatively impact mental health, although indirect bullying seems to have more long-term effects. The most common form of bullying is verbal abuse and name-calling. Swearer's study of ninth- to eleventh-grade boy bullying showed that 48% of the boys were targets of bullying behaviors. Not all the boys were bullied in the same way: 26% of these boys were "gay-baited" (e.g., verbally assaulted with homophobic epithets), while the remaining 74% of the targeted boys were verbally bullied without homophobic remarks. The boys who were bullied because they were perceived as being gay experienced greater psychological distress, greater verbal abuse, and more physical bullying than those boys who were bullied for other reasons.

5. What does the research indicate is the impact on the mental health of those youth who do the bullying?

In addition to symptoms of depression, students who engage in bullying behavior are at increased risk for antisocial behaviors, conduct problems, dropping out of school, and depression. Recent research indicates a connection between being a bully and suicidal ideation and suicidal behaviors.

6. Which group of students involved in bullying seems to have more significant mental health issues?

The students who seem to experience the most significant assault to their mental health are those who are both targets and bullies. These students seem to have more problems with depression, anxiety, loneliness, social relationships, aggressive behaviors, and suicidal thoughts and behaviors. Students who are targets and students who are both targets and bullies seem to have similar behavioral, mental health, and school adjustment problems. Both groups seem to suffer from depression and anxiety and adjustment disorders in the first years of schooling. These negative effects seem to be uniquely linked to the experience of being a target or a target/bully. These students' success in school appears to be at risk because of the bullying. Girls who are targets and target/bullies have been shown to have externalizing problems such as conduct disorders and aggressive behaviors that are hurtful to others. These students seem to be at risk for mental health issues as adults.

7. What does the research indicate about the mental health of student bystanders?

There is a paucity of research in this area of bullying. The few studies that have been done seem to indicate that bystanders, while stressed by witnessing bullying, seem to show fewer mental health diagnoses, appear to feel connected to their school, safe, and less sad than their peers who are targets or provocative targets.

8. What does the research indicate about the long-term effects of bullying?

Olweus found that when boys between the ages of 12 and 16 were targeted for bullying three or more times a month, they had increased levels of depression when surveyed as young adults. His longitudinal study of youth who engaged in bullying behaviors in school were four times as likely to have three or more convictions by the time they were 24 years old. Girls targeted in early adolescence developed more significant emotional problems as adults. When young people have poor social relationships and become the target of bullying, the possibility of emotional problems in adolescence increases. If the school does not address the bullying behaviors, or intervenes in tepid and halfhearted responses, it increases the prospect of serious mental health problems in adulthood. Being targeted can lead to mental health problems in adulthood and may be the root source for some adult psychopathology.

9. What is the effect of cyberbullying on youths' mental health?

Research on this form of school violence show a connection between school violence and adverse mental health, including depression, suicidal ideation, and suicidal behaviors. The most significant adverse impact on mental health seems to be for those students who are targets and those who are target/bullies.

10. What is the mental health sequela of bullying for LGBT and perceived LGBT youth?

LGBT and perceived LGBT youth face significant negative mental health problems because of bullying. Surveys show that over 80% report verbal harassment. Over 40% report being physically harassed and about 19% report being physically assaulted. A study that interviewed LGBT youth indicates that 10% met criteria for post-traumatic stress disorder, 15% met criteria for major depressive disorder, and a third reported having attempted suicide. LGBT youth have a significantly higher chance of attempting or completing suicide than their straight peers. The attempted suicide rate for gay males is 29% compared to 12.6% for their straight peers. According to a study of lesbians, 52.4% attempted suicide compared to 24.8% of their straight peers.

11. What does the research indicate about bullying and suicide in youth?

There is evidence indicating a link between bullying and adverse mental health for youth. In general, these studies demonstrate that involvement in bullying as a target, target/bully, or bully is a significant risk factor for suicidal behaviors.

The relationship between bully victimization, depression, and suicidal ideation and behavior is now seen as correlational. However, correlation does not imply a cause; therefore, the studies do not show that bullying with any certainty causes a person to commit suicide. The connection between bullying and suicidal ideation and behavior appears evident for youths with a mental health diagnosis. However, the bullying behavior is not necessarily the factor for suicide in these cases. Whenever a youth suicide occurs, there are many variables that must be considered when determining a "cause." A single issue or event does not usually predicate suicidal ideation and behavior.

12. What can educators do to address the adverse effects of bullying of youth mental health?

Educators play a major role in helping students' mental well-being by reducing bullying behaviors. Research shows that the implementation of an evidence-based bullying prevention program in schools has a positive impact on reducing bullying and by doing so, enhances mental health in youth. Additionally, creation of student assistance program (SAP) committees that work with students with mental health and substance abuse problems directly addresses youth mental health. Research demonstrates that the creation and support of a gay–straight alliance in the school not only decreases bullying of LGBT and perceived LGBT students but also seems to be effective in decreasing overall bullying behaviors. Educators have expertise on childhood development, normative peer behaviors, and evaluation of academic standards. Records of attendance, grades, behavior, appearance, and class participation are part of every student's school record. Student changes in any of these areas should alert an educator to the possible need for a referral to a mental health professional. School personnel should monitor any student who is involved in bullying. The educator's relationship with the student can be the most powerful method to convey concern, empathy, and respect, thereby influencing behaviors and positive mental health.

REFERENCES

1. Olweus D. *Bullying at School: What We Know and What We Can Do.* Oxford, UK; Cambridge, USA: Blackwell; 1993.

2. Bond L, Carlin JB, Thomas L, et al. Does bullying cause emotional problems? A prospective study of young teenagers. *BMJ*. Sep 1 2001; 323(7311):480–484.

3. Nansel TR, Overpeck M, Pilla RS, et al. Bullying behaviors among US youth: Prevalence and association with psychosocial adjustment. *JAMA*. Apr 25 2001; 285(16):2094–2100.

4. Williams K, Chambers M, Logan S, Robinson D. Association of common health symptoms with bullying in primary school children. *BMJ*. Jul 6 1996; 313(7048):17–19.

5. Rigby K. *Bullying in School—And What to Do About It*. London: Jessica Kingsley; 1997.

6. van der Wal MF, de Wit CAM, Hirasing RA. Psychosocial health among young victims and offenders of direct and indirect bullying. *Pediatrics*. 2003; 111(12777546):1312–1317.

7. Klomek A, Sourander A, Kumpulainen K, et al. Childhood bullying as a risk for later depression and suicidal ideation among Finnish males. *J Affect Disord*. 2008; 109(18221788):47–55.

8. Barker ED, Arseneault L, Brendgen M, Fontaine N, Maughan B. Joint Development of Bullying and Victimization in Adolescence: Relations to Delinquency and Self-Harm. *J Am Acad Child Adolescent Psychiatry*. 2008; 47(9):1030–1038.

9. Hazler RJ, Hoover JH, Oliver RL. Student Perceptions of Victimization by Bullies in Schools. *Journal Humanistic Educ Devel* 1991; 29:143–150.

10. Harkness KL, Stewart JG, Wynne-Edwards KE. Cortisol reactivity to social stress in adolescents: role of depression severity and child maltreatment. *Psychoneuroendocrinology*. 2011; 36(2):173–181.

11. Shalev I. Exposure to violence during childhood is asso... Durham, North Carolina, USA. *Mol Psychiatry*. 2012; PubMed—NCBI. 2012.

12. Sugden K, Arseneault L, Harrington HL, Moffitt TE, Williams B, Caspi A. Serotonin transporter gene moderates the development of emotional problems among children following bullying victimization. *J Am Acad Child Adolesc Psychiatry*. 2010; 49(8):830–440.

13. National Institute of Mental Health. *Depression in children and adolescents (Fact Sheet for Physicians)*. 2001. Available at http://www.nimh.nih.gov/health/publications/depression-in-children-and-adolescents/index.shtml.

14. Fekkes M, Pijpers FI, Verloove-Vanhorick SP. Effects of antibullying school program on bullying and health complaints. *Arch Pediatr Adolesc med*. Jun 2006; 160(6):638–644.

15. Gini G, Pozzoli T. Association between bullying and psychosomatic problems: a meta-analysis. *Pediatrics*. Mar 2009; 123(3):1059–1065.

16. Seals D, Young J. Bullying and victimization: prevalence and relationship to gender, grade level, ethnicity, self-esteem, and depression. *Adolescence*. Winter 2003; 38(152):735–747.

17. Cope WE, Wolke D, Angold A, Costello EJ. Adult Psychiatric Outcomes of Bullying and Being Bullied by Peers in Childhood and Adolescence. *JAMA Psychiatry*. 2013; online first:1–8.

18. van der Wal M. There is bullying and bullying. *Eur J Pediatr*. Amsterdam, The Netherlands. February 1, 2005; 164(2):117–118.

19. Swearer SM, Espelage DL, Napolitano SA. *Bullying Prevention and Intervention: Realistic Strategies for Schools*. New York: Guilford Press; 2009.

20. Nishina A, Juvonen J, Witkow MR. Sticks and stones may break my bones, but names will make me feel sick: The psychosocial, somatic, and scholastic consequences of peer harassment. *J Clin Child Adolesc Psychol, Division 53*. Mar 2005; 34(1):37–48.

21. Kochenderfer B, Ladd G. Peer victimization: cause or consequence of school maladjustment? *Child Dev*. 1996; 67:1305–1317.

22. AB. K, Marrocco F, Kleinman M, Schonfeld IS, S. GM. Bullying, depression, and suicidality in adolescents. *J Am Acad Child Adolesc Psychiatry*. 2007; 26:40–49.

23. Kim YS, Leventhal BL, Koh YJ, Boyce WT. Bullying increased suicide risk: Prospective study of Korean adolescents. *Arch Suicide Res*. 2009; 13:15–30. Available at http://www.ncbi.nlm.nih.gov/pubmed/19123106.

24. Arseneault L, Milne BJ, Taylor A, et al. Being bullied as an environmentally mediated contributing factor to children's internalizing problems: a study of twins discordant for victimization. *Arch Pediatr Adolesc Med*. Feb 2008; 162(2): 145–150.

25. Klomek A, Sourander A, Gould M. The association of suicide and bullying in childhood to young adulthood: A review of cross-sectional and longitudinal research findings. *Can J Psychiatry*. 2010; 55:282–288.

26. Juvonen J, Graham S, Schuster M. Bullying among young adolescents: The strong, weak, and troubled. *Pediatrics*. 2003; 112:1231–1237.

27. Glew G, Rivara F, Feudtner C. Bullying: children hurting children. *Pediatr Rev*. 2000; 21(10854313):183–189.

28. Walsh E, Moran P, Scott C et al. Prevalence of violent victimization in severe mental illness. *British J Psychiatry*. 2003; 183:233–238.

29. Silver E, Arseneault L, Langley J, et al. Mental disorder and violent victimization in a total birth cohort. *Am J Public Health*. 2005; 95:2015–2021.

30. Arseneault L, Bowes L, Shakoor S. Bullying victimization in youths and mental health problems: 'Much ado about nothing'? *Psychol Med*. Vol 40. England 2010:717–729.

31. Prensky M. Digital natives, digital immigrants Part 1. *On the Horizon*. 2001/09/01 2001; 9(5):1–6.

32. Kowalski R, Limber S. Electronic bullying among middle school students. *J Adolesc Health*. 2007; 41: S22–S30.

33. Hinduja S, Patchin J. Cyberbullying: An exploratory analysis of factors related to offending and victimization. *Deviant Behavior*. 2008; 29(2):129–156.

34. Hinduja S, Patchin JW. *Bullying Beyond the Schoolyard: Preventing and Responding to Cyberbullying*. Thousand Oaks, CA: Corwin Press; 2009.

35. Hinduja S, Patchin JW. Bullying, cyberbullying, and suicide. *Arch Suicide Res*. 2010; 14(3).

36. Ybarra ML. Linkages between depressive symptomatology and Internet harassment among young regular Internet users. *Cyberpsychol Behavior: The Impact of the Internet, Multimedia and Virtual Reality on Behavior and Society*. Apr 2004; 7(2):247–257.

37. Annenberg Public Policy C. *Cyberbullying release.pdf (application/pdf Object)*. 2010.

38. Bochenek M. *Hatred in the Hallways: Violence and Discrimination Against Lesbian, Gay, Bisexual, and Transgender Students in U.S. Schools.* New York: Human Rights Watch; 2001.

39. GLSEN. 2009 National School Climate Survey. 2012. Available at http://www.glsen.org/cgi-bin/iowa/all/news/record/2624.html.

40. Mustanski B, Garofalo R, Emerson E. Mental health disorders, psychological distress, and suicidality in a diverse sample of lesbian, gay, bisexual, and transgender youths. *Am Public Health.* 2010; 100:2426–2432.

41. Eisenberg MW, Neumark-Sztainer D. Associations of weight-based teasing and emotional well being among adolescents. *Arch Pediatr Adolesc Med.* 2003; 157: 733–738.

42. Hatzenbuehler M. The social environment and suicide attempts in lesbian, gay, and bisexual youth. *Pediatrics.* 2011; 10(1542):898–903.

43. Centers for Disease Control & Prevention. *Suicide: Facts at a glance.* 2009. Available at http://www.cdc.gov/violenceprevention/pdf/Suicide_DataSheet-a.pdf.

44. Marr N, Field T. *BULLYCIDE: Death at Playtime.* Wesses Press, Wantage, Oxfordshire, United Kingdom: BeWrite Books; 2011.

45. Russell ST, Joyner K. Adolescent sexual orientation and suicide risk: evidence from a national study. *Am Public Health.* Aug 2001; 91(8):1276–1281.

46. Klomek A, Kleinman M, Altschuler E, Marrocco F, Amakawa L, Gould M. High school bullying as a risk for later depression and suicidality. *Suicide Life-Threat Behav.* 2011; 41(5):501–516.

47. Klomek A, Marrocco F, Kleinman J, Schoenfeld I, Gould M. Peer victimization, depression, and suicidality in adolescents. *Suicide Life-Threat Behav.* 2008; 38: 166–180.

5

The Health Consequences of Bullying

Diana Schroeder, MSN, RN

Objectives

1. To discuss physical health consequences of bullying and correlate specific health outcomes relative to whether the child is bullied, bullies others, or is a bystander to bullying.
2. To identify strategies that school officials can employ that will reduce harm and enhance safety related to bullying in schools.
3. To identify the risk factors that predispose children to health consequences of bullying.
4. To provide strategies for parents to enhance communication with schools regarding their child's experience with bullying and expectations of response from the school.

INTRODUCTION

The term *bullying* evokes an emotional response in nearly every adult. Those responses range from a sense of horror that it still occurs to the other end of the spectrum where it is viewed as a natural, albeit unpleasant, rite of passage. Often, those perspectives are derived from the adult's own experience with bullying in school. Over the years of working with schools on the issue of bullying, it is surprising how frequently adults will offer up their personal experiences with bullying as a child. For some, receiving education about bullying from a school as parents will bring clarity to their own childhood experiences. For others, it serves as a reminder of what they experienced, what they may have done to others, or what they failed to do that brings high emotion from an audience. There are clear, vivid memories of what happened, who was involved, how they felt, and what they did or did not do; and as the audience listens to these memories, it is readily apparent that the impact of that bullying has never faded. If a 50-year-old man can still evoke visceral responses of the fear, humiliation, and anger that he felt as a 10-year-old, what are the consequences of carrying that high emotion for those four decades? Does bullying behavior cause health consequences in the immediate and long-term lives of the individuals involved?

WHAT DO WE KNOW ABOUT BULLYING AND HEALTH CONSEQUENCES?

While bullying as a behavior has been studied for decades, it is only in the past 15 years that research has evolved to include its health consequences. The literature review of health consequences of bullying reveals eight broad generalities:

1. The most commonly recorded health outcomes associated with bullying are psychosomatic. *Psychosomatic* for these studies is defined as "relating to, involving, or concerned with bodily symptoms caused by mental or emotional disturbance."[1]
2. The least commonly recorded health outcomes associated with bullying are physical injuries.
3. The majority of the studies looking at bullying's health consequences are based on self-reports from students.
4. The majority of the studies have originated outside of the United States. There is a dearth of available research involving U.S. students.
5. Few of the studies on health consequences evolve from the medical community. The majority of them are from the psychology community.
6. There is an increased awareness of the long-term implications of bullying on health outcomes, but these long-term studies are evolving in current time.
7. There is an increased effort to connect secondary data of "health" to bullying outcomes, (i.e., child maltreatment by adults and how that impacts bullying experiences in school for that child).

8.   There are more studies that document the health effects of children who are bullied than there are on those who bully others or those who are the "bully/victims" (children who are both bullies and victims of bullying).

There is little doubt in the literature that a correlation exists between bullying and mental health issues for children involved in it; either as the bully, the victim, or a bully/victim. Gianluca Gini and Jim Bozigar, in Chapters 3 and 4, address the social and mental health ramifications of bullying quite effectively. The purpose of this chapter is to discuss the general health impact of bullying, the risk factors that influence the health impact to children, and the strategies in which schools might engage to monitor and manage these risk factors and the health consequences.

One of the earliest attempts to assess health consequences of bullying originated in London in 1996. School nurses engaged in health interviews with nearly 3000 children and identified an association between children who reported being bullied and their corresponding health complaints of not being able to sleep well at night, headaches, stomachaches, bedwetting, and feeling sad.[2] Additionally, this study noted an association between increasing risk of symptoms with increased frequency of bullying. In other words, the students who were bullied the most had the most physical complaints.

In 2001, a prospective study of young teenagers found that children who were anxious or depressed at the beginning of the school year were more likely to be victims of bullying later in the school year.[3] This study also revealed an interesting trend: physical symptoms that were visible to other children did *not* increase the risk of being a target of bullying later in the school year, whereas the presence of mental health symptoms did increase the risk. For example, if a child was recovering post-operatively from neurosurgery or was undergoing chemotherapy and had physical symptoms that other children could see, that child was not more likely to be a target later in the school year. A subsequent study by Nishina et al.[4] and Fekkes et al.[5] further supported these findings that psychosocial difficulties were predictive of increased risk of being bullied, whereas the presence of physical symptoms was not. Nishina et al. stated: "In other words, experiencing peer harassment may make youth feel sick, but feeling sick did not increase the risk of being harassed."[4] The conclusions from these studies indicate that behavioral health issues are a risk for children becoming targets of bullying, but do not support the general consensus of public opinion that children who are physically different are more likely to become targets of bullying.

The physical symptoms most frequently identified by students as a result of being targets of bullying include headache, abdominal pain, sleep problems, and bedwetting, and as stated earlier, they are reflective of self-reports by children. Wolke et al.[6] investigated the association of direct and relational bullying with common health problems via parent surveys on their child's health status and then correlating those findings to the children's self-reports of bullying or being bullied. Their findings indicate that children who bullied others have virtually no corollary physical health complaints, while children who were victims of bullying had "significantly more repeated sore throats, colds or coughs, breathing problems, nausea, and poor appetite. They were also more often worried about going to school and were more likely to make up illnesses to stay at home during school days."[6] While it would appear obvious that children who are bullied are more likely to find reasons to stay home from school and would worry about going to school, it is not always considered that these children may have greater risks of becoming physically sick more frequently.

An interesting study has recently been published that looks at the correlation between peer relations in adolescence and its impact on health in adulthood, specifically *metabolic syndrome* in middle age. Metabolic syndrome is defined as increased waist circumference, raised triglycerides, reduced high-density lipoprotein (HDL) cholesterol, raised blood pressure and fasting glucose, and/or diagnosis of type II diabetes mellitus.[7] This 27-year prospective cohort study from Sweden found that "the degree of peer problems in adolescence, as assessed by teachers, is related to a higher risk of the metabolic syndrome in middle age, independently of a range of potentially health-damaging factors in adolescence and adulthood."[7] As I have identified in the introduction of this chapter, the understanding of the impact on childhood bullying to the long-term health and well-being of adults is an evolving body of research, and it will likely take another few decades to definitely state the health consequences in the long term.

RISK FACTORS ASSOCIATED WITH HEALTH CONSEQUENCES OF BULLYING

Risk Factor #1: Student Status as Bully, Bullied, Bully/Victim, or Bystander

Health consequences of bullying can be generally summarized as a stress response to the bullying. When considering factors or circumstances that increase the likelihood of health consequences to bullying, the primary consideration would be the status of the child. Is the child a bully, a victim of bullying, a bully/victim, or a bystander?

Bully

As previously noted in this chapter, the literature supports that physical health consequences are mostly absent in children who bully others. Those same children, while being relatively free of physical health consequences, have a much higher risk of engaging in antisocial behaviors that predispose them to accidental injury as well as substance abuse and violence-related injuries.[8,9]

Bullied

The child who is bullied is at significant risk for the health- and stress-related consequences as previously identified. However, for most children, those physical health consequences tend to be relatively short-lived in duration. Once the bullying situation ends or the child is removed from the situation, the physical health consequences are largely resolved. The research is clear that the health consequences are not as easily resolved if the bullying has been particularly virulent or has persisted for a long period of time.[2,8,9] These children may struggle with ongoing mental health concerns into adulthood.

Bully/Victim

The child who is the bully/victim is the student who is most likely to have both short- and long-term health consequences related to bullying. While this designation of bully/victim represents the smallest percentage of students in any school, they will often occupy the largest percentage of adult time in managing both the bullying and victim behaviors for these students. Consequently, it is not surprising that these children also have the highest degree of physical health consequences. They are not well liked by peers or adults and thus have significant stress in their school lives. Often, there are behavioral health co-morbidities that influence the child's ability to socially interact with other children.[9,10]

Bystanders

There is a corresponding dearth of information on the health consequences to students who are witnesses or bystanders to bullying behaviors in school.

Janson and Hazler[11] note that the psychological distress as measured by changes in perspiration and heart rates for both victims and bystanders to bullying behaviors indicate an elevated emotional arousal when recalling those bullying events. Furthermore, the researchers compare that level of psychological distress to the same intensity of trauma that was experienced by police, firefighters, and paramedics during the 1989 San Francisco Earthquake.[11]

Risk Factor #2: Child's Behavioral or Mental Health Status

As noted previously in this chapter, children who exhibit behavioral or mental health disorders are more frequently targets for bullying. The child's behavioral/mental health state prior to bullying is exacerbated by the bullying that is likely to occur. It is a vicious cycle: The child is depressed or has a behavioral health diagnosis, which predisposes the child to becoming a target of bullying, which increases the behavioral/mental health concerns. The literature is consistent in documenting that children who are bullies/victims are those with the highest negative health-related outcomes. Those same children are also most likely to carry the behavioral or mental health diagnoses that are exacerbated by increased bullying rates.

Risk Factor #3: LBGT Status

Students who are gay or perceived to be gay by their peers have an increased risk of health-related outcomes secondary to being targets of bullying. Chapters 3 and 4 identify the mental health concerns for this group of students, and those concerns need to be reiterated here. The risk of negative physical health outcomes in this population of students is much higher than for their heterosexual peers.[12] It is also important to note that the younger the student who is targeted due to his or her perceived or actual sexual orientation, the greater the health consequences for that student. At particular risk are the students in middle school, as they are most vulnerable to longer-term health consequences. Lesbians have a greater number of negative experiences and tend to score lower on health outcomes as compared to heterosexual females in high school.[12] There are no identified studies that evaluate gay male student physical health outcomes, but mental health concerns are well documented.

Risk Factor #4: Maltreatment at Home

Negative physical health outcomes have been noted in children who are abused in their homes. As I write that statement, I realize that it would seem obvious to anyone who has worked with children. However, in this instance, the negative health outcomes are predisposed by the type of abuse the student experiences. Shields and Cichetti[13] identified that generally children who were maltreated at home were more likely to bully other children. However, a subset of abused children has an increased risk of being bullied at school—children who have been emotionally abused or neglected at home. To suffer that abuse at home, and then to be further victimized at school can lead to significantly higher levels of distress than that experienced by students who are not abused at home, or even compared to those who experience physical abuse at home.[14] The most common health manifestation in this population is post-traumatic stress disorder (PTSD), which results in physical complaints such as headache, stomachache, and sleep disturbances.

STRATEGIES FOR MONITORING AND MANAGING HEALTH-RELATED CONSEQUENCES OF BULLYING

Part of the difficulty in assessing health consequences of bullying is that it requires a two-fold assessment in a school environment in real time. Is the student being bullied and does the student have a health concern? In the school environment, the assessment of behavior and the assessment of health are handled by distinctly separate groups. Teachers and administrators assess school behavior whereas school nurses assess health. If there is not clear communication and shared objectives between health and education, it is easy to lose the connection that results in a better understanding of the health consequences. Both educators and health professionals in a school environment have a shared responsibility to try to connect the dots and enhance the overall well-being of the child. So, how do you do that?

Strategy #1: Ask the Right Question at the Right Time

The first and most important step is to develop a system within your school that encourages adults in the school to ask the right questions at the right time and then to follow through with the findings. When we focus on health consequences associated with bullying, an obvious starting place would be with the school nurse, who assesses each child for their physical well-being and also evaluates them for signs and symptoms of mental health concerns. Your school nurse is a critical partner in assisting your teachers in identifying students who may be experiencing health consequences of bullying. But how do you systematically do this? Williams et al.[2] utilized a brief survey for school nurses that can be modified to routinely gather health data related to bullying. Their survey asks a series of questions in a specific order that allows the student to focus primarily on the physical complaints and secondarily on whether they are experiencing bullying. The Williams and Chambers questionnaire is as follows:[2]

> Do you get headaches? If yes, how often?
> Do you get stomachaches? If yes, how often?
> Do you sleep well?
> Do you sometimes wet the bed? If yes, how often?
> How do you usually feel?
> Do you get bullied? If "sometimes or more":
> Where does the bullying take place?
> What sort of bullying is this?

This survey tool can be modified to meet your school's specific needs. For example, your school nurse may not wish to include a question regarding wetting the bed due to the age of the student population. You could consider adding a question where the student identifies who is engaging in the bullying behavior. However, asking a student to identify another child who bullies may be a difficult question for the student, as many fear retribution from the bully for "snitching." Some schools have decided to routinely ask a child who presents in the school nurse's office if the child "feels safe at school." Asking if the child feels safe at school allows the school nurse to gain insight into the level of concern that the student is experiencing and to determine how immediate his or her response needs to be. School nurses will tell you that they have a high index of suspicion of bullying for some students, as they may be "frequent flyers" who show up in the nurse's office at regular times to avoid a bullying situation or who provide vague responses regarding their illness or injuries. Providing them with an avenue to consistently evaluate those gut instincts and a plan for follow-up would provide that necessary connection between health and education.

Strategy #2: Increase the Communication Between Health Professionals, Parents, and Educators

If your school nurse has identified a child of concern, what steps should he or she take to report that concern? With whom does the nurse communicate, what needs to be reported, and what follow-up is expected? The types of questions that are asked regularly about health and bullying are similar to the types of questions asked in an emergency room when exploring intimate partner violence (IPV). Research on IPV indicates that merely asking the question and not being prepared to take action if a concern is raised is counterproductive and is also potentially harmful to the individual who is revealing those vulnerabilities. More effective strategies include having an action plan if the student identifies concerns about their safety in school.

The action plan should include:

- Notification of concern to the principal who is in touch with the parents.
- Consultation with the parents for more information and development of support to the child.
- Notification of child's teacher(s) regarding the issues identified.
- Investigation of the bullying incidents that are identified to determine the who, what, when, and where of the bullying behaviors.
- Development of a safety plan for the child reflective of the findings of the investigation and consultation with the parents.

A safety plan includes the following:

- Increased surveillance of the student and the perpetrators of the bullying behaviors.
- Reporting methods for the student to safely report continued incidents of bullying.
- Referral to the appropriate support services, including student assistance programs (SAP), mental/behavioral health, or healthcare provider as needed.
- Ongoing dialogue with the school nurse and/or administrator and teacher(s) about the management of the bullying behaviors and the child's health status related to the bullying.
- Ongoing dialogue with the parents regarding their perceptions of the child's health and safety at school related to bullying.

Strategy #3: Perform Exit Interviews for Students Who Are Leaving Your School

Granted, this strategy is a "day late and a dollar short" when it comes to helping students feel safe as the child and/or parent has already decided to leave your school. However, retrospective reviews of the reasons for a student's voluntary exit from a particular school will enhance your understanding of the issues that students are experiencing in your building and help identify systematic changes that may be needed to prevent other students from leaving. If we don't ask the questions, we won't hear the answers about whether a child is leaving school due to bullying. The decision to leave your school has significant ramifications to school climate, budgets, and the individual health of a child who is being bullied. A cost–benefit analysis related to early school leaving stemming from bullying indicates that retaining only two students who would otherwise leave your building due to bullying will provide financial rewards great enough to justify your bullying prevention program (B. Schroeder et al., unpublished manuscript, 2013). But financial considerations are not the sole issue to be considered here. In the exit interviews, it would be appropriate to determine whether the child's health status has been affected by the bullying experienced. Open-ended questions to parents and the child may provide additional insights to the administrative team and teachers about the physical ramifications related to the experience of bullying.

Strategy #4: Engage Your Local Healthcare Providers in Bullying Prevention

Children who experience physical and/or emotional symptoms secondary to bullying will seek medical care from healthcare providers. Those providers include primary care physicians, pediatricians, mental health service providers, nurse practitioners, and others. It is not unusual for the child or parents to tie the health consequences that the child is experiencing to a school issue. The healthcare provider will be able to attend to the physical or emotional conditions, but is often uncertain as to how to assist the child at the school level. Creating an avenue of communication can educate your healthcare providers about the school's policies, programs, and procedures related to bullying, as well as establish a way to talk directly with the school if there is a significant concern about the child's experience with bullying. It will make the most sense for that communication stream to run through your school nurse to the administrative team. The nurse will be able to gather the appropriate health-related information as well as the reported school concerns and serve as the liaison between the provider and the school system.

This system has worked well with our schools in western Pennsylvania and has evolved into a "Regional Coordinated School Health Model" that has been created by the CDC. This model allows schools to incorporate existing health-related data, policies, and procedures into a unified matrix that consolidates procedures and also identifies areas of need and prioritizes those needs. Schools are unable to meet all the healthcare needs of students and already utilize many healthcare providers in their communities to provide support. This process formalizes that collaboration and brings the community resources together to work more effectively for the students in your school.[15]

ADVICE FOR HEALTHCARE PROVIDERS

Healthcare providers are reimbursed to evaluate children, identify disease, and treat disease. Increasingly, there is recognition that prevention of disease is the most cost-effective, proactive way to keep individuals healthy, including children. Based on what has been previously discussed in this chapter, there is little doubt that bullying leads to health consequences for the bully, bullied, and bystander. The strategies outlined in this chapter for schools are easily translatable to healthcare providers: Ask the right question, increase communication between schools, parents, and children, and know what to do when you suspect that bullying is creating a health consequence for your patient. However, that is a lot to ask of the healthcare provider during a 15-minute office visit, especially when the provider is not yet reimbursed for this service. So what should you say and/or do to help your patients? Here are three steps that you can consistently utilize with your patients to quickly assess the impact of bullying on their lives:

1. Ask the child and family if the child has been exposed to bullying or other aggressive behavior in school. Is the child the target of bullying? Does the child participate in the bullying or watch while it occurs? Utilizing the Williams and Chambers survey tool is a quick way of determining physical or emotional health issues while simultaneously assessing whether bullying may be the source of those issues. Recognizing the most common manifestations of illness associated

with bullying is key in your assessment and should prompt you to explore more fully the causes of those illnesses.

2. Ask the child if he or she has been intentionally harmed in school by a peer or anyone else. Healthcare providers routinely assess for evidence of child abuse, and it is appropriate to assess for evidence of peer abuse. When you are seeing a patient who has a physical injury that occurred in school, it is routine to ask how the injury occurred; however, the child is seldom questioned about whether the harm was intentionally caused by a peer.

3. Screening for the health consequences of bullying is only the first step. If you, as the healthcare provider, have opened the conversation, and a situation that needs to be addressed is revealed, you need to have an identified course of action to assist your patient. It is inappropriate to screen only without a plan for follow-up if needed. You should have some awareness of the bullying prevention activities in the area schools and the key school personnel to contact as a follow-up to a patient-related bullying event. If you are uncertain about who would be the most appropriate contact, the principal, school nurse, or guidance counselor would be considerations. You may wonder why this would be helpful—surely the school is aware of the problems of bullying! Indeed they are, but your expertise in assisting them to recognize the health consequences for your patient will heighten the awareness of the needs of your patient and increase his or her safety in school. Additionally, the school might not be aware of the bullying at all, and you will provide an opening for the school to be more responsive to your patient's previously unrecognized difficulties. Your voice has weight in your community. Being an advocate for your patient will increase the chances that his or her situation can be improved.

As the evidence mounts related to the health consequences of bullying, it is important that screening for bullying-related health issues be administered routinely. In order to effectively address these concerns, it is also time for schools, parents, and healthcare providers to lobby for reimbursement for this and other types of prevention services.

CONCLUSIONS

There is little doubt that bullying creates health consequences for children (and their parents). Schools and healthcare providers need to develop strategies that will recognize, treat, and prevent those health concerns. It is also imperative that adults recognize the factors that increase the risk for health consequences and increase screening or monitoring of those children who exhibit the greatest risk. Although we are gaining a perspective on the effects of aggressive behaviors in school, and it is important to recognize and manage those effects, real management comes with prevention of the bullying behaviors in the first place. Effective bullying prevention in your building will not only ensure the ongoing safety of your vulnerable students but also improve your school climate and improve the health and well-being of the students under your supervision.

FREQUENTLY ASKED QUESTIONS

1. What are the most common physical health consequences associated with bullying?

The most common health outcomes are *psychosomatic,* or relating to, involving, or concerning bodily symptoms caused by mental or emotional disturbance. In other words, headaches, abdominal pain, sleep problems, and bedwetting.

2. What are the risk factors associated with health consequences of bullying?

There are four primary risk factors that the literature identifies as an increased risk. Those include:

- Whether the student is the target of bullying, the bully, or the bystander.
- The child's current behavioral or mental health status.
- Lesbian, gay, bisexual, and transgendered (LGBT) status of the child.
- Whether the child suffers maltreatment at home.

3. How are the child's health outcomes affected by being the bully, the target of bullying, or the bystander?

- The child who bullies others has the least impact on their physical health but suffers mental health consequences.
- The child who is the target experiences significant short- and long-term health consequences of bullying, but that is mediated by the length of time and the virulence of the bullying that is experienced.

- The child who is the bystander experiences significant degrees of stress response as an observer and can experience physical symptoms associated with that stress response.

4. How does the child's mental health status predispose the child to bullying and its consequences?

Children who exhibit behavioral or mental health disorders are more frequent targets for bullying. The child's behavioral or mental health state prior to bullying is exacerbated by the bullying that is likely to occur. It is a vicious cycle: The child is depressed or has a behavioral health diagnosis that predisposes the child to becoming a target of bullying, which increases the behavioral and mental health concerns.

5. Is the risk to LGBT students greater than the general population of students?

The risk of negative physical health outcomes in this population of students is much higher than their heterosexual peers. Additionally, the younger the student is who is targeted due to their perceived or actual sexual orientation, the greater the health consequences for that student. Middle-school gay students and lesbians are the most vulnerable to longer-term health consequences.

6. If a child is abused at home, is he or she more likely to be a bully at school?

The type of abuse that the student experiences at home will impact the exposure to bullying at school. A student who is physically maltreated at home is more likely to bully other children, while a child who has been emotionally abused or neglected at home is more likely to be a target of bullying. A student who is mistreated at home and mistreated at school is going to have significantly higher levels of distress than are students who are not abused at home or those who experience physical abuse at home.

7. What can schools do to help these students?

There are four important strategies for schools to do to help their students avoid or minimize the health consequences of bullying:

- Ask the right question at the right time.
- Increase communication between health professionals, parents, and educators.
- Perform exit interview for students who are leaving your school.
- Engage your local healthcare providers in bullying prevention.

8. What is the "right question at the right time"?

Adults in a child's life need to consistently ask about the well-being of the child and asking the right question at the right time increases the likelihood of identifying a developing or ongoing problem that can be addressed. Utilizing a screening tool is an effective strategy to assess both physical symptoms and whether there is a correlation to bullying. The Williams and Chambers survey tool is effectively used in a school nurse's office.[2] If you wish to keep it even simpler, asking every child who presents to the nurse's office with a question as to whether the child "feels safe at school" allows the child to respond as he or she chooses but provides an opening for the child to discuss situations that may make him or her feel unsafe, including bullying.

9. If I am concerned that a child in my school is being bullied or having health consequences related to bullying, what types of communication should I employ to the parents and healthcare providers?

Develop an action plan for the child that is communicated to all appropriate parties. That action plan should include:

- Notification of concern to the principal who is in touch with the parents.
- Consultation with the parents for more information and development of support to the child.
- Notification of the child's teacher(s) regarding the issues identified.
- Investigation of the bullying incidents that are identified to determine the who, what, when, and where of the bullying behaviors.
- Development of a safety plan for the child reflective of the findings of the investigation and consultation with the parents.

10. What is a safety plan?

A safety plan includes the following:

- Increased surveillance of the student and the perpetrators of the bullying behaviors.
- Reporting methods for the student to safely report continued incidents of bullying.
- Referral to the appropriate support services including student assistance programs, mental or behavioral health, or healthcare provider as needed.
- Ongoing dialogue with the school nurse and/or administrator and teacher(s) about the management of the bullying behaviors and the child's health status related to the bullying.
- Ongoing dialogue with the parents regarding their perceptions of the child's health and safety at school related to bullying.

11. What should healthcare providers do when they suspect that their patient has health consequences secondary to bullying in school?

Ask if the child has been exposed to bullying or other aggressive behavior in school. Consider utilizing a screening tool to assess the correlation between bullying and physical and emotional symptoms. Ask if the child has been intentionally harmed at school by a peer. This would include physical injuries as well as stress-related symptoms. Engage with your local schools to determine follow-up plans if you identify a patient who has a health issue that you feel is related to bullying.

REFERENCES

1. Merriam-Webster, Inc. (2012). "Psychosomatic" Retrieved from http://www.merriam-webster.com/dictionary/psychosomatic.

2. Williams K, Chambers M, Logan S, Robinson D. Association of common health symptoms with bullying in primary school children. *BMJ*. 1996; 313: 17–19.

3. Bond L, Carlin J, Thomas L, Rubin K, Patton G. Does bullying cause emotional problems: A prospective study of young teenagers. *BMJ*. 2001; 321 (9):480–484.

4. Nishina A, Juvonen J, Witkow MR. Sticks and stones may break my bones, but names will make me feel sick: The psychosocial, somatic, and scholastic consequences of peer harassment. *J Clin Child Adolesc Psychol.* 2005; 34(1):46.

5. Fekkes, M, Pijpers F, Fredriks M, et al. Do bullied children get ill, or do ill children get bullied? A prospective cohort study on relationship between bullying and health-related symptoms. *Pediatrics.* 2006; 117(5):1568–1574.

6. Wolke D, Woods S, Bloomfield L, Karstadt L. Bullying involvement in primary school and common health problems. *Arch Dis Child.* September 2001; 85(3):199.

7. Gustafsson P, Janlert U, Theorell T, Westerlund H, Hammarstrom A. Do peer relations in adolescence influence health in adulthood? Peer problems in the school setting and the metabolic syndrome in middle-age. *PLOS One.* 2012; 7 (6):1–10.

8. Fekkes M, Pifpers F, Verloove-Vanhorick S. Bullying behavior and associations with psychosomatic complaints and depression in victims. *Pediatrics.* 2004; 44 (1):17–22.

9. Gini G, Pozzoli T. Association between bullying and psychosomatic problems: A meta-analysis. *Pediatrics.* 2009; 123(3):1059–1065.

10. Houbre B, Tarquinio C, Thuillier I, Hergott E. Bullying among students and its consequences on health. *Eur Psychol Edu.* 2006; 22(2):183–208.

11. Janson GR, Hazler RJ. Trauma reactions of bystanders and victims of repetitive abuse experiences. *Violence Vict.* 2004; 19(2):239–255.

12. Gruber J, Fineran S. The impact of bullying and sexual harassment on middle and high school girls. *Violence Against Women.* 2007; 13(6):627–643.

13. Shields A, Cichetti D. Parental maltreatment and emotional dysregulation as risk factors for bullying and victimization in middle childhood. *J Clin Child Psychol.* 2001; 30(3):349–363.

14. Duncan RD. Maltreatment by parents and peers: The relationship between child abuse, bully victimization and psychological distress. *Child Maltreatment.* 1999; 4(1):45–55.

15. Centers for Disease Control and Prevention. (2012). *School Health Index.* Available at http://www.cdc.gov/HealthyYouth/SHI/.

6

Creating Healthy School Climates for Lesbian, Gay, Bisexual and Transgendered Students

Robert A. McGarry, EdD

Objectives

1. To identify strategies to evaluate the safety and well-being of students who are LGBT or identified as LGBT in a school environment, recognizing the health and safety concerns of this segment of the student population.
2. To recognize four school-based interventions that will enhance student safety and well-being related to LGBT issues: supportive school staff, development of school clubs (gay–straight alliances), enumerated school policy, and LGBT inclusive curriculum.
3. To identify specific strategies that will help school staff to support LGBT students in clear, effective ways.

School climate is a term that is used to describe a school's effects on its students (p. 89).[1] It has been suggested that there are various aspects of a school that contribute to how a climate is "constructed." McBrien and Brandt include "teaching practices, diversity, and the relationships among administrators, teachers, parents, and students" among these factors (p. 89).[1] How a school is "experienced," or in the "effects" it has on its students, would seem difficult to qualify as students can have disparate experiences within the same school and describe their experiences very differently. One student might describe the school as a nurturing space where students are well-known, supported, and included, while another might depict it as a hostile, lonely place where students feel excluded, ignored, or bullied.

As Chapter 2 suggests, there is a link between school climate and the prevalence of bullying within a school. Research suggests that one of the most frequent reasons students get bullied is because of their real or perceived sexual orientation or gender identity, or the way they express their gender.[2] When compared to the general student population, the percentage of LGBT (lesbian, gay, bisexual, and transgender) students who report being victimized by bullying-related behaviors—including verbal and sexual harassment, theft or property damage, or rumor spreading—is greater than that of the general population.[2,3] Bullying is a problem for LGBT youth, and given the link between climate and bullying, educators and educational leaders ought to consider how the environment of the school contributes to the problem.

The degree to which students feel "safe" in schools is certainly an indicator of the quality of its climate. For LGBT students, there are a variety of reasons why school can be an unsafe place. Secondary school students (grades 6–12) in the Gay, Lesbian & Straight Education Network's (GLSEN) 2011 National School Climate Survey[4] were asked whether they had ever felt unsafe at school during the prior school year because of a personal characteristic, including: sexual orientation, gender, gender expression (i.e., how traditionally "masculine" or "feminine" they were in appearance or behavior), and actual or perceived race or ethnicity, disability, or religion. More than two-thirds of LGBT students reported feeling unsafe at school during the prior school year because of at least one of these personal characteristics.[2] Sexual orientation and gender expression were the most commonly reported reasons, with 6 in 10 students reporting feeling unsafe at school because of their sexual orientation and 4 in 10 students feeling unsafe because of how they expressed their gender.[2]

At the elementary (K–6) level, GLSEN's[5] national study of elementary school climate reveals a similar school climate effect. That is, that gender nonconforming elementary school students are less likely than other students to feel very safe at school and are more likely than others to indicate that they sometimes do not want to go to school because of these feelings.[5] It's not surprising, then, that gender nonconforming students are more likely than others to be called names, be made fun of, or be bullied at school.[5] Educators who participated in the study also suggest that gender nonconforming students are less likely than other students to feel comfortable at their school.

It seems clear that our nation's schools are often hostile environments for a distressing number of LGBT and gender nonconforming students, almost all of whom commonly hear homophobic/transphobic remarks in the hallways, classrooms, cafeterias, and gymnasiums of their schools. At the same time, these students (and their peers) rarely see positive representations of LGBT people, history, or events in the curriculum. LGBT students face verbal and physical harassment and even physical assault because of their sexual orientation or gender expression. Regardless of whether LGBT students are bullying targets, the kind of school environment described here is surely an unhealthy one.

The consequences for those who are bullied are of even greater concern. LGBT students who face high levels of victimization are more likely to identify that they suffer from depression and anxiety and to have an overall decreased sense of self-esteem. LGBT students are also more likely than other students to lack a sense of belonging to their school and miss classes or even whole days of school to avoid a hostile climate and the lack of safety they feel within it. The outcomes in terms of compromised academic achievement and plans for post-secondary education seem obvious.

There is an urgent need for action to create safer and more inclusive school climates for LGBT and gender nonconforming students. Since 1999 GLSEN has documented the school experiences of LGBT youth across the country in an effort to identify promising practices—conditions in schools that seem to correlate with lower levels of victimization of LGBT and gender nonconforming students and more positive educational outcomes such as higher academic achievement, lower rates of absenteeism, greater sense of school belonging, and increased emotional well-being.[2] This body of research suggests specific actions that educators can take to improve school climates for these students. This chapter describes four evidence-based interventions that school leaders may implement to make their schools safer and more inclusive and affirming for all youth, regardless of sexual orientation or gender identity/expression. Each of these interventions is described in further detail with suggestions for educators on how to incorporate them into school practices. Taken together, such measures can move schools toward a future in which all students will have the opportunity to learn and succeed in school, regardless of sexual orientation or gender identity/expression.

UNDERSTANDING YOUR SCHOOL

Before making changes in a school, it is important to assess the current state of its climate by engaging in strategies drawn from the burgeoning field of practitioner, or action research. Such site-based activity "has the potential for empowerment and the inclusion of a greater diversity of voices in educational policy and social change" (p. 6)[6] It helps focus efforts by identifying areas for improvement, and may lead to the uncovering and exploration of school experiences and the role that educators play in shaping those experiences. It can provide an effective foundation for a deeper look at a school's existing policies, practices, and resources and how these influence the climate, as it is experienced by all students, and LGBT students in particular.

One way to begin this process is to conduct a survey of members of the school community, including students, staff, and parents. Such a survey should include questions that ask about the frequency of biased language, harassment, and assault, as well as the type and level of intervention by educators. GLSEN has a free tool known as the Local School Climate Survey (LSCS), which was designed to help educators and community members assess the climate of a school or community. Conducting the LSCS can provide detailed data to use when planning for change. There are two versions of the LSCS, one that can be conducted in a single school and one that can be conducted within several schools or an entire district. Copies of the survey instrument can be downloaded at www.glsen.org.

Understanding how inclusive a school is of LGBT students, families, and issues can help staff create a plan of action to ensure that a school is safe and welcoming for all students. To assess a school's policies and practices, an LGBT-inclusive school checklist may be applied to the school in question. The checklist helps a school consider policies and practices, course content, school events, and the presence of relevant co-curricular activities. GLSEN's Safe Space Kit includes such a tool. Taken together, the survey and checklist provide a great deal of data from which to begin a discussion and collaboratively identify the priorities and select specific actions the school will take to address the findings. Actions can be as simple as "increasing the school library's collection of LGBT-themed literature and resources" or more complex, such as "revising school or district anti-bullying policy." Actions such as these are related to the following four school-based interventions.

INTERVENTION I: SUPPORTIVE SCHOOL STAFF

The presence of supportive adults within a school has shown to make a positive difference in how LGBT students experience their school climate,[2] and is probably the best place for a school leader to begin the work of improving the climate for LGBT students. Educators can have a profound impact on a school's climate. For many students (both those who identify as LGBT and those who do not), school success can depend on interaction with or awareness of supportive educators. It is not uncommon to hear stories of how a single educator changed the course of a student's life. Supportive teachers, counselors, principals, and other school staff can serve as an important resource for LGBT students. Being able to speak with a caring adult in a school can have a significant positive impact on the school experience for students, particularly for those who feel marginalized or experience harassment. Research has demonstrated that the more supportive educators a student can identify, the more likely it is that levels of victimization will be lessened.[2]

As leaders, school administrators play a particularly important role in determining the school experiences of LGBT youth. Not only might they serve as caring adults to whom the youth can turn, but they also set the school's tone and determine specific policies and programs that affect the school's climate. In 2008, GLSEN released a research report documenting the perspective of principals on issues related to school safety and LGBT students. Among other things, the study suggests that it is principals who determine whether school staff members receive the kind of professional development on LGBT issues that can yield more visibly supportive adults in the school.[5] As with many other topics, when principals see the value it has and deem it important, it is more likely to happen.

It is critical that administrators know and recognize those who already support the LGBT students in their school and make sure that they have the resources they need to continue to do so. It is equally important for administrators to facilitate the growth of the rest of the staff and help them acquire the knowledge, skills, and dispositions they need to be "allies" to LGBT students, as they are known in the LGBT community. In addition, they should serve as role models of respect, tolerance, and inclusiveness for others.

Becoming an ally to LGBT students is not a simple task, and an administrator should not expect to see an increased number of allies as the result of a staff meeting or some minimal professional development event. It is a process that takes time and concerted effort. Administrators cannot proclaim themselves to be a supporter of LGBT students in the same way one might reveal a willingness to mentor students who have a specific career interest or hobby, or to sponsor a co-curricular activity. Taking on the role of a supportive adult presence for LGBT students is a process that requires that an administrator not only devotes time but also practices patience and, in many instances, position him or herself as a co-learner in the work.

In their work, Washington and Evans[7] describe a series of steps that educators should take in the process of becoming allies to LGBT students. These steps provide a developmental framework for consideration of a variety of ally-development strategies. They include (1) developing awareness, (2) gaining knowledge, (3) practicing relevant communication skills, and (4) taking action. A closer examination of these steps can provide insight into the behaviors that supportive school personnel should develop and use on behalf of LGBT students. These steps can also help school leaders develop a "blueprint" for a plan to engage school staff in this work.

Developing Awareness and Gaining Knowledge: The Big Picture and the Local Context

Any discussion of LGBT students and school climate ought to begin with earnest consideration of the most relevant research on the issues. Reading even the "executive summary" of GLSEN's National School Climate Survey can help school staff begin to understand the significant problems that exist as well as the potential research-based solutions that may be implemented in a school. But beyond that general awareness, it is important for school staff to consider the current state of the climate in their school by working with school leaders to consider the survey and checklist already described.

Once a sufficient scan of the school environment has been made, school staff should consider their own beliefs, values, practices, and behaviors and how these do or do not influence their work, and subsequently, the school's climate. Although it is not expected that educators should change their personal beliefs, it is important to acknowledge the part that beliefs play in shaping our behaviors. As such, it is important to understand them, and it is important for school leaders to build in professional development time that provides staff members the opportunity to explore their own beliefs, become familiar with supportive behaviors and strategies that demonstrate support for LGBT youth and ultimately help establish them as an ally.

Giving thoughtful consideration to one's own experiences as an educator and how these relate to LGBT issues, while also assessing personal beliefs, are important parts of the process of becoming an ally and advocate for LGBT students. Formal or informal school leaders or individuals themselves should recall and consider examples of anti-LGBT name-calling, bullying, or harassment that have occurred in the school and think about how they and all of their students (LGBT and non-LGBT alike) are affected by anti-LGBT bias (and may participate in it).

Engaging staff in individual reflection and small-group discussion around these inquiries is a good place to begin the process. Leaders should endeavor to create a safe and supportive space so that faculty and staff feel free to share their experiences, challenges, successes, questions, and doubts on the matter. When done effectively, such a discussion should help reveal how pervasive anti-LGBT bias is and how often educators ignore subtle biases such as anti-LGBT jokes, the exclusion of LGBT-related themes in curricula, and even anti-LGBT name-calling. Subtle or not, bias has the power to hurt and isolate people. Hopefully, this discussion will lead staff members to understand that an ally's work includes consistently recognizing and challenging personal anti-LGBT bias and establishing practices for themselves that help them to avoid it.

Practicing Relevant Proactive and Reactive Communication Skills

One simple, yet important, way for staff to be allies to LGBT students is for them to use LGBT-related terminology accurately and respectfully. Unfortunately, many people do not have the experience or knowledge to use these terms in an accurate or appropriate manner. Language has a huge impact on the way we see others and ourselves, and yet, language is constantly changing. It is important, for example, to understand the differences between sexual orientation (our inner feelings of who we are attracted to) and gender identity (how we identify ourselves in terms of our gender). Far too often, these terms are confused, and the result can be harmful to a student. Familiarizing yourself and keeping up to date with LGBT-related terms and concepts is a key component of being an ally. Conducting an Internet search of respected sites for such information is a good starting point for this process.

Of course, the best way to ensure that you are using the proper terminology when referring to an individual is to find out the terminology he or she prefers. When engaging with students, parents, and other staff, it is important that staff members not assume the sexual orientation or gender identity of anyone, nor use language that assumes that everyone is heterosexual or fits into a prescribed gender role. Educators should try to be open to a great variety of identities and expressions. LGBT students unfortunately live in a very heterosexist society where they constantly receive the message that everyone is supposed to be heterosexual. Allies need to show all students that there is no one way a person "should" be.

Through casual conversation and during classroom time, it is important that staff members use language that is inclusive of all people. When referring to people in general, staff should use words like "partner" instead of "boyfriend/girlfriend" or "husband/wife," and avoid gendered pronouns, using "they" instead of "he/she." Using inclusive language helps LGBT students feel more comfortable being themselves and helps them in their quest to locate the support of an ally.

One of the most effective ways that an ally can demonstrate support is by engaging in communication that disrupts anti-LGBT behavior. In describing their framework for teaching and learning, Bransford, Darling-Hammond, and LePage state, "On a daily basis, teachers confront complex decisions that rely on many different kinds of knowledge and judgment and that can involve high-stakes outcomes for students' futures" (p. 1).[8] In their proposed framework for teaching and learning, these authors include classroom management as one of the critical areas of teacher knowledge. Certainly the disruption of anti-LGBT behavior falls into this category. While lack of knowledge and, more importantly, skill in this area can certainly compromise student learning in terms of content, it also stands to reason that such deficits can yield deleterious effects that might have even higher-stakes outcomes for specific students, including LGBT students.

School leaders need to set an expectation that staff should address name-calling, bullying, harassment, and heterosexist language immediately, concentrating on stopping the behavior in that moment. In doing so, leaders need to be clear that inaction is, in fact, an action— overlooking or ignoring implies acceptance and approval. Leaders should provide opportunities for educators to share examples of student use of such language and develop appropriate responses. Sometimes it's a simple response to hearing a derogatory term like, "That language is unacceptable in this classroom," that sends a clear message to students, while other times the situation might require that educators seize the teachable moment. School staff members need to know that administrators support their doing so and, in fact, expect it.

Incidents such as the kind just alluded to might also require that an educator provide support for a student who has been the target of the name-calling, bullying, or harassment. It is important that staff not label students as victims, and find out from students what they need or want, giving consideration to whether it is best to do so in the moment or at a later time, and whether support should be provided publicly or privately. Lastly, it is important that school staff members hold offending students accountable and impose consequences or means (spelled out in school policy) to make reparation.

Visibility and Support

Educators need to know how to help students develop an awareness of their supportive presence. One of the most important parts of being an ally to LGBT students is being visible. In order for students to come to someone for help, they need to be able to recognize who the allies in their school are. Even if students don't come to an ally directly, research shows that just knowing there is a supportive educator at school can help LGBT students feel safe and included. There are many ways that school staff can make themselves visible as allies. In some cases, staff members need a school leader to invite them to or "grant permission" to do so. Being visible can be as simple a task as posting a sticker that allows students to know up front that a school staff member is supportive. Often these stickers (or posters) also help to make a safe space visible. Making classrooms or offices identifiable as safe spaces for LGBT students will help them identify that the person responsible for that space is someone they can go to for support and that the space as one where they will be safe.

Educators can also post (and maintain the visual dignity of) supportive materials such as quotes from famous LGBT icons, information about the LGBT community, or materials from LGBT organizations. Along with signs for national holidays and months of celebration already in the classroom (e.g., Black History Month or Women's History Month), schools could display information about LGBT History Month in October, LGBT Pride Month in June, or the National Day of Silence in April.

School leaders might also encourage staff to make themselves physically visible as allies, which allows students to easily identify the most supportive educators in their school. Wearing a supportive button or wristband lets students know who supportive allies are without them having to say a word. In an ideal world, all educators would be supportive allies to LGBT students. But the reality is that there may only be a few in a school. Part of being an ally involves letting other educators know that you are a person to whom others can refer students to for support.

While this chapter describes four school-based interventions, none of them are likely to have as positive and healthy an impact on LGBT students as the quality of the supportive educators in the school. Such educators are critical to implementation of the other interventions: student clubs, policy development and implementation, and inclusive curriculum.

INTERVENTION II: STUDENT CLUBS

Schools are often not a safe place for students, particularly those who are LGBT. For many LGBT students, student clubs that address LGBT student issues (commonly called gay–straight alliances, or simply GSAs) offer critical support. These clubs are student-led, usually at the high school or middle school level, and work to address anti-LGBT name-calling, bullying, and harassment in their schools and promote respect for all students.

The existence of these clubs can make schools safer and more welcoming for LGBT students. But despite the evidence of the benefits they offer, many students lack access to the valuable resources GSAs provide. Although the number of GSAs is increasing, less than a quarter of high school students nationally have a GSA in their school, and students in small towns and rural areas are least likely to have access to this type of support. LGBT students of color also have less access to the resources of a GSA than their peers.[2] Educators working to improve school climate need to examine the reasons for this discrepancy and identify strategies to remedy the situation so that all students, regardless of their school context, can access the benefits of a GSA.

The presence of a GSA in a school may mitigate the negative impact of bullying and harassment experienced by some LGBT students. As suggested by the research cited in this chapter, LGBT students in schools with GSAs are less likely to hear biased language, such as homophobic remarks, feel unsafe in school because of their sexual orientation and gender expression, and miss days of school because they are afraid to go. In addition, GSAs may play an important role in helping students identify staff who may be supportive and to whom they can report any incidents of victimization. The presence of a GSA may offer evidence of a school's commitment to LGBT students and their allies, creating a source of perceived support for students even if they are not actively engaged with the GSA themselves. The presence of GSAs may also help to improve the school experiences of LGBT students, by increasing access to education and having a positive impact on LGBT students' academic achievement and aspirations.

GSAs, like all student clubs, must have a faculty advisor. Serving as the advisor for a school's GSA is one of the most effective ways for educators to demonstrate that they are an ally to LGBT students. Not only does being an advisor provide support for the efforts of the GSA, it enhances the ally's visibility and makes it easier for LGBT students to identify supportive school staff, as well as giving other staff the knowledge of a resource person to whom they may refer students. Allies sometimes need to advocate for the rights of students to establish a GSA. Although some opponents of GSAs have attempted to restrict these clubs, the federal Equal Access Act of 1984 requires public schools to allow GSAs to exist alongside other noncurricular student clubs.

As a school-based intervention, the presence of a GSA in school may have considerable benefits for LGBT students and their allies. School leaders should support the formation of GSAs so that all students can learn and pursue an education in a positive and supportive school climate. As part of a comprehensive safe schools initiative, GSAs can create positive changes in school climate that endure over time, outlasting changes in the student body, faculty or administration.

INTERVENTION III: ENUMERATED SCHOOL POLICY

When a law enumerates categories, it usually identifies types of individuals or things that need to be protected. These individuals or things include groups or classes. Anti-bullying and harassment bills are designed to address the needs of students who experience bullying and harassment in their schools. This is best achieved through a policy that both requires that all students are protected from bullying and harassment and also specifies categories of students who must be included by name (e.g., LGBT students).

The two categories most important to creating a safe school for LGBT students are sexual orientation and gender identity. School leaders should make sure these categories are included in policy.

INTERVENTION IV: LGBT-INCLUSIVE CURRICULUM

GLSEN's 2011 *National School Climate Survey* reveals that when educators include positive representations of LGBT people, history, and events in their curricula, students experienced school as a less-hostile place. Beyond fostering a safer school environment, positive representations of LGBT people, history, and events in the classroom may help promote a more welcoming climate for LGBT students. Students in schools with an inclusive curriculum feel a greater sense of connectedness to their school communities than other students. The inclusion of LGBT people, history, and events in the classroom curriculum educates all students about LGBT issues and may help to reduce prejudice and intolerance of LGBT people. When educators work to cultivate greater respect and acceptance of LGBT people among the student body, their efforts can result in a more positive school experience for LGBT students.

Over time, GLSEN research consistently shows that an inclusive curriculum is associated with increased peer support for LGBT students. Educating students to respect all people, regardless of sexual orientation, gender identity, or gender expression is a key component of creating safer and more affirming schools for LGBT youth. When engaging in curriculum revisions or when observing lessons in which LGBT-inclusion seems possible, school leaders should have this on their "radar" and discuss it with staff.

CONCLUSION: MAKING CHANGES

This chapter provides a great deal of guidance for school leaders on the levers (supportive school staff, student clubs, enumerated anti-bullying policy, and LGBT-inclusive curriculum) that research has shown can bring about change in school climate and improved outcomes for LGBT students. While this chapter offers concrete suggestions for action, school leaders who want to make real, sustainable change in how their school's climate is experienced by LGBT students ought to implement a "situated learning"[9] approach in their efforts. Such an approach emphasizes the social construction of knowledge and helps to connect learning and lived experiences. Explicitly technical and personally unexamined approaches to skill development ought to be avoided. Instead, it is self-interrogation of teaching practices that best prepares staff for consideration of their role and the development of the most student-centered approach to the issues in their school.

Regardless of the outcome or action desired, allowing, uncovering, and honoring teachers' uncertainty is an important part of the process for leaders. As a leader, embracing such an approach and taking such a stance provides the opportunity for school staff members to proceed in the most constructive manner possible. Certainly, there are many uncertainties in leading such work, but by publicly navigating through them school staff will witness the kind of courage-informed leadership that is critical in the process.

FREQUENTLY ASKED QUESTIONS

1. How do I know if my school's climate is healthy for LGBT students?

You can do this by surveying members of your school community—students, staff, and parents. Your survey should include questions that ask about the frequency of biased language, harassment, and assault, as well as the level of intervention by educators. GLSEN has a tool, the *Local School Climate Survey* (LSCS), that was designed to help educators and community members conduct a survey to assess the climate of their school or community. Go to glsen.org/research for more information or to download the *Local School Climate Survey*.

2. What is an ally? How can they improve school climate?

An ally is an individual who speaks out and stands up for a person or group that is targeted and discriminated against. An ally works to end oppression by supporting and advocating for people who are stigmatized, discriminated against, or treated unfairly.

For the lesbian, gay, bisexual, and transgender (LGBT) communities, an ally is any person who supports and stands up for the rights of LGBT people. Allies have been involved in almost all movements for social change, and allies can make a significant contribution to the LGBT rights movement. It is important for allies to demonstrate that LGBT people are not alone as they work to improve school climate, and to take a stand in places where it might not be safe for LGBT people to be out or visible. Any educator, LGBT or non-LGBT, can be an ally to LGBT students.

3. Why do allies (supportive educators) matter to LGBT students?

Research has shown that the presence of educators who are supportive of LGBT students can have a positive impact on the school experiences of these students, as well as their psychological well-being. Among the benefits:

- Students with greater numbers of supportive staff had a greater sense of being a part of their school community than other students.
- Students with many supportive staff reported higher grade point averages than other students (3.2 vs. 2.9).
- Students with a greater number of supportive staff also had higher educational aspirations—students with many supportive staff were about a third as likely to say they were not planning on attending college compared to students with no supportive educators (5.1% vs. 14.9%).

4. How do educators demonstrate to LGBT students that they are allies?

There are many main ways to demonstrate that you are or wish to be an ally to LGBT students. For example, responding to anti-LGBT language and behaviors sends a clear message to all students that you are someone who stands up for the rights of LGBT people. There are other, more proactive ways to demonstrate that you're an ally as well, such as supporting student clubs such as GSAs or including LGBT-relevant content in your lessons.

5. Why is it important to respond to anti-LGBT language and behavior?

Anti-LGBT behavior comes in all shapes and sizes: biased language, name-calling, harassment, and even physical assault. GLSEN's National School Climate Survey consistently finds that many LGBT students regularly hear homophobic slurs, such as "faggot" or "dyke," at school, and most students have been verbally or physically harassed in school. Youth who regularly experience harassment can suffer from low self-esteem, high rates of absenteeism, and low academic achievement. Educators can make a difference by intervening in anti-LGBT name-calling, bullying, and harassment every time they witness it. Taking action when you see it occur can help create a safe space for all students. Intervening on the spot will also serve as a teachable moment to let other students know that anti-LGBT behavior will not be tolerated. One of the most effective things you can do as an ally is to respond to anti-LGBT behavior.

6. Why is it important to make curriculum LGBT-inclusive?

LGBT-inclusive curriculum that provides positive representations of LGBT people, history, and events helps to create a tone of acceptance of LGBT people and increase awareness of LGBT-related issues, resulting in a more supportive environment for LGBT students. GLSEN's National School Climate Survey consistently finds that students with inclusive LGBT curriculum in their schools have a greater sense of belonging to their school community, hear fewer homophobic and transphobic remarks, and are less likely to be victimized or feel unsafe at school than those without inclusive curriculum.

7. What resources exist to assist my school in making change?

GLSEN-the Gay, Lesbian & Straight Education Network, provides free resources to educators and community members interested in making schools a healthier place for LGBT students. From professional development materials to model school policies and LGBT-inclusive curricular resources, GLSEN provides the most comprehensive set of tools available, most of which are freely downloadable from it website (www.glsen.org).

8. How do I begin to address issues with faculty and staff?

Deepening our understanding of school life in the service of students is critical to solving problems, and engaging in relevant conversations is a good starting point in many instances. Keep in mind, however, that for many, discourse around LGBT issues is unfamiliar territory. It is important to prepare by reading a comprehensive guide to creating safe schools such as GLSEN's *Safe*

Space Kit (available at www.glsen.org) and to create a safe and supportive space in which faculty/staff will feel free to share their experiences, challenges, successes, questions, and doubts as they pertain to the issues.

REFERENCES

1. McBrien JL, Brandt RS. *The Language of Learning: A Guide to Education Terms.* Alexandria, VA: Association for Supervision and Curriculum Development; 1997.

2. Kosciw JG, Greytak EA, Bartkiewicz MJ, et al. *The 2011 National School Climate Survey: The Experiences of Lesbian, Gay, Bisexual and Transgender Youth in Our Nation's Schools.* New York: GLSEN; 2012.

3. Harris Interactive and GLSEN. *From Teasing to Torment: School Climate in America, A Survey of Students and Teachers.* New York: GLSEN; 2005.

4. GLSEN. *Safe Space Kit: Guide to Being an Ally to LGBT Students,* New York: GLSEN; 2009.

5. GLSEN and Harris Interactive. *The Principal's Perspective: School Safety, Bullying, and Harassment: A Survey of Public School Principals.* New York: GLSEN; 2008.

6. Anderson G, Herr K, Nihlen A. *Studying Your Own School: An Educator's Guide to Qualitative Practitioner Research.* Thousand Oaks, CA: Sage Publications; 1994.

7. Washington J, Evans N. Becoming an ally. In: Evans N, Wall V, editors *Beyond Tolerance: Gays, Lesbians and Bisexuals on Campus.* Alexandria, VA: American College Personnel Association; 1991.

8. Bransford J, Darling-Hammond L, LePage P. *Preparing Teachers for a Changing World.* San Francisco, CA: Jossey-Bass; 2005.

9. Lave J, and Wenger E. *Situated Learning: Legitimate Peripheral Participation.* Cambridge, UK: Cambridge University Press; 1989.

10. Macgillivray IK. *Sexual Orientation and School Policy: A Practical Guide for Teachers, Administrators, and Community Activists.* Lanham, MD: Rowman & Littlefield; 2004.

11. Wessler SL, Prebble W. *The Respectful School: How Educators and Students Can Conquer Hate and Harassment.* Alexandria, VA: Association for Supervision and Curriculum Development; 2003.

7

Best Practices in the Prevention of Bullying: An Example of the Olweus Bullying Prevention Program

Susan P. Limber, PhD

Objectives

1. Identify common strategies to address bullying that are not consistent with current evidence and best practices.
2. Describe principles of best practices in the prevention of bullying.
3. Describe the goals, principles, components, and evidence base of the Olweus Bullying Prevention Program (OBPP).

In the wake of the April 20, 1999, tragic shootings at Columbine High School in Littleton, Colorado, there was a dramatic increase in attention to bullying among the media, the general public, and policy makers. In the span of 13 years, 49 states had passed anti-bullying laws (Montana has policy but no law), the vast majority of which require school districts to develop policies to address bullying in their schools.[1,2] Approximately half of these state laws currently require or encourage school districts to provide training for school staff on bullying prevention, and most require or encourage the implementation of bullying prevention, education, or awareness programs for students.[1-3] Most state laws are silent to the types of education and prevention efforts that are recommended, however, which may leave educators at a loss to know what strategies are likely to help reduce bullying.

This chapter will describe principles of best practice in bullying prevention and intervention, drawing on evaluations of school-based programs, experiences in the field, and recommendations from the federal government.[4] Recognizing that not all well-intentioned efforts are effective, the chapter also will highlight several strategies used by educators where there is no evidence that they actually reduce bullying. Finally, this chapter will describe how the Olweus Bullying Prevention Program serves as an example of an effort that encompasses elements of best practice.

PRINCIPLES OF BEST PRACTICE IN BULLYING PREVENTION

The Federal Partners in Bullying Prevention[5] have identified 10 elements of best practice in bullying prevention and response,[6,7] which were developed based on research on effective educational practice, as well as evaluations of bullying prevention programs and analyses of best practices in the field. These 10 elements can be a useful guide for administrators in planning and assessing their bullying prevention efforts.

1. *Focus on the social environment of the school.* In order to reduce bullying and create positive climates where students feel physically safe, emotionally secure, and connected with other students and educators, it is important to focus on the social environment of the school.[8,9] It must become "uncool" to bully, "cool" to help those who are, and normative for students and adults alike to notice if students are being ignored, marginalized, or bullied by their peers. Doing so requires a comprehensive effort that involves all adults and students within the school community and that is continued over time.

2. *Assess bullying and the need for responses.* Adults are not always very accurate in their assessment of bullying situations in their schools and communities. They can be off in their estimates of the prevalence of bullying, what types of bullying are the biggest worries for students, or what are the hot spots for bullying. As a result, it is critical that community leaders and school administrators collect local data to inform their efforts. There are different strategies that can be used to collect these data,[10] but one of the most common is to administer an

anonymous questionnaire to students. Doing so can help raise awareness of the problem among staff, parents, and students, and motivate adults to take action. It can also help leaders plan training and bullying prevention and intervention strategies, and can serve as a baseline from which to measure progress in efforts to reduce bullying.[11] It also can be helpful to collect data from staff and parents, who often have very different perceptions about the issues than youth themselves. This can be done formally (e.g., written surveys) or more informally (e.g., focus groups, interviews with diverse parents and staff).

3. *Seek support for bullying prevention.* In order for comprehensive bullying prevention efforts to be effective, they must be endorsed and promoted by leaders within the community and school (building-level administrators, district administrators, and school board members). Early, enthusiastic, and ongoing support from leaders is necessary; however, it is not sufficient for the effective implementation of bullying prevention strategies. For bullying prevention efforts to be most effective, they require buy-in from the majority of school staff and support from parents and guardians.[12]

4. *Coordinate and integrate prevention efforts.* School personnel expend considerable time, energy, and resources to address and prevent a wide variety of social and emotional problems among students, not just bullying. As a result, it is important to coordinate and, where appropriate, integrate these prevention efforts. Doing so will help to ensure that messages are consistent and that the limited human and financial resources are well spent. School safety efforts seem to work best when they are coordinated by a representative group of staff, including administrators, teaching staff, nonteaching staff, and parents.

5. *Provide training in bullying prevention and response.* It is critical to train all school staff so that they have a common and accurate understanding of the nature and prevalence of bullying, its effects, the school's policies and rules, and how to work as a team to prevent bullying. Training also is important to prepare every adult who interacts with students to respond appropriately if they observe or suspect bullying. Designated adults need training to follow up with

involved students and parents to stop the behavior and provide or arrange additional support services, as needed.

6. *Establish and enforce anti-bullying rules and policies.* Although many school behavior codes implicitly address bullying behavior, many do not explicitly use the term, define it, or clarify what behavior adults should expect of their students. It is important to establish rules that make clear to students that bullying behaviors are prohibited and that explain how students should react if they are aware of bullying or sense that another student is troubled. These rules should be discussed regularly with students and parents and posted widely. If students violate the rules and bully others, nonhostile, developmentally appropriate consequences may be needed to stop the behavior. When students help others who are bullied or troubled, adults should notice and reinforce this behavior. In a meta-analysis of school-based bullying prevention programs, those programs that had classroom rules and clear discipline for violations were more likely to produce reductions in bullying.[13]

7. *Increase adult supervision where bullying is most likely.* Bullying flourishes in locations where adults are absent or are not as observant as they might be. Therefore, it is important to redouble supervision in those locations where bullying most often occurs. Because adults are not always aware of these bullying "hot spots," it is useful to collect this information from students through formal or informal means (e.g., student surveys, focus groups, class discussions). Adults should keep in mind, however, that bullying may migrate to new locations once adults increase their supervision in known hot spots, so they should be vigilant to possible bullying throughout the school.

8. *Respond consistently and appropriately when bullying occurs.* Not only should adults be watchful for possible bullying, but they also should be ready to respond appropriately and immediately when they observe it. Designated staff should follow up (separately) with involved students after a bullying incident, and, whenever appropriate, with the students' parents. Referrals may be needed to mental health professionals within or outside of the school setting.

9. *Spend time discussing bullying with students.* Bullying prevention efforts should include time for small group facilitated discussions,

during which time students can learn about what bullying is and the harms that it causes, learn how to better respond to bullying that they experience or witness, and build empathy toward others. Student benefits from social and emotional learning include gains in critical thinking, academic achievement, school connectedness, empathy, and positive interactions with peers.[14]

10. *Continue efforts over time.* Bullying prevention efforts should have no end-date but should become integrated into the life of the school. Sustaining these efforts over time requires careful planning and a strong commitment from administrators and staff.

STRATEGIES INCONSISTENT WITH CURRENT EVIDENCE AND BEST PRACTICES

Not all strategies used by well-intentioned school personnel are effective in reducing bullying, and some, unfortunately, may have unintended negative effects. Due to these concerns, the Federal Partners in Bullying Prevention have identified four misdirections in bullying prevention and intervention:[15,16]

1. Zero tolerance for bullying.
2. Conflict resolution and peer mediation.
3. Group treatment for children who bully.
4. Simple, short-term solutions.

Zero Tolerance for Bullying

Some school districts or individual schools have adopted zero tolerance policies toward bullying, in which children who bully receive harsh punitive consequences, including suspension, expulsion, or transfer to alternative settings.[15,16] Such policies raise a number of serious concerns. First, they have the potential to affect a large number of students. For example, in a nationally representative sample of students in the United States, almost 1 in 10 of the 11-, 13-, and 15-year-olds surveyed (8% of girls and 13% of boys) indicated that they had bullied another student at school at least twice in the past couple of months.[17] Second, these policies may actually erode the climate within a school and ultimately have a negative effect on academic outcomes. The American

Psychological Association (APA) Task Force on Zero Tolerance (2008)[18] reviewed the research literature and concluded the following:

> [S]chools with higher rates of school suspension and expulsion appear to have less satisfactory ratings of school climate, less satisfactory school governance structures, and to spend a disproportionate amount of time on disciplinary matters. Perhaps more importantly, recent research indicates a negative relationship between the use of school suspension and expulsion and school-wide academic achievement (p. 855).

Threats of harsh punishment for students who bully may have a chilling effect on the willingness of students and adults to report known or suspected bullying if they feel these consequences are unfair or detrimental. Finally, recognizing that bullying can be an early indication of other problem behaviors,[17-21] children who bully need to be exposed to positive, prosocial role models, including fellow students and adults in their school. Unfortunately, students who are suspended are more likely to exhibit problem behavior and be suspended in the future.[18]

Conflict Resolution and Peer Mediation

Conflict resolution and peer mediation are strategies that many school personnel use to address conflicts between students. Some staff also use these strategies to address bullying, but this practice is not advisable.[15,16,22,23] In bullying situations, unlike in cases of conflict, there is an imbalance of power among the students involved. Bullying is a form of victimization. It should be considered no more of a "conflict" than domestic violence or child abuse.[16] As a result, attempts to mediate a bullying situation may send unacceptable messages to students who are involved, such as, "We need to work on this conflict between you two," or, "You're both partly right and partly wrong."[15,16] In some cases, mediation may also cause harm to a child who has been bullied. Some children are terrified at the thought of having to face their tormentors. In some cases, restorative practices may be appropriate to address bullying. Restorative practices include a focus on repairing the harm done to people and relationships by others.[24] They may include a meeting between children who bully, children who are bullied (if they are willing to participate and are well prepared), and parents. However, such practices may require considerable time and training by professionals—conditions that are not common to most peer mediation programs in schools.

Group Treatment for Children Who Bully

Other approaches have focused on providing therapeutic treatment for children who bully. Individual or family treatment may be useful in changing the behavior and addressing other problems, but group treatment for children who bully is not advised.[15,16] Group interventions with antisocial youth, although well-intentioned, are often counterproductive, as members of the group may reinforce each others' antisocial behavior.[25,26]

Simple, Short-Term Solutions

Given the many demands placed on educators, it is not surprising that while they may recognize the importance of preventing bullying, many are searching for simple, short-term, or inexpensive solutions. As a result, it is not uncommon for educators to adopt a piecemeal approach to bullying prevention,[15,16] whereby bullying may be the topic of just a half-day staff in-service training, a single schoolwide assembly, lessons taught by individual teachers, or a parent–teacher association meeting. Although such efforts may help raise awareness about the problem and may represent important steps toward a more comprehensive effort, it is unlikely that they will measurably reduce bullying.[15,16] They may also frustrate students and parents if it appears that the members of the school staff are merely paying lip service to the issue.

THE OLWEUS BULLYING PREVENTION PROGRAM

With these principles of best practice (and misdirections) in mind, it may be useful to examine the underlying principles and program components of one particular evidence-based bullying prevention program. The Olweus Bullying Prevention Program (OBPP) was the first bullying prevention program in the world to be implemented and systematically evaluated. Developed by Dan Olweus in the early 1980s, during a time of heightened concern about bullying in Norway, the program was first implemented within the context of a national campaign to reduce bullying in Norwegian schools.[12,20,27] Since this time, it has been widely disseminated. The book, *Bullying at School: What We Know and What We Can Do*[20] details the elements and outcomes of the program in

Norway, and has been translated into 20 languages.[28] The OBPP has been implemented in hundreds of Norwegian schools and, with cultural adaptation, to several thousand schools within the United States. It also has been influential in the development of other bullying prevention efforts worldwide. In a recent meta-analysis of 16 different bullying prevention programs, Ttofi and Farrington[13,29] concluded that bullying prevention programs could be effective in reducing bullying but that there was variability in findings. Those programs "inspired by the work of Dan Olweus worked best" (p. 72).[29]

Goals and Principles of the OBPP

The OBPP is a schoolwide, comprehensive bullying program, whose goals are to reduce existing bullying problems within a school environment, prevent the development of new problems, and improve peer relations.[12,20,27,30] Several key program principles, which were derived from research on aggressive behavior among youth,[30–34] guided the program's development. To reduce bullying in school, adults within a school environment must: (1) show warmth and interest in students; (2) establish firm but reasonable rules for unacceptable behavior; (3) use consistent and non-hostile consequences when rules are violated; and (4) act as positive role models for youth.[11,20]

Program Components

Specific program components are built upon these program principles, and are implemented at several levels: schoolwide, within the classroom, with individuals involved in bullying, and with the broader community. A listing of all program components, as implemented in the United States, is provided in Table 7.1. Although it is beyond the scope of this chapter to describe each in detail, several key components will be discussed. For a detailed description of all program components, see Olweus et al., 2007; Olweus & Limber 2010.[11–13]

Establishment of a Bullying Prevention Coordinating Committee (BPCC)

In keeping with the comprehensive nature of the OBPP, a number of interventions are implemented schoolwide, reaching all school staff, students, and parents. Key to the implementation of the program with fidelity and sustaining the program over time is the establishment of a Bullying Prevention

Table 7.1. Components of the OBPP

School-level Components
- Establish a Bullying Prevention Coordinating Committee.
- Conduct trainings for the committee and all staff and engage in ongoing consultation.
- Administer the Olweus Bullying Questionnaire to students in grades 3–12.
- Engage all staff in ongoing learning through regular meetings of staff discussion groups.
- Introduce the school rules about bullying.
- Review and refine the school's supervisory system.
- Hold a schoolwide kick-off event.
- Engage parents.

Classroom-level Components
- Post and enforce schoolwide rules against bullying.
- Hold regular class meetings to discuss bullying and related topics.
- Hold class-level meetings with parents.

Individual-level Components
- Supervise students' activities.
- Ensure that all staff intervene immediately when bullying is observed.
- Meet with students involved in bullying (separately for those who bully and those who are bullied).
- Meet with parents of students involved in bullying.
- Develop individual intervention plans for involved students, as needed.

Community-level Components
- Involve community members on the Bullying Prevention Coordinating Committee.
- Develop school-community partnerships to support the school's program.
- Help to spread bullying prevention messages in the community.

Adapted from Olweus & Limber (2010b).

Coordinating Committee (BPCC). The BPCC typically includes 8 to 15 members, with one or more members representing each of the following groups of individuals within a school: administrators, teachers, nonteaching staff, counseling/mental health professionals, parents. Other staff who bring particular expertise, such as a school nurse, school resource officer, Title IX representative, also are frequently involved, as well as one or two members of the broader community (e.g., after-school program coordinator). In some cases, students may be represented on the committee where developmentally appropriate (e.g., middle or high school students); in other cases, separate student advisory committees may be formed to provide input into development of their school's program. After receiving two days of training from a certified OBPP trainer, members of the BPCC (in consultation with their trainer) develop a plan to implement the OBPP within their school;

communicate the plan to staff, students, and parents; coordinate the OBPP with other initiatives at their school; and monitor the implementation of the program over time.[11,12,35] The BPCC is chaired by an on-site OBPP coordinator (e.g., a school counselor, prevention specialist, administrator), who engages in regular consultation with the OBPP trainer during at least the first year of the program's implementation. An engaged committee, which meets on a regular basis throughout the life of the program, has proven to be a key piece to successful and long-term implementation of the OBPP.[16]

Training for the Bullying Prevention Coordinating Committee and All School Staff

Members of the BPCC receive two days of intensive in-person training by a certified OBPP trainer, who also provides at least one year (typically 12–18 hours per year) of in-person or telephone consultation to the committee members of the BPCC. In turn, those committee members provide at least one full day of training to all school staff prior to the launch of the program. Periodic booster trainings for staff are held, as needed, on topics of particular interest to staff, and yearly trainings for new staff are encouraged.

Administration of an Anonymous Questionnaire

Another key schoolwide component of the OBPP is the administration of the Olweus Bullying Questionnaire (OBQ),[36] a 42-item anonymous questionnaire designed for students in grades 3–12. The OBQ assesses students' experiences with and perceptions of bullying in their school environment. It is recommended that the OBQ be administered prior to the implementation of the OBPP and on a yearly basis thereafter.[11,37] A comprehensive building-level report of students' responses to questions on the OBQ (typically broken down by grade and gender) is made available to schools. The Bullying Prevention Coordinating Committee is encouraged to use these data to raise awareness about bullying among staff, students, and parents; plan for the implementation of their own program; and assess their progress in reducing bullying over time.[11,12]

Ongoing Learning Through Staff Discussion Groups

Although the initial training in the OBPP provides a solid basis of knowledge about bullying and administration of the program, it is important to put structures in place for ongoing learning and sharing among staff. Schools are encouraged to develop discussion groups of teachers and other staff that meet on a regular basis (ideally monthly throughout the first year of the program). Groups consist of relatively small numbers of staff (no more than 15) and typically are led by a member of the BPCC.[11,12,16,35] The goals of these meetings are to provide more detailed information about particular program components, as well as an opportunity for colleagues to share experiences and trouble-shoot problems. The meetings help keep staff engaged and sustain the program over time.

Establishment and Enforcement of School Rules About Bullying

To help ensure that students and adults have clear and consistent expectations about appropriate behavior at school, school administrators are encouraged to adopt four specific rules about bullying: (1) We will not bully others. (2) We will try to help students who are bullied. (3) We will try to include students who are left out. (4) If we know that somebody is being bullied, we will tell an adult at school and an adult at home.[11] These rules are not only directed at children who bully or who may be tempted to bully (rule 1), but they also are meant to guide the behavior of those who may witness bullying or be in positions to prevent bullying (rules 2–4). These rules are posted widely throughout the school and discussed with students and parents. The Bullying Prevention Coordinating Committee sets guidelines for applying consistent negative consequences (when rule 1 is violated) and positive consequences (for following rules 2–4). Olweus and colleagues[38,39] observed that greater reductions in bullying were found in classrooms that had adopted these rules.

Classroom Meetings With Students

Among the classroom-level components of the OBPP (see Table 7.1),[12] the cornerstone is regular classroom meetings, where teachers facilitate discussions around bullying and related issues.[11,12] The purposes of class meetings are to build a sense of community among students and adults in the class, provide an opportunity for students to learn about bullying and the school's expectations for their behavior, and enable them to problem-solve and practice solutions to everyday bullying problems they may encounter. Topics of class meetings naturally move beyond the topic of bullying to address other related issues of concern to teachers and students and provide an ongoing opportunity for social and emotional learning. Schools are encouraged to schedule class meetings once per week at a predictable time. Olweus et al. observed that those classrooms that held regular class meetings and that used role play as a strategy to address bullying had greater reductions in bullying than those that did not.[38]

Interventions With Students Involved in Bullying

If school-level and classroom-level interventions are implemented well, it is less likely that individual students will be bullied. Nevertheless, school personnel must have in place appropriate strategies to address bullying when it is observed or suspected. To this end, school staff receive training to know how to respond appropriately on-the-spot if they observe or suspect bullying.[11,12] Training is also provided for follow-up meetings with students who are bullied and (separately) with students who bully others. Parents are involved in these meetings whenever possible and appropriate. The focus of these meetings is to support bullied students and stop the behavior. School personnel also assess all students' needs for further assistance (including outside referrals where appropriate) to cope with bullying they may have experienced or to help reduce aggressive behavior in children and youth who bully.

Community Involvement

Recognizing that bullying doesn't stop at the doors of the school, members of the Bullying Prevention Coordinating Committee are encouraged to engage the broader community in bullying prevention efforts.[11,12] School staff are encouraged to include one or more community members on the school's committee, look for ways the community may be made aware and supportive of the school's efforts (e.g., through financial, human, or material resources), and spread consistent bullying prevention messages and strategies to youth organizations and other settings where youth gather.

Training and Implementation

Print and video resources are available to support administrators, members of schools' BPCCs, and teachers in implementing the program.[42] School personnel are also strongly encouraged to work with a Certified Olweus

Trainer/Consultant to help ensure that the program is effectively introduced and implemented with fidelity.[41]

OVERVIEW OF EFFECTIVENESS OF THE OLWEUS BULLYING PREVENTION PROGRAM

The Olweus Bullying Prevention Program has been evaluated in a number of studies in Norway and the United States. An in-depth review of this research is beyond the scope of this chapter, but highlights from these studies will be presented. (For a detailed summary of current research see Olweus & Limber, 2010; Limber, 2011.)[27,35]

There have been seven outcome evaluations of the OBPP in Norway, involving more than 20,000 students. Olweus and his colleagues found large reductions in the likelihood that students were bullied and had bullied others among students in grades 4–8, based on students' self-reports, peer ratings, and teacher ratings.[12,27] They also found that fidelity of implementation mattered. Those classes that implemented key components of the program (such as rules about bullying, class meetings, and role playing) showed the greatest reductions in bullying.[38,39] Significant reductions in antisocial behavior (such as involvement in vandalism, theft, and truancy) were observed and attributed to the OBPP. Moreover, positive program effects were found with regard to students' perceptions school climate.[12,20,27,43]

Several studies have evaluated the OBPP in diverse school settings in the United States, and a large-scale evaluation of the program in Pennsylvania is still underway. In the first evaluation of the OBPP in the United States, Limber and colleagues[44,45] assessed the effectiveness of the program in elementary and middle schools in primarily rural, low socio-economic, predominantly African-American school districts in South Carolina. Comparing intervention and nonintervention schools after seven months of program implementation, researchers found significant reductions in students' reports of bullying others in schools implementing the program (a 16% decrease) and increases in bullying among students in the nonintervention schools (12% increase), resulting in a 28% relative reduction of bullying between OBPP and non-OBPP schools. Significant program effects were also observed for self-reported delinquency, vandalism, school misbehavior, and sanctions for school misbehavior, but not for being bullied.

Black and Jackson[46] evaluated the OBPP in six large public elementary and middle schools in Philadelphia, Pennsylvania, over four years. Using an observational measure that assessed physical, verbal, and emotional bullying, researchers reported a decrease in bullying incidents by 45% over those four years, from 65 incidents per 100 student hours, to 36 incidents.

Bauer and colleagues[47] evaluated the OBPP using a nonrandomized, controlled study with seven intervention and three control middle schools. Researchers found significant program effects for relational victimization and physical victimization among white students but not for students of other races and ethnicities. They also observed positive program effects regarding students' perceptions that their peers actively intervened in bullying incidents.

Limber and colleagues[48] evaluated the OBPP in a large-scale study in Pennsylvania involving students in grades 3–12 from 194 schools. Using a selection cohorts design and assessing students at baseline and again after at least one and one-half years of program implementation, the researchers observed significant reductions in elementary, middle, and high school students' self-reports of being bullied and bullying others (whether measured by global variables, three individual forms of bullying that are most prevalent among the youth [verbal bullying, social exclusion, physical bullying], or scale score of 10 specific forms of bullying). They also observed positive changes in students' perceptions of their own behavior as witnesses to bullying (e.g., propensity to try to help stop bullying), and their perceptions of the actions of others in the school environment to help stop bullying. Positive findings were largely consistent for boys and girls across grades (elementary, middle, and high school grades), and among students of different racial/ethnic groups. The study design allowed the researchers to examine whether results might be the result of "historical effects" (such as historical trends over time or other broad bullying prevention efforts within the state). Analyses indicated that "historical effects" could be ruled out as an explanation for the findings.

CONCLUSIONS

With the recent increased attention to bullying among the American public, and with mandates in many states to address bullying in public schools through training and prevention, many educators are searching for effective strategies to reduce bullying. Administrators may be guided in their efforts by descriptions of 10 best practices in bullying prevention, which have been developed based on research and experiences in the field and promoted by the Federal Partners in Bullying Prevention. Similarly, administrators will benefit from learning which strategies have *not* proven effective in reducing bullying, and which may, in fact, have unintended negative outcomes, such as zero tolerance policies or simple, short-term efforts to reduce bullying. The Olweus Bullying Prevention Program, which encompasses these key principles of best practice, has been shown to be effective in preventing bullying, evidenced by studies such as a recent large-scale evaluation of efforts within the Commonwealth of Pennsylvania.

FREQUENTLY ASKED QUESTIONS

1. In what ways have there been changes in attention to bullying in recent years, on the part of the general public, media, and policy makers?

In the wake of the tragic shootings at Columbine High School, there was a dramatic increase in attention to bullying among the media, the general public, and policy makers. In the span of 13 years, 49 states had passed anti-bullying laws, the vast majority of which require school districts to develop policies to address bullying in their schools. Approximately half of these state laws currently require or encourage school districts to provide training for school staff on bullying prevention, and most require or encourage the implementation of bullying prevention, education, or awareness programs for students.

2. Why is it critical to assess bullying among children and youth in educational settings?

Adults are not always very accurate in their assessment of bullying situations in their schools and communities. They can be off in their estimates of the prevalence of bullying, what types of bullying are the biggest worries for students, or what are the hot spots for bullying. As a result, it is critical that community leaders and school administrators collect local data to inform their efforts.

3. What training is needed for educators to address and prevent bullying?

It is critical to train all school staff so that they have a common and accurate understanding of the nature and prevalence of bullying, its effects, the school's policies and rules, and how to work as a team to prevent bullying. Training also is important to prepare every adult who interacts with students to respond appropriately if they observe or suspect bullying. Designated adults need training to follow up with involved students and parents to stop the behavior and provide or arrange additional support services, as needed.

4. What classroom-level practices are considered best practices in bullying prevention?

Bullying prevention efforts should include time for small group facilitated discussions, during which time students can learn about what bullying is and the harms that it causes, learn how to better respond to bullying that they experience or witness, and build empathy toward others. Student benefits from social and emotional learning include gains in critical thinking, academic achievement, school connectedness, empathy, and positive interactions with peers.

5. Some schools have adopted zero tolerance policies to address bullying. What are these?

These policies typically involve administering inflexible, harsh punitive consequences for children who bully, including suspension, expulsion, or transfer to alternative settings.

6. Why are zero tolerance policies not recommended in cases of bullying?

First, they have the potential to affect a large number of students. Second, these policies may actually erode the climate within a school and ultimately have a negative effect on academic outcomes. Threats of harsh punishment for students who bully may have a chilling effect on the willingness of students and adults to report known or suspected bullying if they feel these consequences are unfair or detrimental. Finally, recognizing that bullying can be an early indication of other problem behaviors, children who bully need to be exposed to positive, pro-social role models, including fellow students and adults in their school.

7. Why is it not advisable to engage children who bully in group treatment?

Group interventions with antisocial youth, although well-intentioned, are often counterproductive, as members of the group may reinforce each other's antisocial behavior.

8. What are the goals and principles of the Olweus Bullying Prevention Program (OBPP)?

The OBPP is a schoolwide, comprehensive bullying program, whose goals are to reduce existing bullying problems within a school environment, prevent the development of new problems, and improve peer relations. Several key program principles, which were derived from research on aggressive behavior among youth, guided the development of the program. To reduce bullying in school, adults within a school environment must: (1) show warmth and interest in students; (2) establish firm but reasonable rules for unacceptable behavior; (3) use consistent and nonhostile consequences when rules are violated; and (4) act as positive role models for youth.

9. What research has been conducted to assess the OBPP in Norwegian schools?

There have been seven outcome evaluations of the OBPP in Norway, involving more than 20,000 students. Olweus and his colleagues found large reductions in the likelihood that students were bullied and had bullied others among students in grades 4–8, based on students' self-reports, peer ratings, and teacher ratings. They also found that fidelity of implementation mattered. Those classes that implemented key components of the program (such as rules about bullying, class meetings, and role playing) showed the greatest reductions in bullying. [40,41] Significant reductions in antisocial behavior (such as involvement in vandalism, theft, and truancy) were observed and attributed to the OBPP.

10. What recent evidence is there on the effectiveness of the OBPP in U.S. schools?

The most recent evaluation of the OBPP is a large-scale effort involving nearly 200 schools, to date. Researchers observed significant reductions in elementary, middle, and high school students' self-reports of being bullied and bullying others. They also observed positive changes in students' perceptions of their own behavior as witnesses to bullying (e.g., propensity to try to help stop bullying), and their perceptions of the actions of others in the school environment to help stop bullying. Positive findings were largely consistent for boys and girls, across grades (elementary, middle, and high school grades), and among students of different racial/ethnic groups.

REFERENCES

1. Sacco D, Silbaugh K, Corredor F, et al. *An Overview of State Anti-Bullying Legislation and Other Related Laws.* 2012.

2. U.S. Department of Education. Dear Colleague Letter. Available from http://www2.ed.gov/about/offices/list/ocr/letters/colleague-201010.html. Accessed on October 26, 2010.

3. Cornell DG, Limber SP. Legal and policy considerations in bullying intervention. *Under review.*

4. Federal Partners in Bullying Prevention. 2013; www.stopbullying.gov.

5. Federal Partners in Bullying Prevention. Community Action Planning; 2013. Available at http://www.stopbullying.gov/prevention/in-the-community/community-action-planning/index.html.

6. Limber S. What works (and doesn't work) in bullying prevention and intervention. *Stud Assist.* 2004:16–19.

7. Limber SP, Snyder M. What works and doesn't work in bullying prevention and intervention. *The State Education Standard.* 2006, July:24–28.

8. Mulvey E, Cauffman E. The inherent limits of predicting school violence. *Am Psychol.* 2001; 56:797–802.

9. Nation M, Crusto C, Wandersman A, et al. What works in prevention: Principles of effective prevention programs. *Am Psycholog.* 2003; 58:449–456.

10. Centers for Disease Control and Prevention. Measuring bullying victimization, perpetration, and bystander experiences: A compendium of assessment tools; 2011.

11. Olweus D, Limber SP, Flerx V, et al. *Olweus Bullying Prevention Program: Schoolwide Guide*. Center City, MN: Hazelden; 2007.

12. Olweus D, Limber SP. The Olweus Bullying Prevention Program: Implementation and evaluation over two decades. In: *The Handbook of School Bullying: An International Perspective*. New York: Routledge; 2010:377–402.

13. Ttofi MM, Farrington DP. What works in preventing bullying: Effective elements of anti-bullying programmes. *J Aggression, Conflict Peace Res*. 2009; 1:13–24.

14. Durlak JA, Weissberg RP, Dymnicki AB, et al. The impact of enhancing students' social and emotional learning: a meta-analysis of school-based universal interventions. *Child Dev*. Jan–Feb 2011; 82(1):405–432.

15. Federal Partners in Bullying Prevention. *Misdirections in Bullying Prevention and Intervention*.

16. Limber SP. Implementation of the Olweus Bullying Prevention Program: Lessons learned from the field. In: *Bullying in North American Schools: A Social-Ecological Perspective on Prevention and Intervention*. 2nd ed. New York: Routledge; 2010: 291–306.

17. Molcho M, Craig W, Due P, et al. Cross-national time trends in bullying behaviour 1994–2006: Findings from Europe and North America. *Int Public Health*. Sep 2009; 54 Suppl 2:225–234.

18. American Psychological Association Zero Tolerance Task Force. Are zero tolerance policies effective in the schools? *Am Psychol*. 2008; 63(9)852–862.

19. Nansel TR, Overpeck M, Pilla RS, et al. Bullying behaviors among US youth: Prevalence and association with psychosocial adjustment. *JAMA*. April 25 2001; 285(16):2094–2100.

20. Olweus D. *Bullying at School: What We Know and What We Can Do*. Oxford, UK; Cambridge, MA: Blackwell; 1993.

21. Ttofi MM, Farrington DP, Losel F, Loeber R. The predictive efficiency of school bullying versus later offending: a systematic/meta-analytic review of longitudinal studies. *Crim Behav Mental Health: CBMH*. Apr 2011; 21(2):80–89.

22. Limber SP. Addressing youth bullying behaviors. Proceedings of the Educational Forum on Adolescent Health: Youth Bullying, American Medical Association; 2002 Chicago.

23. Cohen R. Stop mediating these conflicts now! The School Mediator: Peer Mediation Insights from the Desk of Richard Cohen. *The School Mediator.* 2002. Available at www.schoolmediation.com/.

24. Amstuta LS, Mullet JH. *The Little Book of Restorative Discipline for Students.* Intercourse, PA: Good Books; 2005.

25. Dishion TJ, Poulin F, Burraston B. Peer group dynamics associated with iatrogenic effects in group interventions with high-risk young adolescents. *New Dir Child Adolescent Dev.* Spring 2001; (91):79–92.

26. Dishion TJ, McCord J, Poulin F. When interventions harm. Peer groups and problem behavior. *Am Psychol.* September 1999; 54(9):755–764.

27. Olweus D, Limber SP. Bullying in school: Evaluation and dissemination of the Olweus Bullying Prevention Program. *Am J Orthopsychiatry.* January 2010; 80(1):124–134.

28. Olweus, D. Personal communication. September 2012.

29. Ttofi MM, Farrington, DP, Baldry, AC. *Effectiveness of Programmes to Reduce Bullying.* Stockholm, Sweden: Swedish National Council for Crime Prevention; 2008.

30. Baumrind D. Child care practices anteceding three patterns of preschool behavior. *Genet Psychol Monographs.* 1967; 75:43–88.

31. Loeber R, Stouthamer-Loeber M. Family factors as correlates and predictors of juvenile conduct problems and delinquency. *Crime Justice* 1986; 7:29–150.

32. Olweus D. *Aggression in the Schools: Bullies and Whipping Boys.* New York: Hemisphere Publishing Corporation; 1978.

33. Olweus D. Familial and tempermental determinants of aggressive behavior in adolescent boys: A casual analysis. *Dev Psychol.* 1980; 16:6444–6660.

34. Olweus D. Stability of aggressive reaction patterns in males: a review. *Psychol Bull.* July 1979; 86(4):852–875.

35. Limber SP. Development, evaluation, and future directions of the Olweus Bullying Prevention Program. *J Sch Violence*. 2011; 10:71–87.

36. Olweus D. *Olweus Bullying Questionnaire*. Center City, MN: Hazelden; 2007.

37. Solberg M, Olweus D. Prevalence estimation of school bullying with the Olweus Bully/Victim Questionnaire. *Aggressive Behav*. 2003; 29:239–268.

38. Olweus D, Alsaker FD. Assessing change in a cohort longitudinal study with hierarchical data. In: D Magnusson, LR Bergman, G Rudinger, and B Torestad, eds. *Problems and Methods in Longitudinal Research*. New York: Cambridge University Press; 1991:107–132.

39. Olweus D, Kallestad JH. The Olweus Bullying Prevention Program: Effects of classroom components at different grade levels. In: K Osterman, ed. *Indirect and Direct Aggression*. New York: Peter Lang; 2010.

40. Hazelden Foundation. The World's Foremost Bullying Prevention Program 2013. Available at http://www.violencepreventionworks.org/public/ olweus_bullying_prevention_program.page.

41. Olweus Bullying Prevention Program U. Olweus Bullying Prevention Program. 2013. Available at http://www.clemson.edu/olweus/.

42. Olweus D. Bully/victim problems at school: Facts and intervention. *European Journal of Psychology of Education*. 1997; 12:495–510.

43. Olweus D. Bully/victim problems among school children: Basic facts and effects of a school based intervention program. In: DJ Pepler and KH Rubin, eds. *The Development and Treatment of Childhood Aggression*. Hillsdale, NJ: Erlbaum; 1991:411–438.

44. Limber SP, Nation M, Tracy, AJ, et al. Implementation of the Olweus Bullying Prevention Program in the Southeastern United States. In: PK Smith, D Pepler, and K Rigby, eds. *Bullying in schools: How Successful Can Interventions Be?* Cambridge, UK: Cambridge University Press; 2004:55–79.

45. Melton GB, Limber SP, Cunningham P, et al. *Violence Among Rural Youth*. 1998.

46. Black SA, Jackson, E. Using bullying incident density to evaluate the Olweus Bullying Prevention Programme. *Sch Psychol Int*. 2007; 28:623–638.

47. Bauer NS, Herrenkohl TI, Lozano P, et al. Childhood bullying involvement and exposure to intimate partner violence. *Pediatrics*. Aug 2006; 118(2):E235–E242.

48. Limber SP, Olweus D, Masiello M, et al. Evaluation of the Olweus Bullying Prevention Program in a large scale study in Pennsylvania. *In preparation*.

8

Readiness and Bullying Prevention

Stacie Molnar-Main, EdD and Heather Cecil, PhD

Objectives

1. Provide an overview of the construct of readiness, drawing from the public health and educational literature.
2. Provide an overview of research on readiness, with particular focus on the Olweus Bullying Prevention Program (OBPP) and recent Pennsylvania Creating Atmospheres of Respect in Every School (PA CARES) fidelity data.
3. Describe the Center for Safe Schools/Highmark readiness support process (three tiers).
4. Address lessons and future directions for research and practice.

The case for bullying prevention has been made convincingly by experts in health promotion, delinquency prevention and youth development.[1–3] Consistent with the response to other public health issues,[4] America has approached the epidemic of bullying in an incremental way, reflecting a growing awareness of the issue and the importance of coordinated, systemic responses.[5,6] When viewed from a historical perspective, America's progress in addressing the issue of bullying has actually been quite impressive. For instance, in the past 10 years, there have been over 2000 research articles published on this topic, 49 U.S. states have passed legislation on bullying,[7,8] and countless schools have adopted bullying prevention programs.[9]

While the issue of bullying is relevant to all youth development practitioners, educators are among the professionals most affected by the issue. Not only have media accounts frequently implicated educators in the aftermath of tragedies associated with bullying[10,11] but also research indicates that most bullying occurs in schools or during school-associated activities.[12,13] The effects of peer victimization in an educational setting can be serious. Specifically, research indicates that children who are involved in bullying tend to suffer academically[14,15] and are at greater risk of negative social and emotional outcomes.[16,17] In addition, schools with high rates of bullying tend to perform lower on state mandated tests than schools without "bullying climates."[18]

Based on the prevalence of bullying and its negative effects, many school administrators feel compelled to implement programs to address bullying.[19,20] Yet, not all anti-bullying programs implemented in schools result in the intended outcomes.[21,22] Some programs do not have adequate research to demonstrate their effectiveness and, therefore, may not be wise investments.[23] Other programs may have ample evidence of their effectiveness but are difficult to implement with fidelity.[24] Successful implementation requires extensive planning, wherein school personnel carefully select intervention strategies, prepare for implementation, provide ongoing training for key staff, and engage in monitoring of the intervention and its effects.[25,26] It is important for school personnel to understand this process so that they can support effective decision making and sustainability of bullying prevention efforts over time.

This chapter addresses the issue of site readiness, a factor known to affect the quality of program implementation.[27–29] It begins with a brief summary of the barriers to implementation of prevention programs with fidelity and then continues with an overview of the readiness construct as it relates to research on prevention programming in schools. It then describes three dimensions of school readiness that influence the success of school-based interventions. In order to demonstrate the relationship between readiness and implementation fidelity, we provide a case study of a readiness intervention. The chapter concludes with a series of practical recommendations for school adminis-trators, teachers, and support staff who are interested in improving their school's readiness for comprehensive bullying prevention efforts.

BARRIERS TO EFFECTIVE PREVENTION PROGRAMMING

As the other chapters in this book detail, bullying is a complex phenomenon that cannot be addressed through simple solutions.[2] Bullying is a socio-ecological problem[30,31] that occurs as individuals interact in social systems and with contextual factors.[22,32,33] As a result, the most effective approaches to bullying prevention take a comprehensive view of the problem.[34] These programs go beyond teaching content and skills to combat bullying and focus on changing the social culture of schools by affecting norms, systems, and practices at the peer, family, school, and community levels.[2,22,35]

Schools are considered ideal settings for implementing prevention programs because they offer ready access to students, staff, and many resources necessary to implement youth programs.[36,37] Nonetheless, research indicates that schools often employ prevention strategies ineffectively.[38,39] For example, school personnel might select strategies that are not research-based or they might fail to implement proven interventions with fidelity.[23] The former is of concern because research clearly indicates that some strategies are more effective at producing outcomes than others. The latter is problematic, as programs that are known to be effective must be implemented as designed in order to produce the intended results.[40–44]

The extent to which a program is implemented as designed is known as the level of *implementation fidelity*.[24,40,45] High fidelity is widely recognized as the goal of intervention programs because greater program fidelity is associated with better youth outcomes.[24,42,45] A program is implemented with high fidelity when the organization executes all intervention components with integrity and adheres to guidelines related to duration, dosage, and methods of intervention.[24,41,45,46]

At times, programs implemented with high levels of fidelity may fail because they have not been institutionalized into school systems and practices.[47] These failures are often due to ineffective planning for *sustainability* of the effort.[28,48] Sustainability can be threatened when schools do not provide needed resources to the program, align school policies with the program, plan effectively for transitions in program leadership, engage key stakeholders, and address staff development needs.[28,49–51] Although ineffective planning for sustainability may occur at any stage of program implementation, Adelman and Taylor[28] note, "One of the most fundamental errors related to facilitating systemic change is the tendency to set actions in motion without taking sufficient time to lay the foundation needed for substantive change" (p. 12). This issue is at the heart of the readiness construct.

READINESS AND SUCCESS OF SCHOOL-BASED PREVENTION PROGRAMS

In general, readiness refers to a willingness and preparedness to implement or adopt a program.[36,52,53] It is reflected in the systems and resources of the organization and in the commitments, skills, and characteristics of people involved in the implementation effort. While it has been recognized as a moderator of program implementation in numerous studies on organizational change,[54,55] readiness is a relatively new area of inquiry and theorizing in educational literature.

Preliminary studies suggest that readiness is an important predictor of successful implementation of school improvement strategies.[36] Implementation efforts are more likely to succeed when the underlying philosophy of the program and its methods align with the educational philosophy and resources of the school, its staff, and the community.[37,56,57] This conclusion suggests that interventions that focus on changing the norms or culture of a school may be more difficult to implement than interventions that have a more instrumental focus. Comprehensive bullying prevention programs, for example, require schools to do more than implement policies curricula. Educators and other school staff must also commit to responding to peer aggression differently and demonstrating an enhanced level of care for students involved.[58]

While there is no consensus as to which readiness variables influence the implementation of school-based bullying prevention programs, current research has begun to identify readiness variables related to the implementation of other prevention programs in schools.[59] For the purposes of this review, these readiness variables are organized into three broad categories: *organizational capacity, implementer characteristics,* and *leadership factors.*

Organizational Capacity

Organizational capacity refers to the ability of an organization to support change over time.[54] It includes *resources, structures,* and organizational *practices* that support the functioning of a school.[60] To expand, organizational capacity refers to the availability of financial and material resources to support adopted programs, the alignment of policies with programmatic goals, and the presence of systems to support effective planning and communication.[37,61,62] Readiness is also reflected in school infrastructures that allow for the efficient delivery of staff training, program elements, and oversight.[59,63,64]

Existing resources, infrastructure, and practices can enhance the capacity of leaders and implementers to fulfill the requirements of research-based programs and make necessary adjustments to the implementation plan. For example, a school that organizes its teachers into teams or professional learning communities may use that structure to deliver staff development and coaching associated with the prevention program. Existing systems of stakeholder engagement and communication, similarly, may be used to share information about the program with constituents and gather feedback to inform the implementation effort.

Several features of organizational capacity are particularly relevant to a school's readiness for comprehensive bullying prevention programming:

- District policies that mandate anti-bullying and anti-harassment programming at the school level.
- Space within the formal curricula to address social–emotional learning components of the bullying prevention program.
- Availability of financial resources to purchase prevention materials.
- Adequate personnel resources to fulfill program requirements.
- Adequate staff development time dedicated to building-level initiatives, such as bullying prevention.
- Effective systems of facilitating communication among implementers and stakeholders in bullying prevention.

In addition, schools that intend to implement comprehensive bullying prevention programs should have adequate resources available to support the implementation of the program *over time*.[65] Inadequate facilities and financial resources are among the main barriers to program implementation identified by implementers.[61] Research also suggests that new programs are particularly susceptible to failure in the first two years of implementation.[66,67] Thus, it is particularly important for schools to allocate sufficient resources for programmatic efforts during the early years of implementation to bolster initial implementation efforts and establish conditions for sustainability.[47,59]

Implementer Characteristics

Another important aspect of site readiness is embodied in the characteristics of the people responsible for implementing the program.[45,61,68] According to Armenakis and colleagues,[29] individual readiness is "the cognitive precursor to the behaviors of either resistance to, or support for, a change effort" (pp. 681–682). From this perspective, readiness is manifest in individuals' beliefs, attitudes, and intentions regarding the extent to which changes are needed and the organization's capacity to successfully undertake these.[29,55]

In the case of prevention programs, the faculty and staff of schools are often responsible for delivering the program to students.[69] Research indicates that *participant buy-in, commitment,* and *self-efficacy* are important predictors of successful programmatic implementation.[29,48,57] In other words, staff who have a role in implementing prevention programs must recognize the need for the intervention and understand the value of implementing a comprehensive, evidence-based approach.[70,71] Second, readiness efforts should ensure that educators are committed to implementing the prevention program as designed.[72] This level of commitment is critical to support fidelity of implementation.[44] Finally, change agents need to ensure that educators are confident in their ability to implement the required prevention strategies effectively.[29,55,70] That is, implementers need to believe that they can perform the program's activities and that the activities will influence students' behaviors.[70,73]

Educator buy-in, commitment, and efficacy can be influenced by teachers' past experience with school improvement programs,[74] training,[45,75] program features,[45,48] and external conditions.[76–78] When educators have experienced multiple failed implementation efforts, they may be reluctant to support other initiatives because they do not believe the school can succeed. In addition, teachers' beliefs about their own competence to implement an intervention can serve as a barrier to implementation if they have not had adequate training or the intervention strategy appears too complex. Finally, external conditions, such as the policy environment and the availability of supportive resources, can influence implementers' commitment to the intervention.

Applied to comprehensive bullying prevention programming, the following participant characteristics are indicators of readiness:

- Teachers, administrators, and support staff believe bullying is a significant problem that negatively affects their students and the school.
- Teachers and administrators recognize social and emotional learning as an educational priority linked to the mission of the school.
- The majority of implementers (teachers, support staff) have a positive or neutral view of the selected program.
- Most implementers believe they can implement program elements successfully.

Leadership Factors

While organizational and participant factors play a direct role in the change processes, leadership is a mediating factor. Research suggests that prevention programs are more likely to be fully implemented in schools where leadership is shared and stable, professional development and learning are the norm, and administrative support for the program is clearly present.[37,79] Conversely, it can be difficult to implement a prevention program in schools that have a history of leadership instability, high staff turnover, and frequent curriculum changes.[48,57]

Regardless of a school's history, principals and other leaders play a significant role in organizational readiness for prevention programs.[26] A program is more likely to succeed if the school principal makes it a high priority and school staff perceive the principal as highly engaged in its implementation.[26,79,80] Further, program developers often recommended that a separate program leader oversee the implementation of research-based programs in schools.[48,81] This leadership structure can help to ensure that adequate attention is given to the coordination, monitoring, and institutionalization of the program over time. Finally, many prevention programs require educators to adopt new practices or change existing practices. In order to support these changes, research suggests that leaders and implementers should have access to high-quality training,[45,75] ongoing technical assistance,[26] and coaching throughout the implementation process.[27]

The following indicators of leadership capacity are relevant to educators and parents interested in implementing schoolwide bullying prevention program:

- The school has a history of leadership stability and low rates of staff turnover.
- There is an ethos of shared leadership in the school and a commitment to ongoing improvement among staff.
- The principal understands the requirements of the program and supports high fidelity implementation.
- A coordinator and leadership team are identified to oversee the program's implementation.
- Leaders have identified a trainer or coach who is an expert in the designated program and available to provide support during the first three years of implementation.
- Parental involvement is encouraged to provide support to the school-based prevention program.

CASE STUDY IN READINESS FOR BULLYING PREVENTION

In order to demonstrate how the readiness construct applies to bullying prevention in schools, we discuss a case study of a statewide bullying prevention initiative that addressed readiness issues as part of its implementation strategy. Pennsylvania Creating Atmospheres of Respect in Every School (PA CARES) is a public health initiative, funded by the Highmark Foundation. It has been responsible for overseeing the implementation of the Olweus Bullying Prevention Program[82] (OBPP) in more than 200 schools in Pennsylvania since 2008.

The OBPP was selected for broad-scale implementation by PA CARES because it is an evidence-based, comprehensive program.[58,82,83] Although the OBPP is recognized as effective, it is a complex intervention that can be difficult to implement with fidelity and sustain over time.[58,84–89]. In a review of OBPP studies conducted in the United States, Olweus and Limber[58] proposed that successful implementation of the OBPP is dependent on the school being ready for the program, the program's compatibility with other school-based initiatives, and school leaders' ability to provide needed resources and support (e.g., training, time for meetings, etc.[84,90,91]).

Since its inception, PA CARES has used readiness as one of the criteria for selecting schools to participate in OBPP. In 2011, leaders of PA CARES extended readiness support to schools that did not meet readiness criteria on the PA CARES grant application. The readiness support process involved a structured site visit from a certified Olweus trainer, who reviewed program requirements with the school principal, answered questions about implementation, and established criteria for the school to meet in order to be ready to implement the program. As part of the site visit process, the school administrator had to commit to implementing all program components with fidelity, identify staff who would serve on an OBPP leadership team, and establish dates for necessary trainings, data collection, and program monitoring activities. The site visitor/trainer submitted this information to PA CARES along with a letter of recommendation, in which the trainer provided a narrative description of the school's readiness for OBPP. Fully 97% (37/38) of schools that received a readiness intervention eventually received a PA CARES acceptance and implemented OBPP. Each school received program materials, Olweus Bullying Questionnaires, and technical assistance from a certified Olweus trainer for a period of 12 months.

In an effort to assess the impact of readiness support on programmatic success, we compared schools that received a readiness site visit to schools that did not receive a site visit on key measures of program fidelity. Specifically, schools that received readiness support were compared to 66 schools that did not receive readiness support because they had already met readiness criteria at the time of the grant application. Using an online teacher survey designed for programmatic monitoring, teacher and staff self-reports and perceptions of key program activities were assessed after approximately six months of implementation. More specifically, teachers and staff were asked whether specific OBPP programmatic activities had been implemented at the school-wide, classroom, or individual-level. Response options for these items are "completed," "making good progress," "progress needed," or N/A (not applicable) (note that N/A responses are excluded from all analyses). Responses were aggregated at the school level for these items.

A series of t-tests were conducted to assess whether schools that received a fidelity visit ($N = 37$) reported higher levels of fidelity to the OBPP model than did schools that did not receive a fidelity visit ($N = 66$).

Results, reported in Table 8.1, reveal some notable differences in teachers and staff reports of implementing key program elements at the school-level and individual level among the readiness support group versus the control group. While there were no significant differences between the two groups in

Table 8.1. Results from t-tests[1] to Determine Whether Percents of Teachers and Staff at the School Level Who Had "Completed" or Were "In Progress" of Performing Specific OBPP Activities Varied as a Function of Having Received a Site Visit

School-Level Components Have you...	% Completed	% in Progress
participated in 6 hours of OBPP training?	$t(101) = -1.22, p = 0.22$	$t(101) = 0.27, p = 0.78$
read the OBPP Teacher's Guide?	$t(100.94) = -0.91, p = 0.36$	$t(100.94) = -1.04, p = 0.26$
read the materials on the OBPP Teacher's Guide CD-ROM?	$t(98.45) = -0.32, p = 0.75$	$t(94.52) = -2.48, p = 0.015$
viewed the OBPP Teacher's Guide DVD?	$t(101) = -0.62, p = 0.54$	$t(101) = -1.16, p = 0.25$
attended the school kick-off event?	$t(101) = -1.27, p = 0.20$	$t(101) = -1.21, p = 0.23$
participated at least once a month in a staff discussion group?	$t(101) = -0.35, p = 0.73$	$t(101) = 0.18, p = 0.85$
viewed and discussed the scenarios on the teacher guide DVD with students?	$t(101) = -0.57, p = 0.57$	$t(101) = -2.40, p = 0.018$

Classroom-Level Components Have you...	% Completed	% in Progress
held two to three classroom-level meetings with parents about bullying?	$t(101) = -1.31, p = 0.19$	$t(101) = 0.13, p = 0.90$
posted the anti-bullying rules in your classroom?	$t(100.94) = -1.11, p = 0.27$	$t(100.94) = 0.71, p = 0.48$
explained and discussed the anti-bullying rules with your students?	$t(98.45) = -0.86, p = 0.39$	$t(94.52) = 0.22, p = 0.82$
explained and discussed the anti-bullying rules with the parents of your students?	$t(101) = -0.22, p = 0.83$	$t(101) = 0.06, p = 0.95$
held regular (weekly) class meetings to discuss issues related to bullying, peer relations, and other related topics?	$t(101) = -1.19, p = 0.24$	$t(101) = 0.67, p = 0.51$
on several occasions had students engage in role-playing about bullying and related follow-up discussions?	$t(101) = -0.97, p = 0.34$	$t(101) = 0.20, p = 0.84$
used literature to explain key concepts related to bullying?	$t(101) = -1.26, p = 0.21$	$t(101) = 1.62, p = 0.11$

(continued on next page)

Table 8.1. (*continued*)

Individual-Level Components Have you...	% Completed	% in Progress
• consistently enforced negative consequences for students who did not follow rule 1?	$t(101) = -2.10, p = 0.038$	$t(101) = 1.33, p = 0.19$
• given positive consequences for students who followed rules 2–4?	$t(100.94) = -2.17, p = 0.032$	$t(100.94) = 0.28, p = 0.79$
• consistently intervened on-the-spot in situations where you observed bullying?	$t(98.45) = -1.68, p = 0.096$	$t(94.52) = 1.40, p = 0.16$
• consistently intervened on-the-spot in situations where you suspected bullying?	$t(101) = -1.68, p = 0.095$	$t(101) = 1.60, p = 0.11$
• investigated all incidents of bullying that you observed (where appropriate)?	$t(101) = -1.86, p = 0.066$	$t(101) = 1.81, p = 0.073$
• investigated all incidents of bullying that you suspected (where appropriate)?	$t(101) = -1.39, p = 0.17$	$t(101) = 1.42, p = 0.16$

[1]When Levene's Test for Equality of Variances was significant, t for unequal variance is reported.

their ability to meet school-level programmatic milestones (e.g., training, kick-off) and engage in complex implementation tasks (e.g., working with parents, using role play in the classroom), significant or near significant differences were noted between the groups in their self-reported use of programmatic materials and processes, as well as in the teachers' and staff self-reports of intervening in bullying situations. More specifically, teachers and staff who worked in schools that had received readiness support from a certified Olweus trainer were more likely to report that they had "completed" or were "making good progress" performing the following activities: reading the OBPP Teachers' Guide, viewing and discussing program videos with students, enforcing negative consequences for students who bully others (rule #1), giving positive consequences to positive bystanders (rules #2–4), and investigating all observed bullying incidents.

As indicated in Table 8.2, group differences suggest that pre-implementation support from a program expert can contribute to greater implementation

Table 8.2. Average Percents of Teachers and Staff at the School Level Who Had "Completed" or Reported "In Progress" Regarding Specific OBPP Program Activities as a Function of Having Received a Site Visit

School-Level Components	% Completed		% In Progress	
Have you...	Received site visit ($N = 37$)	No site visit ($N = 66$)	Received site visit ($N = 37$)	No site visit ($N = 66$)
participated in 6 hours of OBPP training?	73.07 (15.36)	68.50 (19.61)	16.97 (9.51)	17.60 (11.98)
read the OBPP Teacher's Guide?	48.47 (10.03)	45.92 (18.47)	33.98 (8.85)	31.68 (11.61)
read the materials on the OBPP Teacher's Guide CD-ROM?	37.09 (11.22)	36.20 (17.13)	33.39 (9.15)	28.01 (12.67)*
viewed the OBPP Teacher's Guide DVD?	45.56 (13.21)	43.49 (17.70)	27.98 (9.98)	25.57 (10.21)
attended the school kick-off event?	90.75 (12.56)	86.59 (17.46)	4.45 (4.40)	6.15 (7.81)
participated at least once a month in a staff discussion group?	46.49 (17.81)	45.06 (21.15)	23.81 (9.86)	24.22 (11.47)
viewed and discussed the scenarios on the teacher guide DVD with students?	37.84 (19.42)	35.29 (22.75)	32.50 (13.23)	26.75 (10.72)*

Classroom-Level Components	% Completed		% In Progress	
Have you...	Received site visit ($N = 37$)	No site visit ($N = 66$)	Received site visit ($N = 37$)	No site visit ($N = 66$)
held two to three classroom-level meetings with parents about bullying?	28.26 (14.61)	24.40 (14.21)	17.18 (11.43)	17.48 (11.57)
posted the anti-bullying rules in your classroom?	86.70 (13.81)	83.16 (16.42)	6.65 (5.89)	7.59 (6.80)
explained and discussed the anti-bullying rules with your students?	85.74 (13.38)	83.07 (16.11)	10.35 (8.79)	10.77 (9.36)
explained and discussed the anti-bullying rules with the parents of your students?	32.36 (16.94)	31.46 (21.42)	23.42 (10.19)	23.58 (14.16)
held regular (weekly) class meetings to discuss issues related to bullying, peer relations, and other related topics?	63.27 (24.34)	56.76 (27.74)	24.03 (14.04)	25.98 (14.33)

(continued on next page)

Table 8.2. (*continued*)

Classroom-Level Components	% Completed		% In Progress	
Have you...	Received site visit ($N = 37$)	No site visit ($N = 66$)	Received site visit ($N = 37$)	No site visit ($N = 66$)
on several occasions had students engage in role-playing about bullying and related follow-up discussions?	38.50 (18.07)	34.57 (20.71)	33.28 (10.39)	33.78 (12.76)
used literature to explain key concepts related to bullying?	47.52 (19.48)	42.60 (18.71)	33.63 (10.62)	37.60 (12.56)

Individual-Level Components	% Completed		% In Progress	
Have you....	Received site visit ($N = 37$)	No site visit ($N = 66$)	Received site visit ($N = 37$)	No site visit ($N = 66$)
consistently enforced negative consequences for students who did not follow rule 1?	58.65 (16.05)	51.78 (15.88)[*]	32.55 (11.09)	35.77 (12.21)
given positive consequences for students who followed rules 2–4?	55.46 (15.03)	48.06 (17.45)[*]	35.80 (9.70)	36.48 (12.80)
consistently intervened on-the-spot in situations where you observed bullying?	62.97 (13.48)	57.71 (16.12)	30.43 (9.73)	33.97 (13.47)
consistently intervened on-the-spot in situations where you suspected bullying?	58.48 (13.01)	53.27 (16.04)	34.28 (9.04)	38.30 (13.65)
investigated all incidents of bullying that you observed (where appropriate)?	64.41 (13.38)	58.38 (17.00)	29.40 (10.34)	34.26 (14.36)
investigated all incidents of bullying that you suspected (where appropriate)?	58.25 (12.51)	54.00 (16.03)	33.76 (9.64)	37.53 (14.37)

[*]indicates significance

fidelity for some programmatic activities. The results also suggest that when formal leaders participate in readiness activities, it resonates with teachers. Within schools whose principals successfully completed the readiness process, teachers reported greater progress in fulfilling programmatic obligations. This is particularly true for program elements that involved teachers' use of program materials, teachers' involvement in reinforcing anti-bullying rules, and teachers' responsiveness to bullying that they witnessed.

CONCLUSIONS AND RECOMMENDATIONS

While there are many good reasons for implementing bullying prevention programs in schools, educators' good intentions and the availability of resources cannot guarantee program success. Existing organizational capacities, participant characteristics, and leadership factors influence a school's readiness to implement research-based programs with high fidelity. In order to moderate the potential negative effects of these factors on implementation, it is important to attend to issues of readiness when selecting bullying prevention strategies and planning for their implementation. Educators who wish to implement schoolwide bullying prevention programs should attend to the readiness indicators bulleted in this chapter, as many of these indicators can be addressed through planning and stakeholder engagement strategies.

The case study provided in this chapter suggests that implementers should have access to high-quality technical assistance before a program is selected to ensure that there is adequate site readiness to support successful implementation of the program. As other investigators have suggested, proactive technical assistance can support implementation fidelity when it is delivered by an expert trainer[19] and it is focused on issues relevant to implementation fidelity.[59] Readiness support can also aid schools and other implementation sites in determining whether an intervention strategy is appropriate for their context and can help school leaders identify strategies that may increase the school's readiness for future implementation of prevention programs.

For policy makers and funders, this chapter underscores the need to attend to issues of site readiness when designing and evaluating implementation projects. We concur with previous researchers that readiness assessment should be a part of any competitive award process involving implementation of evidence-based programs. We go further, however, in suggesting that on-site readiness support is beneficial and may enhance the likelihood of program success. Future research is needed to determine if the apparent benefits of readiness support are enduring and if readiness support, at the school level, results in any measurable improvements in student-level outcomes.

FREQUENTLY ASKED QUESTIONS

1. What is organizational readiness?

Organizational readiness refers to a willingness and preparedness of an organization and its members to implement a program or adopt best practices. Readiness is reflected in the systems and resources of the organization and in the commitments, skills, and characteristics of people involved in supporting and implementing programs and practices.

2. Why is organizational readiness relevant to bullying prevention in schools?

Bullying is a complex phenomenon that responds best to comprehensive interventions that improve the overall climate of schools and promote effective bystander responsiveness to peer aggression. The best approaches to violence prevention involve the implementation of evidence-based programs and practices. In order to increase the likelihood that evidence-based programs and practices produce the intended effects, educators need to implement them with fidelity—as designed by the program author. Organizational readiness is an important predictor of implementation fidelity. In other words, schools that are ready to implement a program are more likely to implement the program as it was intended, which in turn increases the likelihood that the program will be successful in changing behaviors. Thus, educators should attend to readiness factors when selecting and planning bullying prevention strategies.

3. How can a school improve its readiness to implement a comprehensive bullying prevention program?

School leaders may enhance organizational readiness for bullying prevention by attending to specific indicators of readiness that are bulleted in this chapter. In addition, data from the readiness intervention described in this chapter suggest that schools benefit from technical assistance during the earliest stages of planning bullying prevention efforts. In our experience, the individuals who are most effective at providing readiness-related technical assistance to schools have expertise in bullying prevention, an in-depth understanding of the requirements of various bullying prevention programs/curricula, and skills in school-based consultancy.

4. What are the implications of organizational readiness for policy makers and funders concerned about bullying prevention?

Assessing organizational readiness is difficult to do from afar. Yet, there is a desire by many stakeholders to support efficient, broad-scale implementation of evidence-based violence prevention efforts in schools. Given the relationship between readiness and fidelity, and the positive relationship between fidelity and programmatic outcomes, there is a need for greater attention to improving school readiness. In particular, our research suggests that proactive, on-site technical assistance can lead to better implementation fidelity than more remote approaches. Administrators and funders should consider making investments in organizational readiness as part of plans to scale-up implementation of violence prevention programs.

REFERENCES

1. Spivak H, Prothrow-Stith D. The need to address bullying—An important component of violence prevention. *JAMA*. 2001; 285:2131–2132.

2. Williams K, Rivera L, Neighbours R, Reznik V. Youth violence prevention comes of age: Research, training and future directions. *Annu Rev Public Health*. 2007; 28:195–211.

3. Zagar RJ, Busch KG, Hughes JR. Empirical risk factors for delinquency and best treatments: Where do we go from here? *Psychol Rep*. 2009; 104:279–308.

4. Brownson RC, Fielding JE, Maylahn CM. Evidence-based public health: A fundamental concept for public health practice. *Annu Rev Public Health*. 2009; 30:175–201.

5. Anthony BJ, Wessler SL, Sebian JK. Commentary: Guiding a public health approach to bullying. *J Pediatr Psychol*. 2010; 35:1113–1115.

6. Children's Safety Network. Preventing bullying: The role of public health and safety professionals. Newton, MA: CSN National Resource Center; 2011.

7. Srabstein JC, Berkman BE, Pyntikova E. Antibullying legislation: A public health perspective. *J Adolesc Health*. 2008; 42:11–20.

8. Stanton L, Beran T. A review of legislation and bylaws relevant to bullying. *McGill J Educ*. 2000; 44:245–260.

9. Limber SP, Small MA. State laws and policies to address bullying in schools. *School Psychol Rev.* 2003; 32:445–455.

10. Muschert GW, Peguero AA. The Columbine effect and school antiviolence policy. In: Peyrot M, Burns SL, eds. *New Approaches to Social Problems Treatment.* 17 ed. Emerald Group Publishing Limited; 2010:117–148.

11. Warnick BR, Johnson BA, Rocha S. Tragedy and the meaning of school shootings. *Educ Theory.* 2010; 60:371–390.

12. Rivers I, Smith PK. Types of bullying behaviour and their correlates. *Aggress Behav.* 1994; 20:359–368.

13. Turner HA, Finkelhor D, Hamby SL, Shattuck A, Ormrod RK. Specifying type and location of peer victimization in a national sample of children and youth. *J Youth Adolesc.* 2011; 40:1052–1067.

14. Konishi C, Hymel S, Zumbo BD, Li Z. Do School bullying and student–teacher relationships matter for academic achievement? A multilevel analysis. *Can J Sch Psychol.* 2010; 25:19–39.

15. Carlson LW, Cornell DG. Differences between persistent and desistent middle school bullies. *Sch Psychol Int.* 2008; 29:442–451.

16. Arseneault L, Bowes L, Shakoor S. Bullying victimization in youths and mental health problems: 'Much ado about nothing?' *Psychol Med.* 2010; 40:717–729.

17. Beaty LA, Alexeyev EB. The problem of school bullies: What the research tells us. *Adolesc.* 2008; 43:1–11.

18. Lacey A, Cornell D. The impact of bullying climate on schoolwide academic performance. 119th Annual Convention of the American Psychological Association, 11 Aug 4, Washington, D.C.: 2011.

19. Smith JD, Ryan W, Cousins JB. Antibullying programs: A survey of evaluation activities in public schools. *Studies Educ Eval.* 2007; 33:120–134.

20. Dillon J. No place for bullying. *Principal Magazine.* 2010; 90:20–23.

21. Lund EM, Blake JJ, Ewing HK, Banks CS. School counselors' and school psychologists' bullying prevention and intervention strategies: A look into real-world practices. *J Sch Violence.* 2012; 11:246–265.

22. Swearer SM, Espelage DL, Vaillancourt T, Hymel S. What can be done about school bullying?: Linking research to educational practice. *Educ Res.* 2010; 39:38–47.

23. Armstrong TA, Webb V. The School–based violence prevention planning program: A Pilot test. *J Sch Violence.* 2006,5:79–97.

24. Durlak JA, DuPre EP. Implementation matters: A review of research on the influence of implementation on program outcomes and the factors affecting implementation. *Am J Commun Psychol.* 2008; 41:327–350.

25. Saldana L, Chamberlain P, Wang W, Brown CH. Predicting program start–up using the stages of implementation measure. *Adm Policy Ment Health Ment Health Serv.* 2011; 39:419–425.

26. Fagen MC, Flay BR. Sustaining a school–based prevention program: Results from the Aban Aya sustainability project. *Health Educ Behav.* 2009; 36:9–23.

27. Bumbarger BK, Perkins DF, Greenberg M. Taking effective prevention to scale. In: Doll B, Pfohl W, Yoon J, eds. *Handbook of Youth Prevention Science.* New York: Routledge; 2010:433–444.

28. Adelman HS, Taylor L. On sustainability of project innovations as systemic change. *J Educ Psychol Consult.* 2003; 14:1–25.

29. Armenakis AA, Harris SG, Mossholder KW. Creating readiness for organizational change. *Human Relations.* 1993; 46:681–703.

30. Bronfenbrenner U. *The Ecology of Human Development: Experiments by Nature and Design.* Cambridge, MA: Harvard University Press; 1979.

31. Lee C–H. An ecological systems approach to bullying behaviors among middle school students in the United States. *J Interpersonal Violence.* 2011; 26:1664–1693.

32. Astor RA, Guerra N, Van Acker R. How can we improve school safety research? *Educ Res.* 2010; 39:69–78.

33. Swearer SM, Espelage DL. Introduction: A social–ecological framework of bullying among youth. *Bullying in American schools: A Social-Ecological Perspective on Prevention and Iintervention.* Mahwah, NJ, US: Lawrence Erlbaum Associates Publishers, 2004:1–12.

34. Limber SP, Snyder M. What works and doesn't work in bullying prevention and intervention. *The State Education Standard*. 2006; 7:24–28.

35. Farrell AD, Flannery DJ. Youth violence prevention: Are we there yet? *Aggress Violent Behav*. 2006; 11:138–150.

36. Flaspohler PD, Anderson–Butcher D, Bean J, Burke RW, Paternite CE. Readiness and school improvement: Strategies for enhancing dissemination and implementation of expanded school mental health practices. *Adv Sch Ment Health Promot*. 2008; 1:16–27.

37. Short KH, Weist MD, Manion IG, Evans SW. Tying together research and practice: using rope for successful partnerships in school mental health. *Adm Policy Ment Health*. 2012; 39:238–247.

38. Fagan AA, Hanson K, Hawkins JD, Arthur MW. Bridging science to practice: Achieving prevention program implementation fidelity in the Community Youth Development Study. *Am J Commun Psychol*. 2008; 41:235–249.

39. Fagan AA, Arthur MW, Hanson K, et al. Effects of communities that care on the adoption and implementation fidelity of evidence–based prevention programs in communities: Results from a randomized controlled trial. *Prev Sci*. 2011; 12:223–234.

40. Proctor E, Silmere H, Raghavan R et al. Outcomes for implementation research: Conceptual distinctions, measurement challenges, and research agenda. *Adm Policy Ment Health Ment Health Serv*. 2011; 38:65–76.

41. Carroll C, Patterson M, Wood S et al. A conceptual framework for implementation fidelity. *Implement Sci*. 2007:2.

42. Dariotis JK, Bumbarger BK, Duncan LG, Greenberg MT. How do implementation efforts relate to program adherence? Examining the role of organizational, implementer, and program factors. *J Commun Psychol*. 2008; 36:744–760.

43. Dumas JE, Lynch AM, Laughlin JE, et al. Promoting intervention fidelity: Conceptual issues, methods, and preliminary results from the EARLY ALLIANCE prevention trial. *Am J Prev Med*. 2001; 20:38–47.

44. Fixsen DL, Naoom SF, Blase KA, et al. *Implementation Research: A Synthesis of the Literature*. Tampa, Florida: National Implementation Research Network at the Louis

de la Parte Florida Mental Health Institute, University of South Florida, 2005. FMHI Publication #231.

45. Dusenbury L, Brannigan R, Falco M, Hansen WB. A review of research on fidelity of implementation: Implications for drug abuse prevention in school settings. *Health Edu Res.* 2003; 18:237–256.

46. O'Donnell CL. Defining, conceptualizing, and measuring fidelity of implementation and its relationship to outcomes in k–12 curriculum intervention research. *Rev Edu Res.* 2008; 78:33–84.

47. Greenberg MT. Current and future challenges in school-based prevention: The researcher perspective. *Prev Sci.* 2004; 5:5–13.

48. Fagan AA, Mihalic S. Strategies for enhancing the adoption of school–based prevention programs: Lessons learned from the blueprints for violence prevention replications of The Life Skills Training Program. *J Commun Psychol.* 2003; 31:235–253.

49. Grimes J, Kurns S, Tilly WD, III. Sustainability: An enduring commitment to success. *Sch Psychol Rev.* 2006; 35:224–244.

50. Noell GH, Gansle KA. Moving from good ideas in educational systems change to sustainable program implementation: Coming to terms with some of the realities. *Psychol Schools.* 2009; Special Issue: Building systems to support students at risk for failure in schools. 46:78–88. .

51. Webster–Stratton C, Reinke WM, Herman KC, Newcomer LL. The Incredible Years Teacher Classroom Management training: The methods and principles that support fidelity of training delivery. *Sch Psychol Rev.* 2011; Special series: Developing social-emotional and behavioral interventions with school communities: Systematic and collaborative processes. 40:509–529.

52. Ball A. Educator readiness to adopt expanded school mental health: Findings and implications for cross–systems approaches. *Adv Sch Ment Health Promot.* 2011; 4:39–50.

53. Hull PS, Canedo J, Aquilera J, et al. Assessing community readiness for change in the Nashville Hispanic community through participatory research. *Progress Community Health Partnerships: Res Educ Action.* 2008; 2:185–194.

54. Goh SC, Cousins JB, Elliott C. Organizational learning capacity, evaluative inquiry and readiness for change in schools: Views and perceptions of educators. *J Educ Change.* 2006; 7:289–318.

55. Rafferty AE, Simons RH. An examination of the antecedents of readiness for fine-tuning and corporate transformation changes. *J Bus Psychol.* 2006; 20:325–350.

56. Miao T–A, Umemoto K, Gonda D, Hishinuma ES. Essential elements for community engagement in evidence-based youth violence prevention. *Am J Commun Psychol.* 2011; 48:120–132.

57. Thaker S, Steckler A, Sánchez V, Khatapoush S, Rose J, Hallfors DD. Program characteristics and organizational factors affecting the implementation of a school-based indicated prevention program. *Health Edu Res.* 2008; 23:238–248.

58. Olweus D, Limber SP. The Olweus Bullying Prevention Program: Implementation and evaluation over two decades. In: Jimerson SR, Swearer M, Espelage DL, eds. *Handbook of Bullying in Schools: An International Perspective.* New York: Routledge/Taylor & Francis Group; 2010:377–401.

59. Bumbarger BK, Perkins DF. After randomised trials: Issues related to dissemination of evidence-based interventions. *J Child Services.* 2008; 3:53–61.

60. Sobeck J, Agius E. Organizational capacity building: Addressing a research and practice gap. *Eval Program Plann.* 2007; 30:237–246.

61. Gugglberger L, Dür W. Capacity building in and for health promoting schools: Results from a qualitative study. *Health Policy.* 2011; 101:37–43.

62. Payne AA, Gottfredson DC, Gottfredson GD. School predictors of the intensity of implementation of school-based prevention programs: Results from a national study. *Prev Sci* 2006; 7:225–237.

63. Dane AV, Schneider BH. Program integrity in primary and early secondary prevention: Are implementation effects out of control? *Clin Psychol Rev.* 1998; 18:23–45.

64. Coyle HE. School Culture Benchmarks: Bridges and barriers to successful bullying prevention program implementation. *J Sch Violence.* 2008; 7:105–122.

65. Cassidy EF, Leviton LC. The relationships of program and organizational capacity to program sustainability: What helps programs survive? *Eval Program Plann.* 2006; 29:149–152.

66. Fagan AA, Brooke–Weiss B, Cady R, Hawkins JD. If at first you don't succeed...keep trying: Strategies to enhance coalition/school partnerships to implement school–based prevention programming. *Aust N Z J Criminol.* 2009; 42:387–405.

67. Zins JE, Elias MJ. Social and emotional learning: Promoting the development of all students. *J Edu Psychol Consult.* 2006; 17:233–255.

68. Hirschstein MK, Edstrom LVS, Frey KS, Snell JL, MacKenzie EP. Walking the talk in bullying prevention: Teacher implementation variables related to initial impact of the "steps to respect" program. *Sch Psychol Rev.* 2007; 36:3–21.

69. Gottfredson DC, Wilson DB. Characteristics of effective school–based substance abuse prevention. *Prev Sci.* 2003; 4:27–38.

70. Dake JA, Price JH, Telljohann SK, Funk JB. Teacher perceptions and practices regarding school bullying prevention. *J Sch Health.* 2003; 73:347–355.

71. Ellis AA, Shute R. Teacher responses to bullying in relation to moral orientation and seriousness of bullying. *Br J Edu Psychol.* 2007; 77:649–663.

72. Forman SG, Smallwood DL, Nagle R. Organizational and individual factors in bringing research to practice: What we know, where we need to go. *Psychol Sch.* 2005; 42:569–576.

73. Bandura A. *Self-Efficacy: The Exercise of Control.* New York: Worth Publishers; 1977.

74. Kaniuka TS. Toward an understanding of how teachers change during school reform: Considerations for educational leadership and school improvement. *J Edu Change.* 2012; 13:327–346.

75. Langberg JM, Smith BH. Developing evidence–based interventions for deployment into school settings: A case example highlighting key issues of efficacy and effectiveness. *Eval Program Plann.* 2006; 29:323–334.

76. Furlong M, Paige LZ, Osher D. The Safe Schools/Healthy Students (SS/HS) Initiative: Lessons learned from implementing comprehensive youth development programs. *Psychol Sch.* 2003; 40:447–456.

77. Gingiss PM, Roberts–Gray C, Boerm M. *Bridge–It:* A system for predicting implementation fidelity for school–based tobacco prevention programs. *Prev Sci.* 2006; 7:197–207.

78. Weiner BJ. A theory of organizational readiness for change. *Implement Sci.* 2009; 4:n/a.

79. Domitrovich CE, Bradshaw CP, Poduska JM et al. Maximizing the implementation quality of evidence–based preventive interventions in schools: A conceptual framework. *Adv Sch Ment Health Promot.* 2008; 1:6–28.

80. Roberts–Gray C, Gingiss PM, Boerm M. Evaluating school capacity to implement new programs. *Eval Program Plann.* 2007; 30:247–257.

81. Olweus D, Limber SP. *Olweus Bullying Prevention Program: Teacher guide.* Center City, MN: Hazelden, 2007.

82. Olweus D, Limber S, Mihalic S. *Blueprints for Violence Prevention: Vol. 9. The Bullying Prevention Program.* Boulder, CO: Institute of Behavioral Science, University of Colorado; 1999.

83. Olweus D. *Bullying at School: What We Know and What Can We Do.* Oxford, UK: Blackwell Publishers; 1993.

84. Black S, Washington E, Trent V, Harner P, Pollock E. Translating the Olweus Bullying Prevention Program into real–world practice. *Health Promot Prac.* 2010; 11:733–740.

85. Edmondson L, Hoover J. Process evaluation of a bullying prevention program: A public school-county health partnership. *Reclaiming Children and Youth: The J Strength-based Interventions.* 2008; 16:25–33.

86. Limber SP. Implementation of the Olweus Bullying Prevention Program in American Schools: Lessons learned from the field. In: Espelage DL, Swearer SM, eds. *Bullying in American Schools: A Social-Ecological Perspective on Prevention and Intervention.* Lawrence Erlbaum Associates; 2004:351–363.

87. Olweus D, Limber SP. Bullying in school: Evaluation and dissemination of the Olweus Bullying Prevention Program. *Am J Orthopsychiatry.* 2010; 80:124–134.

88. Black S, Washington E. Evaluation of the Olweus Bullying Prevention Program in nine urban schools: Effective Practices and next steps. *ERS Spectrum.* 2008; 26:7–19.

89. Edmondson L, Hoover J. Process evaluation of a bullying prevention program: A public school–county health partnership. *Reclaiming Children and Youth: The J Strength–based Interventions.* 2008; 16:25–33.

90. Berger C, Karimpour R, Rodkin PC. Bullies and victims at school: Perspectives and strategies for primary prevention. In: Miller T, ed. *School Violence and Primary Prevention.* New York: Springer-Verlag; 2008:287–314.

91. Kallestad JH, Olweus D. Predicting Teachers' and schools' implementation of the Olweus Bullying Prevention Program: A multilevel study. *Prev Treat.* 2003; 6:np.

9

Developing Organizational and Educational Capacity for Ongoing Implementation

Shiryl Barto, MEd

Objectives

1. To identify and discuss helpful conditions that exist in schools where programs are sustained successfully over time.
2. To illustrate the importance of continuing education as a reinforcement of effective program implementation.
3. To identify a few specific continuing education opportunities that can be utilized by schools or learning networks involved in program implementation.

Over the past two decades, awareness of bullying as a problem for American children and families has increased. This is due, in part, to the popular press invoking the term *bullying* (or *bully*, or *bullied*) when instances of school violence and aggression or student self-harm point to social maladjustment or dysfunctional behavior. The popularization of the term, however, has created an umbrella effect that has taken in all forms of negative interaction, both in and outside of school and between adults as well as students, with little regard to the socioecological root of the individuals' behavior. At times, this publicity has been misdirected and misinforming. Nonetheless, many negative interactions, some violent, occur daily between students and can rightly be classified as bullying, and we know that schools have an obligation to facilitate a climate that is safe and supportive. Engaging in universal bullying prevention[1] is an important step toward safe and supportive schools.

Once a school commits to the implementation of a comprehensive, schoolwide bullying prevention program, there are conditions that can be observed that influence the ongoing success of the program.[2] Previous chapters have established that the decision to undertake bullying prevention should not be made independently by a single administrator or school official, but rather, in consensus following a full discussion among school leadership, teachers, and other stakeholders. Agreeing that program implementation is a priority is a good start, but what does a supportive school environment for bullying prevention look like? Experts suggest that the support system is critical in reducing variations in program outcomes and maintaining the overall identity of the intervention itself.[3] Let's look at some conditions that can add to or detract from successful implementation and support.

SUPPORT FROM LEADERSHIP

Almost always, school administrators are involved in the decision to implement a program in their school. After the initial decision, however, an administrator's role in program implementation can vary from significant to nonexistent. Some programs, especially those that are not systemic and instead rely on only one or two staff to carry out most of the implementation,[4] might do well with simplistic backing from leadership (e.g. approval). Whole school approaches, however, are likely to require a more layered endorsement from school administrators, inclusive of responsibilities and protocols found only at their level of the system. For bullying prevention efforts to be successful at school, administrators need to make it a priority for themselves.

In his book *No Place for Bullying: Leadership for Schools That Care for Every Student,* Jim Dillon asserts that school leaders often reveal what is important to them through the topics they discuss with faculty and staff.[5] Are faculty meetings more about policy and the logistics of running the school, or are they about relating, learning together, and achieving positive outcomes at school? When staff see and hear leadership prioritizing a positive school climate for all, undertaking prosocial efforts seems to fit. In addition, it is often helpful for school personnel to come to understand their own "personal stake" in bullying prevention. This is especially true for school officials. Why does the issue of bullying matter to them? Does it matter personally? Perhaps they or a family member have experienced bullying first hand. Does it matter to them professionally? Are they charged with implementation in their school because of legislation or as a response to a previous incident? Regardless of its origins, any root of personal motivation should be tendered in the most positive light, keeping the benefit of students and school climate in mind. Developing a meaningful personal rationale for bullying prevention efforts needs to be an essential first step for administrators who are expected to lead these efforts in their school. Although this seems like an informal step, and one that shouldn't need to be verbalized or explained, research has shown that in the absence of other barriers, some principals simply do not employ bullying prevention activities.[6] And many schools' bullying prevention efforts fail because of a change in leadership, where new leadership does not prioritize bullying prevention.

When readiness for bullying prevention has been established, school leadership should research programs that are available for implementation and that "fit" best within their school's organizational framework. This upfront work allows school decision makers to become familiar with the time and material requirements of a program to ensure that those requirements can be met before plans are shared with all staff, students, and parents. Depending on the program, principals and assistant principals may need to be trained with the school committee. Due to their busy role in school, they should not head the bullying prevention committee, but rather, attend meetings and provide the support to carry out the decisions of the committee. They should employ a distributed leadership approach to the prosocial and bullying prevention efforts in their school. This is not unlike what is recommended in cases of school safety planning, where there are often lines of succession in terms of responsibility for carrying out plans. It is important to note that freeing up staff to meet and carry out the work of the committee is of paramount importance and should be supported by administration if implementation is to succeed.

In cases when administrators are not involved in the original decision to implement (for instance, if the plans were in place when the administrator was hired) every attempt should be made to learn as much as possible about the program and its reach across the school environment. Transitioning administrators can have negative effects on program fidelity,[7] making it all the more important for principals and assistant principals to positively support any bullying prevention efforts. Principals who oversee more than one school should also be careful to show active support to specific efforts in each school and to grow leadership for the program among faculty and staff.

Principals and assistant principals, even head teachers, can be rationalized as their school's intervention protocol at work. The translation of districtwide policy into meaningful and correct action at the school level is critical to the effectiveness of any bullying prevention program. Most systemic approaches to bullying prevention involve a consistent response by any staff member who witnesses the bullying behavior, and clear and graduated sanctions adopted schoolwide that are applied by teachers or staff members when they intervene. Supporting teachers and staff in these efforts and providing them with feedback after a referral is made are both effective ways for school leadership to convey that bullying prevention efforts are important.

Principals should be aware that the boundaries of information sharing are dictated by the Family Educational Rights and Privacy Act (FERPA)[8] and other regulations. However, these laws do not circumvent the development of an open communication arrangement with teachers and staff. If the adults in the school are to accurately and adequately follow through on an intervention protocol, they deserve to know that the appropriate follow-through has been taken by the administration and that no outside influence or judgment has precluded the use of the agreed-upon system of response.

It can be more problematic for administrators to respond when a bullying report is made without anyone witnessing the behavior or in cases when reports come from parents or guardians and describe a pattern of peer abuse that is continuing despite intervention. Harmful behaviors being carried out online that meet the definition of bullying and interrupt the school life of a child[9] warrant a consistent and fair response from school but sometimes prove tricky for principals.

When the administrator becomes involved in a specific report of bullying, as outlined in the school's protocol or as requested, the primary goal should be to stop the behavior from recurring. However, this should be done in a way that protects the safety of the target while also taking every effort to prevent similar future behavior by the offender. When these types of reports reach administration, and parental contact has been made, it can be natural for leadership to assume a defensive stance.

Chapter 11 talks more about effective parent strategies, but it's noteworthy to mention here that effective bullying prevention administrators show understanding and willingness to help, and above all are sincere, apologetic, and empathetic. For those who provide structure and regulation to busy and chaotic school days to pause for a moment and admit that something went wrong in their school, and that a student is suffering as a result, can feel like defeat. Resist the urge, as leaders, to assume this disappointment, but rather, seize these opportunities to recall your personal stake in bullying prevention. Listen without assigning blame (to students, parents, teachers, or yourself). Use this as an occasion to learn more about securing your school against bullying, and less about the motivation or origin of the specific behavior.

What systems worked or didn't work in this particular instance and for these particular students and families? What action can you and your committee take to ensure the systems are corrected? These are all important questions to consider when you are challenged to ensure that school life gets better for the student or students in question.

STUDENT AND STAFF TIME

As mentioned earlier in this chapter, carving time from the school schedule to carry out bullying prevention planning and activities is essential to program success. During the upfront research on a particular program, note the *minimal* amount of time recommended for staff involvement. Typically, the training of teaching staff is the very least commitment involved. This can be accomplished in a single in-service day or carried out over several learning opportunities, depending on which prevention model your school employs. Although it can be a challenge to find time during the school day for staff to meet and plan, this step is imperative to the success of program efforts.

Typically, committees[10] meet twice monthly for a minimum of 30 minutes at a time. Committee functioning is dictated by the tenets of each bullying prevention program. In some cases, schools may choose to align bullying prevention as a responsibility to a standing committee already in place, such as student assistant program teams or child study teams.

Schools that exhibit a highly supportive climate may experience relative ease in melding bullying prevention efforts with other student support efforts. No current research exists on the effectiveness of such practices, but administrators should thoughtfully approach delegating responsibility for program leadership. If your school is highly structured, with little or no time built in for staff interaction around bullying prevention, it will be more difficult to find a program that staff will find workable and effective. Aside from committee meeting time, most researched programs also request time for staff to communicate with each other about bullying and the progress of implementation, as well as time for staff to dialogue with students about bullying and other school climate issues.

In the time since the enactment of No Child Left Behind, schools have felt increasing pressure to highly achieve on standardized tests. This has led to a severe winnowing of time for prosocial and civic education, extracurricular activities, and even teacher planning time during the school day. Ironically, current research demonstrates that bullying and a negatively perceived school climate likely affect student engagement in learning and performance on standardized tests.[11,12] Schools that choose to devote time for students and staff to engage meaningfully with one another, and in doing so show caring and concern for student and staff safety and belonging, fare better academically.[11] Ultimately, the decision to devote time during the school day for social and emotional learning—of which bullying prevention is a part—is one that administrators should not dismiss in the face of pressure to perform academically. Gauging school climate perceptions of students and staff can aid school leaders in taking effective measures for addressing school climate.

Current literature is uncovering the necessity of school-based bullying prevention efforts to mobilize students toward positive actions[13] and points to more positive outcomes when bystanders are engaged to intervene.[14] However, this is difficult to achieve when instructional time leaves little room for additions to the schedule. Schools that have committed to bullying prevention should work to build discussion and activities, pointed toward skill building, into the school day.

TEACHER BUY-IN

Most schools, both public and private, have been afforded opportunities to increase their faculty's knowledge about bullying and to provide them with basic resources. Many work to provide some type of bullying prevention activity during the school year but stop short of the commitment that is needed to truly create change. Research tells us that bullying is more likely to occur in places with limited supervision and also in classrooms where classroom management is lacking.[15] Oftentimes, a deterrent to a whole-school approach is the lack of staff buy-in or the reluctance of the adults in the school to support a systems-change program. Bullying prevention researchers suggest that this hesitancy for teachers to commit is sometimes grounded in the belief that bullying is not a significant problem at their school, or that childhood bullying is in some way a normal or beneficial part of growing up.[15] Additionally, it is possible that some schools' efforts to prevent or respond to bullying behavior utilize methods that have no evaluated benefit, which may actually do more harm than good.[15,16] Some of these methods require little to no additional action on the part of the teaching staff and are counted as meeting the requirement of "bullying prevention" because they are easy to enact and perceived as minimally disruptive. The implications of these factors on bullying prevention in a school can be damaging. Administrators should act to provide consistent messages about the importance of effective bullying prevention, as well as communicate to teachers the absolute necessity of consistent action to prevent and respond to bullying. Teachers should be aware that their own beliefs about bullying often predict how (or if) they will support and advise students in their charge who are being bullied.[17] Involving staff in the decision-making process when choosing a program or updating policies is a necessary step in gaining the support and future compliance of teachers.

Every effort should be made not only to educate teachers on effective bullying prevention but also to provide time for them to hone the skills necessary to become effective at intervention and follow-up when faced with bullying situations. Anecdotally, most educators practicing in schools involved in our project have no formal training or experience with appropriate intervention and thus rely on the strategies that have been modeled for them— either in their student-teaching experiences or during their time as students themselves. The growth of knowledge and research on bullying prevention in the past decade alone dictates that common practices in the classroom should reflect what is now known, and not necessarily what has been passed down. In other words, "Teachers don't know what they don't know." Time, resources, and encouragement are needed to become comfortable with any change in the classroom, especially in junior high and secondary school settings, where possibly even less of the school day is spent in a prosocial context.

CONTINUING EDUCATION

Expanding the bullying prevention effectiveness of teachers requires growth and development over time. By nature, the field of education is one where standards change frequently based on new research and the progression of discovery in general. Teachers are required to remain abreast of current developments within their content area and also topics that affect the overall school environment, such as classroom management techniques or the most current technology. Without continuing teacher education, classrooms would become stagnant and lessons would lose their relevance. So important is the career-long learning of teachers that federal legislation under the Elementary and Secondary Education Act consistently upholds that teachers become and remain "highly qualified." "Highly qualified" teachers produce academically successful students. It may be important to stop here and actually examine what leads to academic success. Staying in school is essential. So is the ability to synergize the knowledge from daily lessons into something that can be meaningfully retained, thus achieving at least a passing grade or better.

When considering how a school day unfolds, for teachers and students alike, we can certainly see that, along with time scheduled for academic pursuits, there are also less structured times when students are left "relating." During these times, students learn how to be social. They figure out dynamics of personalities and the effects those personalities can create. Relating happens in other places as well—in the neighborhood, on teams, or in community-sponsored groups—but the interactions that occur in school most directly impact the learning environment. When these interactions among students are positive and nondisruptive, the learning environment has been enhanced. When the interactions have a negative effect on students or are disruptive, they present a barrier to learning. Although there can be several nonacademic barriers to learning,[18] those manifesting from negative interactions among students (such as bullying) can be effectively addressed and managed by the adults in the school if they act with pointed consistency, using a set of skills rooted in accurate knowledge; in other words, if they become "highly qualified" to respond to bullying.

Although it is absolutely imperative that all teachers or school staff members respond to bullying when they see it or receive a report, the response should be consistent among staff and based on the school's policy and protocol. Schools should not encourage each individual teacher or staff member to develop their own personal response to a bullying situation. The individual actions of school personnel translate the school (and district) policy to parents and to the community. Can schools be sure their staff are taking into consideration current knowledge and best practices when they intervene? After intervention, are staff prepared to follow up with students, as is currently recommended?[19] Can you be sure that all of your staff members would even notice bullying or prioritize intervention, or react, based on their own critical thinking about the topic and not merely model what they remember from their school experience?

So what is the best way for teachers and staff to gain access to information upon which they can build their own bullying prevention repertoire? Schoolwide systemic approaches to bullying prevention often include teacher training, which is a good start. However, just as teachers and other staff members are consistently given opportunities to add to their basic professional education, they should likewise be afforded time to acquire deeper knowledge and sharpen their skills related to bullying prevention. Depending on school and teacher preference, these opportunities can span many delivery models, from independent study through the offering of in-service courses. What's important is that the philosophy behind continuing education should extend beyond academics and into the realm of school climate and student safety.

As already stated, a primary reason for teachers and staff to have access to continuing education pertaining to bullying is to increase their knowledge and skills for prevention and intervention. However, there are many secondary purposes achieved when faculty spend time learning more about this topic. For instance, allowing the school committee (or other personnel who lead the school's bullying prevention efforts) to attend continuing education opportunities together is a way to encourage good committee functioning. When this group of individuals is responsible for bringing new and valid information back to the school and formulating a plan for weaving that information into everyday practices, there is life in the committee. Too many times we've heard from schools that their committees have stopped meeting because, "there just wasn't anything to talk about anymore." Even the most basic efforts in a school should always be examined and refreshed, at least yearly. Interviewing students can reveal what is good and what needs to be improved about the school's prosocial efforts. Parent sessions or newsletters can be reworked with the newest school data or research from the field. Activities or events that highlight student service or volunteering can be planned. New teaching or support staff should be trained in the school policy and protocol. The committee driving bullying prevention can encourage all of these things and more, and all of them require knowledge of current recommendations and best practices from the field. To reiterate, school leadership needs to prioritize and support the viability of bullying prevention by allowing time for committee functioning and continuing education.

Continuing education can also be connected within regions so that schools can share resources and support each other. Currently, 49 states have laws pertaining to bullying (Montana has policy but no law).[20] Some of these laws describe programming within schools and teacher training on bullying specifically, while others concentrate mainly on policy. Concurrent with the passing of legislation, bullying has become a topic of discussion among school personnel. While the quantity and quality of that discussion varies widely among U.S. schools, it is unlikely for a school to be the only one in a region doing some kind of bullying prevention programming. Schools that reach out to one another and partner on in-service opportunities, share costs for learning sessions, or host networking meetings for committee members from several schools are all providing growth opportunities for staff, and likely they are doing so with fiscal conservancy. When neighboring schools pull together, learn from, and enrich each other's bullying prevention efforts, children and families benefit more. Students and adults are reaffirmed when they hear of successful bullying prevention activities from people they know in different districts. It validates the efforts of their own school even more by making them part of a greater effort to address this particular form of school violence. The idea of regional collaboration between schools is fairly easy to achieve when school leaders begin conversations and allow their staffs to set up common times for beneficial interactions.

In many communities, there are several agencies that provide direct services and programming within schools. Many times, the services provided by the agencies are free of charge, making them great resources for schools. Before the onset of these services or sessions inside the school, it is important that school leaders inform outside agencies about the nature and protocol of bullying prevention within the school. Agency employees working inside the school should utilize the prevention and intervention methods agreed on by school staff, and they should be careful that any resources they use are a good "fit" with the school's philosophy of bullying prevention. Although it may be easier for schools to count on an "outside" presence for bullying prevention, the services these agencies have to offer should only compliment the school's efforts and should never be the entirety of a school's "program."

In Pennsylvania, project schools have been encouraged to be involved in several opportunities for continuing education, some of which have been supported and convened over the course of the large-scale implementation. The following types of continuing education can be and should be considered by schools with an interest in effective and institutionalized bullying prevention.

ADMINISTRATORS' RETREAT

An administrators' retreat is directed toward principals, assistant principals, and superintendents, allowing for a dedicated period of time for these school leaders to refine the bullying prevention philosophy of their schools. Although a school committee typically drives the everyday bullying prevention efforts of the school, it is important for these administrators to come to see bullying prevention as a priority and to leverage their position in the district to ensure that bullying prevention is undertaken with fidelity and synergy. When an administrators' retreat is hosted regionally, all school leaders from the area can come together and learn from one another. Typically, an outside agency can arrange or host the event, but schools can work together to pool resources and rotate the hosting of the retreat yearly.

Regardless of site or host, there are some topics that should consistently be a part of the agenda at these retreats. First, an overview of bullying and the current research surrounding bullying and prevention and intervention should be provided. Schools might consider trainers from bullying prevention models to provide this overview. As mentioned earlier, it is likely that state legislation has required districts in your state to have a specific policy pertaining to bullying and/ or cyberbullying. Second, reviewing that policy is another important undertaking of administrators at the retreat. They should not only review the overall policy to ensure that it adequately reflects the current body of bullying prevention knowledge, principals should compare the district policy to their individual school's discipline code and other systemic protocols. Schools should take care to ensure that the language in their policy is not vague and goes far enough in explaining consequences, parent notification guidelines, and measures of support for students involved in bullying. When individual school buildings count on the district's policy to represent them, with no plan for making that policy operational in their smaller system, important fundamentals of bullying prevention can be overlooked. Third, principals should spend time with their committees to ensure their schools employ consistent rules against bullying, an adequate reporting system, reliable steps of investigation, graduated sanctions for students who break the rules, a priority on following up with all students who were involved in an incident, and an agreed-on timeframe to notify parents that their child is involved in bullying. Fourth, notification of parents, and strategies for general parent communication regarding bullying (and bullying prevention efforts), should also be a topic for discussion during administrator meetings.

Administrators play a crucial role in ensuring that school programming meshes and that programs are not being introduced that are competitive with one another or that, in tandem, overwhelm the faculty and staff with their implementation. It is the job of administrators to best decide which programs best fit the needs of the school. In those cases when programming might be mandated, administrators should look to combine efforts as much as possible to the benefit of both programs. All of these areas are important for administrators to grasp if they are to serve as true leaders of bullying prevention in their school. And although bullying prevention is not classroom management or leadership training, we've heard time and again from our program schools that the overall school climate improved, even for adults, when priority was placed on the prosocial aspects of school improvement and strategic planning. Recent studies also suggest that academics improve when comprehensive bullying prevention is in place. This kind of prioritizing can only come from the top down in each and every school. Allowing time for administrators to focus on these issues is of critical importance and can be accomplished through dedicated retreats.

COMMITTEE NETWORKING SESSIONS

A best practice in bullying prevention is the formation of a committee to plan and drive the bullying prevention efforts at school. This committee should not meet once or twice to achieve a laundry list of activities and then disband, but should become a consistent working entity that plans for initial bullying prevention implementation and makes sure a school's bullying prevention platform is sustained and remains effective over time. To this end, committee members need to have time to meet, and they need to be exposed to current strategies and resources to bring back to their school. It can be extremely effective for school committees to network with one another regionally. As with the administrators' retreat, these networking sessions can be hosted by outside agencies or can be held in partnership among schools on a rotating basis. We find that schools usually benefit from meeting once early on in the school year and again before school ends so that they can carry momentum into next year's efforts. During these sessions, schools share their successes and seek help with challenges surrounding bullying prevention and intervention within their schools. Some networking topics include: creative activities or ideas for student discussion about bullying, effective strategies for communicating with parents, the use of positive rewards for students "caught being good," and the weaving of bullying prevention and prosocial themes across the curriculum.

TRAINING FOR ALL STAFF

Schools should offer continuing education on bullying and related topics frequently, as has been established. If there are teachers who are new to the school, it is important that they be trained thoroughly on the philosophy, policies, and protocols of bullying prevention in the school. This is especially important if teachers are new to the profession or are in their first teaching experience, as exposure to best practices and evidence-based bullying prevention are often not reflected in pre-service teacher feedback.[21] Even if the new staff member has transferred from a school where bullying prevention was also a priority, setting aside time to train and communicate your school's specific bullying prevention nuances reinforces your school's standards and expectations.

Another very important group of adults in the school is the ancillary staff. Positions such as bus drivers, cafeteria workers, classroom aides, secretaries, and custodians are all important adults at school who see, hear, and interact with students on a daily basis. These staff members sometimes underestimate their role in bullying prevention or have their potential roles minimized. Yet research shows that they often witness bullying behavior and are sought out by students who report.[22] Schools that are most effective at bullying prevention prioritize their involvement by educating, communicating with, and supporting these individuals as they would the teaching staff.

SINGLE-FOCUS SESSIONS

It is important to concentrate on a systems approach to bullying prevention, which embeds the interaction and education of the teachers and staff on a consistent basis. It is unlikely that a one-time in-service training will adequately prepare your staff to respond appropriately to the epidemic of bullying, or even meets the legal requirement in some states. However, there are times when a single-focused training may boost your school's bullying prevention efforts. Training events like these can supply committee members with information they need to craft a more effective overall program, or they can come in response to a specific incident that might uncover a lack of resources available to staff. Single-focus topics that can be especially pertinent include: cyberbullying, bullying and suicide, sports bullying or hazing, and the bullying and harassment of students who are lesbian, gay, bisexual, and transgendered. Increasingly, single-focus sessions are available online, making them a convenient and cost-effective way to provide staff with continuing education.

CONCLUSION

School-based bullying prevention cannot be undertaken lightly. Schools that communicate their intentions to address bullying must uphold program commitments, address legislation through policy, and support the professional development of teachers in the social-emotional learning realm. School leadership must weave the issue into overall strategic planning and refrain from viewing this and other prosocial efforts as "extra." Maslow taught us long ago the pathway to building healthy, well-adjusted adults. Although we acknowledge that students should feel safe in school, are our actions matching are sentiments? The social construct of bullying behavior and victimization as a school-based problem with a school-based solution has permeated the discussion about bullying, but all segments of society have a responsibility for action. Schools can and should serve as community leaders in bullying prevention.

FREQUENTLY ASKED QUESTIONS

1. What is the administrator's role in addressing bullying prevention?

It is crucial that school leaders display active support for bullying prevention in their district and schools. In addition to educating themselves on proper bullying prevention, effective administrators ensure that district policy fully meets state or federal legislation and at the very least, corresponds with researched best practice. They should work to ensure that the district policy is properly translated and put in place. Administrators should lead their staff in effective implementation and build capacity for ongoing continuing education. This includes allowing for adequate planning time for committees, as well as ongoing communication about the progress and status of bullying prevention. Also, administrators need to formulate effective and empathetic parent engagement strategies, especially when a family has been involved with a bullying situation.

2. Why is teacher "buy-in" an important factor for successful bullying prevention?

Without the support of teachers, school reform measures, whether academic or behavioral, are likely to fail. Teachers know their students best. They are in positions to notice changes in individual moods or group relationships, and they often witness bullying first hand. Students also report that bullying happens in the presence of teachers, uncovering the need for additional strategies and a proactive approach to bullying prevention.

3. How much information should administrators share with staff after a report of bullying is made?

Schools should work to create a system of reporting, investigation, and follow-up in situations of alleged bullying. Although care should be taken to protect student rights under FERPA, schools that succeed in bullying prevention do well at communicating internally about how their protocols are working, generally and more specifically after an incident.

4. What are some prime functions of school committees that should remain ongoing?

In cases where schools have formed committees to head prosocial and/or bullying prevention efforts, those committees should meet consistently (at least monthly) to discuss implementation progress, training of new staff, the ongoing collection of data, and the use of the data to inform practice. Committee members should be given the chance to rotate on or off every two years.

5. What types of continuing education should be sought for sustainable bullying prevention?

Allowing members of school staff to consistently learn and grow in their job is important. This applies not only to academic content but also to prosocial and school climate content aimed at a safer school culture. Administrators, coordinating committee members, and teachers should seek opportunities to network with their counterparts in nearby districts. Single-focus sessions are not recommended as overall strategies for bullying prevention, but can be used to reinforce the efforts of a school, especially when devoted to related topics such as cyberbullying, class meetings, and student mental health.

6. How can schools work together to regionalize bullying prevention?

Cooperation among regional schools to hold continuing education events, community forums, and other bullying prevention events can strengthen individual school efforts. This partnership allows schools to draw greater attention to their efforts and reinforces the message that bullying is a public health issue for all and not just a problem in a particular school.

7. We have a district policy on bullying prevention; isn't that enough?

Bullying is a systemic problem with complicated etiology. As such, there is no simplistic solution to prevent bullying. Publishing the district policy in a handbook or online should be accompanied by the school changing the systems involved so that it becomes "hard to bully" in that school. Is the district policy translated properly for the age of the students in every school? Does your policy meet the needs of any state legislation? Are teachers trained to understand bullying and to respond to the benefit of all students? Are parents aware of what your school is doing to prevent and intervene in situations of bullying? Policies are only the beginning of a comprehensive bullying prevention program.

8. Which staff should be trained in bullying prevention?

All staff, including ancillary staff (custodians, cafeteria servers, secretaries, and classroom aides) should be involved in bullying prevention training. All of the adults in the school have a responsibility to intervene when they witness bullying. Schools whose staff intervene in a consistent manner send the message to students, parents, and communities that a safe school climate is prioritized.

REFERENCES

1. Flaspohler PD, Elfstrom JL, Vanderzee KL, et al. Stand by me: The effects of peer and teacher support in mitigating the impact of bullying on quality of life. *Psychol Schools.* 2009; 46(7):636–649.

2. Kallestad J, Olweus D. Predicting teachers' and schools' implementation of the Olweus Bullying Prevention Program: A multi-level study. *Preven Treatment.* 2003; 6(1):3–21.

3. Domitrovich CE, Bradshaw CP, Poduska JM, et al. Maximizing the implementation quality of evidence-based preventive interventions in schools: A conceptual framework. *Adv Sch Mental Health Promotion.* 2008; 1(3).

4. Lynam D, Milich R, Zimmerman R, et al. Project DARE No effects at ten-year follow-up. *J Consul Clin Psychol.* 1999; 67(4):590–593.

5. Dillon J. *No Place for Bullying: Leadership for Schools That Care for Every Student.* Thousand Oaks, CA: Corwin Press; 2012.

6. Dake JA, Price JH, Teljohann SK, Funk JB. Principals' perceptions and practices of School bullying prevention activities. *Health Educ Behav.* 2004; 31(3):372–387.

7. Center for Safe Schools. *Olweus Bullying Prevention Program: Fidelity and School Characteristics.* 2010.

8. Family Educational Rights and Privacy Act (FERPA.) Available at http://www2.ed.gov/policy/gen/guid/fpco/ferpa/index.html. Accessed June 20, 2012.

9. Educator Resources for Cyberbullying. Available at http://www.cyberbullying.us/resources.php. Accessed May 14, 2012.

10. Limber SP. What works (and doesn't work) in bullying prevention and intervention. *Stud Assist J.* 2004; Winter:16–19.

11. Cornell D, Lacey A. *The Impact of Bullying Climate on Schoolwide Academic Performance.* Charlottesville: Curry School of Education, University of Virginia; 2011.

12. Ripski M, Gregory A. Unfair, unsafe, and unwelcome: Do high school students' perceptions of unfairness, hostility, and victimization in school predict engagement and achievement? *J Sch Violence.* 2008; 8(4):355–375.

13. Polanin JR, Espelage DL, Pigott TD. A meta-analysis of school-based bulling prevention programs' effects on bystander intervention behavior. *Sch Psych Rev.* 2012; 41(1):47–65.

14. Ttofi MM, Farrington DP. Bullying prevention programs: The importance of peer intervention, disciplinary methods and age variations. *J Exp Criminol.* 2012; 8(4):443–462.

15. Olweus D, Limber SP. Bullying in school: Evaluation and dissemination of the Olweus Bullying Prevention Program. *Am J Orthopsychiatry.* Jan 2010; 80(1): 124–134.

16. American Psychological Association Zero Tolerance Task Force. Are Zero Tolerance Policies Effective in the Schools? An Evidentiary Review and Recommendations. 2008; 63(9):852–862.

17. Kochenderfer-Ladd P. Teachers' views and beliefs about bullying: Influences on classroom management strategies and students' coping with peer victimization. *J School Psychol.* 2008; 46(4):431–453.

18. Ohio Mental Health Network for School Success. OMNSS Information Brief: Non-academic Barriers to Learning; 2012.

19. Limber SPS, M. What works and doesn't work in bullying prevention and intervention. *The State Education Standard.* 2006; July:24–28.

20. Policies & Laws. Available at http://www.stopbullying.gov/laws/index.html. Accessed July 6, 2012.

21. Bauman S, Del Rio AP. Preservice teachers' responses to bullying scenarios: Comparing physical, verbal, and relational bullying. *J Edu Psychol.* 2006; 98(1):219–231.

22. Bradshaw CP, Waasdorp TE, Figiel K. *Education Support Professionals' Perspectives on Bullying and Prevention: Contrasting 2010 and 2012 Survey Responses.* Iowa State Education Association; 2012.

10

Foundations of Coalition Building to Reduce Bullying: A Pennsylvania Case Example

Janice Seigle, MPM

Objectives

This chapter will help the reader better understand how the following success factors contribute to the progress and the ultimate, positive impact of a wide-scale collaborative effort:

1. To understand the importance of shared vision, mission, and goals in forming productive partnerships.
2. To identify the role of an evidence-based or best practice model in focusing and cementing coalition partner efforts.
3. To facilitate the willingness of coalition partners to surrender or suspend—to varying degrees—individual agendas while bringing singularly unique forces or skills to the effort.

Alone we can do so little; together we can do so much.-Helen Keller

Coalitions are nothing new. Even children learn early in life that there is strength in numbers and joining forces with like-minded allies is a quicker way to achieve goals than struggling on alone. As simple as the idea is, building one among many organizations or entities quickly becomes more complicated. However, when a few basic principles are applied, coalitions can be highly effective in bringing about change. Mothers Against Drunk Driving (MADD), a coalition to end drunk driving, has helped change laws and push into practice the concept of the *designated driver*. The ultimate goal of reducing drinking and driving has been the result.

A coalition works to reach goals that cannot be achieved by organizations working alone by leveraging resources and getting out more than was put into the effort.[1,2] Through a coalition, or a process of collaboration and cooperation among disparate entities, significant progress has been made in reducing the incidence of bullying behavior in Pennsylvania. The following shows an example of how a small but effective coalition was formed to address in-school bullying, and discusses some of the success factors and challenges in achieving those goals.

GETTING STARTED: HOW THE PENNSYLVANIA COALITION BEGAN

Although there appears to be no single best way to form a coalition, the general consensus often calls for a structure that begins with gathering interested and appropriate organizations and then creating a mission, vision, and goals.[1,3,4] However, when the Highmark Foundation, a private health foundation funded solely by Highmark Inc. and headquartered in Pittsburgh, Pennsylvania, determined it would focus on bullying prevention, its primary intent was not necessarily to form a coalition. It had already created a vision of widespread reduction in bullying across its service region, but it quickly realized it would need to engage partners to achieve that vision and change the behavior of schoolchildren across a broad and diverse geographic area: 49 of Pennsylvania's 67 counties.[5]

The Pennsylvania coalition that subsequently formed, with the Foundation operating as lead agency and funder, was not a large one; it is not necessary for a coalition to be large to be successful.[6,7] Nevertheless, the coalition adhered to many of the tenets considered essential to successful coalition building. The Foundation found these elements of coalition building most relevant:

- Rallying around a shared vision.
- Agreeing on goals, strategies, and tactics.
- Fostering participation among key individuals and/or organizations.
- Working to influence or institutionalize change.
- Communicating successes.

In addition, the Foundation sought to apply a public health approach to the issue of bullying, an issue affecting the well-being of millions of schoolchildren across the nation.[5] The public health model called for the formation of a coalition as its starting point. The public health approach that the Foundation applied to Pennsylvania efforts was most evident in terms of gathering data to understand the depth of the problem and using data to monitor, evaluate, and validate the work. The coalition grew organically and became a stabilizing and organizing mechanism that provided an efficient way to address bullying in schools.

UNDERSTANDING THE PROBLEM

In 2004, in a meeting room at a regional Sheraton Hotel, several superintendents representing school districts throughout western Pennsylvania gathered for a breakfast meeting. Invited by Highmark, they sat over coffee, yogurt, and carrot and wheat muffins to discuss how Highmark could best help schools improve the health of children.

While this engaged group of men and women sincerely cared about student health and listened politely to ideas about health promotion and disease prevention, they voiced their issues and reservations. They understood the importance of good health in ultimately producing effective learners and fully appreciated the connection between student health and academic performance, but they also made it clear that these are among many, many priorities they juggle every day. The superintendents talked about their struggles just to help their students achieve basic academic standards. They complained about lack of hours in a school day to cover all the material that are so vital for all children to learn. Most of all, they described the difficulty they routinely face with disruptive student behavior and student emotional well-being, and their ability to overcome, in some cases, extreme deficits. These overshadowed all other issues, from too few hours to a lack of resources and deficiencies in the physical plant. These tangible and nearly universal issues caused wariness among those present. While grateful for Highmark's interest, they all warned, "Don't give us another program that is here to today and gone tomorrow," adding, "We often know what to do. We lack the resources to do them."

This early meeting began a process of investigation at Highmark to find solutions to the serious problems schools face. It was the beginning of understanding how not to impose solutions, but to discover where and how resources can best be brought to bear to help schools create more healthy environments so that good health and well-being are promoted and ingrained in every school's culture.

In tandem with the superintendents, Highmark had also contracted a marketing firm to conduct research on the drivers that undermine the well-being of children and put their health at risk. Through literature searches and mining sources of children's health data, the firm uncovered bullying as a significant issue affecting children's ability to succeed in school and thrive emotionally and, ultimately, physically. The firm also identified likely partners that had expertise in bullying prevention who were ultimately engaged through individual grants to participate in the coalition.

The early investigative work conducted by Highmark constituted an important component to coalition building, particularly in the planning stages (i.e., assessing the problem and the barriers that stand in the way of addressing it).[1,6,8] It was important to acknowledge and honor the schools' insistence on autonomy and control, which are often not addressed by simply introducing a new program. These are vital ingredients for building collaborative working relationships that translate to real change in schools.

Armed with the investigative work initiated by Highmark, the Highmark Foundation, solely funded by Highmark, identified bullying prevention as a major goal under its $100 million, five-year initiative launched in 2006 to address issues important to the health of children.[9] The dollars made available over an extended period afforded focus on building capacities and putting in place important programs that met the demands of schools. The Highmark Foundation, through many years of experience in providing grant dollars to individual school buildings, had learned that money alone, without a solid programmatic approach and administrative practices to support it, has a poor track record of solving problems relating to overall student health.

Understanding the problems schools face, as well as the need to support schools rather than tell them what to do, were vital in addressing in-school bullying. But questions remained: How could the Foundation best translate dollars committed to bullying prevention into solutions that already-stressed schools could embrace? What would it take to institutionalize bullying prevention so that it becomes part of a school's culture and not a simply a program that would meet resistance or be short-lived?

The coalition was a natural evolution in the search for workable, scalable answers to these questions. The Foundation recognized it needed help. Success would depend on the input of those who knew the ins and outs of school-based health promotion and prevention and knew how schools operate, as well as their limitations and potential. The Foundation, while it had relationships with individual schools, did not have the capacity within itself to address them. The efforts to reduce bullying in Pennsylvania were successful in no small measure due to collaboration and cooperation among an effective group of individuals who brought with them expertise and capacities of the organizations they represented.

RECRUITING COALITION MEMBERS: THE FORMATION OF A POWER BASE TO AFFECT CHANGE

The formation of an expert panel served as the nucleus of the Highmark Foundation–led coalition that eventually took shape and continued to evolve over a 6-year period. A small group of individuals with a strong interest and influence in bullying prevention were invited to participate. They were asked to agree to meet biannually for the purpose of brainstorming on how the Foundation's resources could be brought to bear to help prevent in-school bullying. It comprised commonwealth, national, and international experts with acumen in research, school safety, and program implementation across large school systems. It grew out of a need to engage people with expertise who would be essential if the Foundation were to realize its vision.

An important aspect of coalition building is to engage the appropriate participants. Coalitions form most effectively when participants agree that a problem exists. This important first step leads to a second: bringing into the coalition those who have the ability and capacity to play a substantial role in helping solve that problem.[10] The Foundation, once its vision was determined, pulled together people who shared that vision and who could help shape it. The capacity to create change on a wide scale was a high priority because of the Foundation's far-reaching, Pennsylvania service region that encompasses more than 3000 school buildings over a geographic area spanning 49 of the state's 67 counties.

Those who have analyzed best practices in coalition building conclude that assembling those with deep and varied expertise is a critical factor in influencing social change on a large scale.[11] With little first-hand knowledge of how to end bullying behavior, the Foundation sought coalition partners who, above all, had knowledge but also influence. In *The Tipping Point: How Little Things Can Make a Big Difference,*[12] author Malcolm Gladwell talks in depth about how "social epidemics," from deadly diseases to desire for the hottest new footwear, are able to spread and "infect" an entire society. One crucial aspect is the importance of engaging "connectors, mavens and salesmen." These are people who set trends because others watch what they do, have extensive networks or connections with people who can facilitate spreading ideas and trends, and are articulate and persuasive in advocating their position. An effective coalition will have among its participants those who have a broad sphere of influence and are able, either directly or through others in their network, to enact policy and ultimately change.

The Foundation engaged those renowned in the sphere of bullying prevention. They were all known for their previous work and their depth of experience and capacity. The coalition partners and their respective organizations had expertise and many of the necessary resources it would take to work with schools, helping them through the learning curve as they instituted a new approach that could alter school climate. Being realistic about and willing to overcome implementation barriers is also important if schools are to be successful in dealing with bullies, victims, and bystanders who fall into neither category but are essential players in bullying prevention. The coalition partners are those connectors, mavens, and salespeople with convincing credentials, with successes to point to and to whom school educators and administrators could relate through common language and practice. Above all, the experts chosen were those people school personnel could trust.

Supported by Highmark Foundation grants, each coalition member included those within their organizations who carried out day-to-day tasks: they comprised the operations teams, translating strategic goals into achievable tactics or tasks. Those involved worked directly with schools and other experts across the United States, including at Clemson University, to monitor outcomes and develop enhancements as the data indicated. While staff was responsible for executing tactics and strategies, leaders at the highest levels of the coalition organizations met biannually to discuss vision, long-term goals, and resource issues. The leaders were those individuals with authority to make decisions, allocate resources, and make or influence policy decisions inside and outside of their respective organizations.

The Pennsylvania bullying prevention initiative was successful precisely because of organizations that were already established within the commonwealth, nationally and internationally, and that had begun the process of testing the most promising and evidence-based bullying prevention practices and building a wealth of experience. They also possessed other virtues essential to effective coalitions, namely: constituencies among the community, solid relationships with other professionals in the field and direct ties to major systems within Pennsylvania with power to change policy.[7,13] The major coalition partners in the Pennsylvania bullying initiative included:

- Pennsylvania Department of Education: under the auspices of the Center for Schools and Communities/Center for Safe Schools, charged with statewide dissemination of safe school policy and advocacy that includes close association with the network of Olweus Bullying Prevention Program (OBPP) certified trainer network, well established in the commonwealth.

- Clemson University, Institute on Family & Neighborhood Life: through agreements with Dr. Dan Olweus, program creator, it is responsible for OBPP evaluation and monitoring and training of trainers throughout the United States.

- Windber Research Institute, Center for Health Promotion and Disease Prevention: expertise and success with OBPP implementation and evaluation at the micro-, county-wide scale that included a mix of rural, urban and suburban schools. The Center also afforded a strong public health approach to overall coalition direction and program evaluation, which were essential in determining coalition direction.

- The Highmark Foundation: a private health foundation serving 49 of Pennsylvania's 67 counties. It acted as the lead agency with the expressed mandate from its board of directors of working to reduce incidence of bullying in its service region and improving health outcomes among children.

The partners that the Foundation engaged are representative of entities or potential partners that can be found in most states. Once again, the underlying principles of coalition building can be applied to bring together the best candidates who share a concern about the problem as well as the vision of what a coalition could achieve. The strength of the Pennsylvania coalition was manifest in the individual partner organizations and the people associated with them and their willingness to participate through channeling staff and resources in reaching the vision.

SUCCESS FACTORS AND BARRIERS IN REACHING OBJECTIVES

Coalitions seem to function smoothly when each participating member organization is willing to commit to and be accountable for common objectives while maintaining autonomy and not allowing turf issues to derail efforts. Turf issues have potential to surface when organizations' missions overlap or there are perceived or real territorial conflicts.[8,14,15] A factor that contributed to the success of the Pennsylvania coalition was appointing a person to act in a coordination role. In addition to working to stay abreast of the day-to-day activities of individual partners, the coordinator was able to gain awareness of any disputes and work to alleviate them. A coalition, mainly through the work of the lead agency, needs to strive to maintain equal power among partners and not assign accountability that leads to competition among them.[8,16] Also contributing to success were regular—though not often—structured meetings with the organization heads, decision makers, and those with authority to hold their organization and staff accountable to act in a cooperative manner day to day. The Foundation was fortunate to have as its partners highly professional and proficient members, skilled in navigating partner relationships. Each was very familiar with working under the parameters of the grantee/grantor relationship. While some models for coalition building call for a formal governance system,[14] in the case of the Pennsylvania coalition, the terms of the grants to individual partners dictated their participation including reporting and other requirements that called for regular meetings and collaborative interaction.

CORE COMPONENTS OF COALITION BUILDING AND THEIR RELEVANCE TO THE PENNSYLVANIA BULLYING PREVENTION INITIATIVE

- *Participation:* Leaders at the highest level of the member organizations convened twice yearly or less often to discuss overarching goals, and to direct and further sharpen the vision for the initiative. At the operations level, the organizations' staff responsible for day-to-day activities and achieving goals met on a more regular basis via phone conference or face-to-face to update each other and collaborate on tasks.

- *Communication:* Each member had responsibility for tracking or monitoring, and then sharing outcomes data, throughout the coalition and also to external audiences in health care, schools, and others. Many publications for peer-reviewed, trade, and general media have arisen from the work of the coalition with the intent of informing a variety of audiences from school administrators to policy makers of successes and documenting processes and outcomes.
- *Governance and rules for operation:* Most conditions were initially expressed in grant terms by the Foundation when awards were made by it to coalition partners. The terms also included templates to be used for reporting as well as reporting schedules.
- *Staff/coalition member relationships:* The Foundation named a designee to convene meetings and act as coordinator and liaison between coalition members and the Foundation.

THE IMPORTANCE OF AN EVIDENCE-BASED MODEL IN THE HIGHMARK FOUNDATION COALITION

As part of his process, composer Ludwig van Beethoven had notebooks in which he devoted page after page to exploring simple three- or four-note motifs. He turned them upside down, right side up, left to right, and right to left. They later became the backbone upon which he based his great symphonies. Leonardo da Vinci, too, is famous for his notebooks and portfolios bursting with ideas and renderings, ranging from inventions or mental fabrications years ahead of their time to meticulous anatomical models that informed the science of medicine of his day, not to mention his paintings and sculptures. These careful musings caught first on paper, almost as a blueprint, preceded the actual work of these colossal masters and acted as guides and as models to copy, enlarge, and perfect in their actual art.

When it came to the Pennsylvania bullying prevention initiative, the Olweus Bulling Prevention Program (OBPP) acted in a similar way. It provided a tested model that delineated a clear path, leading to a highly predictable and successful outcome. It eliminated risk and, if the model were followed faithfully, all but ensured a significant return on investment in reduced bullying behavior and improved school climate. Adhering to the Olweus model hastened the coalition's work.

In coalition building, a necessary component is for participants to agree on goals and objectives, and the strategies and tactics to reach them.[4,6,15] Having the OBPP model as the jumping-off point for the coalition precluded what otherwise would have been a lengthy but essential process to both a public health approach and coalition work: namely, the need to discover or develop strategies from scratch, test them with a pilot program, tweak them based on evaluation, and retest until positive results were achieved. That work had already been done through the OBPP development process.[17]

Beginning with an evidence-based model enabled a fast track to action to reduce bullying behavior and became the basis for coalition efforts to create change in individual buildings, entire school districts, and eventually the entire state in a broad implementation that touched thousands of school-aged children in Pennsylvania.[5]

In an important sense, the OBPP model was not another program, here today and gone tomorrow. The model is widely recognized by educators and violence prevention experts as the leading bullying prevention program available today. Over decades of implementation and evaluation in Norway and the United States, Olweus has perfected a methodology to change student behavior based on today's school structure, with the classroom as the nucleus and forum for student understanding and open discussion on bullying. His model equips educators and students with specific tactics and tools to help them in these discussions, engender empathy and, most importantly, begin to affect a school's culture.

The Highmark Foundation, as with many other funding institutions, made its decisions on where and how to invest dollars more and more often on outcomes data. The Foundation determined early on to devote resources to disseminating the OBPP model and excluded less tested approaches; though given time and testing, others may prove effective. Focusing on the OBPP also made it clear which partners were needed. The result of sticking to one approach and using the capabilities of coalition partners with expertise in OBPP served to consistently reduce bullying behaviors and create healthier learning environments across a broad spectrum of school size, locale, and demographics.[5]

The decision to focus on the OBPP offered several advantages. It allowed a deep and broad scientific approach to implementing the OBPP that was possible only because of the partners involved. Advantages and benefits resulting from the coalition members contributing to the PA effort include the following:

- Evaluation tools, especially the Olweus Bullying Questionnaire, a validated instrument, were in place to gather data on student perceptions at the individual school building level.
- An extensive database of OBPP nationwide outcomes data maintained by Clemson University afforded benchmarking, checking, and validating progress.
- A train-the-trainer model and trainer certification process afforded consistent technical support through trainers positioned across the state to serve schools adopting the OBPP for the first time and those implementing the program over time.
- A shortened learning curve: schools working independently to implement the model obviously had similar yet different experiences. Coalition members created content for and facilitated workshops and other scheduled educational opportunities for administrators and others. These face-to-face and online opportunities facilitated information sharing and networking among those responsible for school-level implementation.

COALITION EVOLUTION OVER TIME

As activities of the coalition progressed and OBPP implementation grew from years one through five, the coalition's focus and direction evolved. Data collected at each phase of the initiative and the maturing relationship among members, along with shared experiences, informed and led to consensus on how to proceed with efforts. Based on data and lessons learned, efforts focused on streamlining and creating efficiencies in program adoption in schools (i.e., quickly surmounting the learning curve). Additional surveys of teachers and trainers shed insight on how faithfully the OBPP was being implemented, and where schools tended to take shortcuts or were ineffective. These types of observations were facilitated greatly by the collaborative interaction of the coalition agencies. Quality assurance and fidelity of the program implementation within schools, for instance, appeared to affect outcomes. The decision by the Foundation and coalition partners to devote more resources to understanding the role of fidelity was an easy one. Once again, the collaboration that was necessary to develop and monitor a quality assurance initiative was made possible through spreading responsibility across the partners, with each partner bringing its unique capabilities to bear in the effort.

IMPORTANCE OF SHARED OBJECTIVES: AN EXAMPLE

An example of the productivity that results when goals are shared and of high priority within individual agencies is seen in the Pennsylvania coalition. As part of its charter under the auspices of the Center for Schools and Communities and affiliation with the Pennsylvania Department of Education, the Center for Safe Schools already had responsibility for developing the network of OBPP certified trainers within the state. It also had responsibility for advocating for and making available certain resources to support schools in their mandated, school safety efforts. However, as is often the case in state-funded programs, the Center lacked necessary resources to accommodate the needs of an entire state. Although it worked efficiently with the resources at hand, significant gaps existed. An important one was the network of available, certified trainers to provide the technical support needed for a large number of schools to adopt the OBPP.

Through scholarships provided by the Highmark Foundation and the ability and constituency in place at the Center to promote and provide training, new trainers were quickly recruited and trained, allowing the network to expand and meet the demand for them. In turn, the technical support the trainers ultimately provided has been crucial to allowing an implementation at the scale needed to serve 14% of the schools found across the 49 Pennsylvania counties and individual school districts that adopted the OBPP through the initiative.[5]

In effect, the coalition partners, prior to the Highmark Foundation's catalytic entrance on the stage of PA bullying prevention efforts, had been laying important foundations upon which a committed and determined statewide bullying prevention effort could be built. Convening the members hastened a quick start that gained immediate traction and momentum across the wide and disparate geographic region involved, encompassing urban, suburban, and rural school districts.

However, the successes of the Pennsylvania bullying prevention initiative were realized over time. In one sense, the 5 years of collaboration it took to reach demonstrable reductions in bullying seems like a long time, especially in the reality of today's financial climate and uncertainty. However, a coalition should plan to be involved for a term reasonable to reach its stated objectives and that often requires a long-term commitment.[16] Time also influenced the Pennsylvania effort in another way. The coalition was also highly bound by the vagaries associated with the September to May school year, and planning and decision-making and setting yearly goals were dictated by the school calendar. The resiliency and responsiveness of all partners, including the Highmark Foundation, were important to keeping the coalition operations on track. In many instances, coalition partners were required to go above and beyond the extra mile to accommodate tight timelines. To their credit, they were willing to do so. This type of commitment, from the Foundation's experience, was absolutely critical to the coalition's success.

IMPACT AT THE SCHOOL AND COMMUNITY LEVELS

Greek philosopher Aristotle (384–322 BC) has given us the adage, "The whole is greater than the sum of its parts." The truth of his statement has survived the millennia and applies to the synergy and impact an effective coalition can have. The Pennsylvania coalition to reduce bullying, through the work of individual participating organizations and individuals, has been felt in meaningful ways at the school level.

A dramatic account of the impact of the OBPP bullying prevention implementation comes from Woodland Hills School District outside of Pittsburgh, an urban OBPP adopter with a diverse student population plagued by racial tensions and disruptive behavior, particularly in its high school. The district saw dramatic change among its 4400-member student body. At the beginning of the 2008–2009 school year when its bullying prevention efforts began, it had seen 333 expulsions, 487 in-school suspensions, and 947 out-of-school suspensions. By the end of the third year of implementing OBPP, expulsions had been reduced to zero. District Superintendent Walter Calinger,

PhD, states that the experience in his district "has strong implications for cultural changes and change in policy at the local, regional and national levels."[9]

A pastor at a local church tells a story about how a suburban, western Pennsylvania high school's culture is reflected in behavior within the community. One spring afternoon, the pastor looked out from his office window to see what appeared to be a white cloth lying in the church parking lot among the parked cars. The church was adjacent to the high school that at the time was undergoing major renovation, and the church had given permission for students and faculty of the school to use the church parking lot while theirs was occupied with heavy machinery and construction trailers. Intrigued by the white cloth, the pastor went out to investigate. As he approached the white glob, he realized it was a mass of toilet tissue that had been used, he surmised, to prank a car, perhaps of a graduating student. The tissue lay in a sizable heap, four cardboard tubes giving testimony to the number of rolls used in the process. He gathered up the mess to take to the trash, and as he walked back toward the church two boys came walking into the lot.

"Hi, guys," the pastor said to them. "What do you suggest I do with this?" he asked, holding out the tangle of white tissue.

The boys, embarrassed and understanding in an instant from where the tissue most likely had come, weren't sure how to respond. But one boy finally spoke up. Pulling himself up a little taller and sticking his chest out somewhat, he said, "Pastor, on behalf of all the students in our school, we want to apologize for causing any trouble for the church."

In today's post-modern society, the idea of individual freedom has begun to erode a sense of greater community. The belief that personal behavior is just that, concerning and affecting only the individual, with little concern for greater good, is pervasive. The boys could have just as easily said, "We had nothing to do with it," and left it at that. The fact that this school district has adopted the OBPP is an anecdotal footnote. The example of a relatively harmless prank is mild when compared to the Woodland Hills example. But the boys' taking responsibility for actions beyond their own, seeing themselves as representative of a larger whole, speaks to an important aspect of effective, long-term efforts by schools to address bullying behavior. When students grow to understand that their behavior affects not just a few but all, and that each has a responsibility and role to play, students' behavior begins to change. That change ripples through or infects a student body and is reflected in improved school culture.

CONCLUSION

Forming a coalition need not be a daunting task. Coalitions are effective when they are able to focus on common objectives while allowing for the autonomy of each participating organization, making certain that common coalition objectives are strongly tied to individual organizational objectives. There is not one set formula for creating a coalition. The size and activities will depend on the problem being addressed, the resources needed, and the ability of various members to provide them. The Highmark Foundation, PA-based coalition succeeded by applying basic tenets of coalition structure and reliance on an evidence-based program as its key rallying point.

With a plan of reducing bullying behavior at its nucleus, the PA coalition grew organically as needs were discovered and the coalition gained experience. Along the way, as relationships matured and trust developed, the coalition was able to overcome turf issues and arrive at an operational system that allowed for open discussion and collaboration.

The result has been realization of an initial vision, a reduction in bullying across very wide geographic and demographic divides. Tens of thousands of Pennsylvania's schoolchildren have benefited. Through much work, collaboration, and cooperation at many levels along the coalition's chain of committed participants, the results have been felt in thousands of school hallways, classrooms, and communities as attitudes, behaviors, and the ultimate health of students has improved.

FREQUENTLY ASKED QUESTIONS

1. What are the advantages of forming a coalition?

Coalitions are a way to pool resources and leverage impact. The result of several like-minded organizations and individuals working together efficiently can achieve a much greater result than any one organization operating alone, especially if the problem they attempt to address is widespread and pervasive, as was the case with bullying in Pennsylvania. The PA coalition was able to conserve resources and often reduce costs in the process, which are attractive attributes to grantmakers who may be more readily disposed to provide funding to a coalition project than to one proposed by a single organization.

2. Where should a coalition begin?

A successful coalition is formed when participants are engaged who each recognize and agree on a significant problem, are aligned in their organizational mission to solve the problem, and have expertise or resources available to do so. There is a temptation, in order to swell the ranks, to involve organizations or individuals who have none of the above requisites. Involving them can lead to loss of focus and ultimate frustration.

3. What are key attributes to look for in coalition partners?

Common mission and agreement on the problem are essential, but also of importance are the resources needed to achieve the coalition's goals. Some participants may bring important networks or constituents who need to be involved, expertise in solving the problem, or leadership capability that paves the way to influencing policy or swaying opinion in favor of the coalition's efforts. The PA coalition partners brought all of these. The coalition should comprise entities that are in the best position to help the coalition reach its objectives. These can include community leaders, foundation and other institution heads, media representatives, parents, and others.

4. Why is an investigation or assessment phase important?

Understanding the extent of the problem a coalition seeks to address and being aware of the barriers to solving the problem constitute important information the coalition will need as it formulates its strategies and plan of attack. Highmark Foundation's relationship with schools, for instance, and knowledge of their challenges in adopting or changing new policies, was a key factor in investing resources in the Olweus Bullying Prevention Program, an evidence-based, proven solution. The initial assessment phase also provided base-line data against which coalition progress was measured over time as OBPP was adopted by schools and evaluated.

5. What are some of the key organizational issues a coalition faces?

A significant challenge for any coalition is the need for disparate and otherwise independent organizations to stay connected and to act in a concerted way. The partners in the PA coalition were bound by terms of grants they had received from the Highmark Foundation. The terms dictated a structure for participation, an important component of an effective coalition. The partners designated staff who were responsible for staying connected and collaborating with other partners on an as-needed basis, which at some points was weekly. A staff person designated as coordinator set agendas for meetings and was in a position to detect abrasions in individual relationships and stay ahead of any fractures in purpose or collaboration.

6. Does the size of a coalition matter?

In the case of the Highmark Foundation coalition, participating members were few but their influence, skills, and capacities were sufficient for success. The size of the coalition depends on the actual problem it seeks to address and the needed resources. Obviously, as a coalition grows there is more energy and time necessary for management. More important than numbers of members is the willingness of members to commit to the coalition's objectives and stick with the effort over both smooth and bumpy ground. The coalition should also encompass and reflect the population it hopes to serve, both in terms of diversity and interests.

7. What is the role of an evidence-based program as it relates to coalition building?

In the case of the Highmark Foundation coalition to address bullying prevention, the evidence-based Olweus Bullying Prevention Program served as a rallying point for engaging participants. Inviting into the coalition those with expertise in program training, dissemination, and evaluation gave instant focus to efforts, provided a basis for consistency in benchmarking efforts and informing future direction and objectives. All of these are essential components in an effective coalition endeavor.

8. Why is shared mission and vision among coalition partners so important?

In the experience of the Pennsylvania bullying prevention coalition, partners were gathered initially based on a shared vision and common goals; therefore, working cooperatively was far less of a strain on each organization's capacity. They were already highly tooled for and engaged in addressing bullying prevention work. If these partner organizations were attempting to meet coalition goals *in addition* to their own, individual ones, it is likely that coalition goals would have been relegated to a lower priority and the coalition's efforts not as effective.

9. Where is a coalition initiative likely to break down?

Priorities can sometimes shift within participating organizations, despite best intentions. As a result, interest, resources, and personnel can be siphoned away from the coalition's project. As organizations are recruited into a coalition endeavor it should be with the understanding that they are committed for the long-term or until agreed-upon objectives for which they are responsible are met.

REFERENCES

1. *We Did It Ourselves: A Guide Book to Improve the Well-Being of Children Through Community Development.* Sierra Health Foundation; 2000. Available at http://www.sierrahealth.org/assets/files/other_pubs/WDIO-We-Did-It-Ourselves.pdf. Accessed Feb. 23, 2013

2. Smith P, Bell C. *Building Coalitions: Structure. University of Florida Extension, Institute of Food and Agricultural Sciences, FY504-P12, H12-A.* Columbus: The Ohio State University; 1992.

3. *Working Collaboratively: Some Principles to Assure Effective Functioning.* Sacramento, CA: Public Health Institute Center for Collaborative Planning; Available at: http://www.connectccp.org/library/title/collaboration Accessed: Feb. 23, 2013

4. Foster DL, Wolff TJ. *Building Coalitions That Work: Lessons from the Field.* Amherst, MA: AHEC/Community Partners; 1993.

5. *Bullying Prevention: The Impact on Pennsylvania School Children.* Pittsburgh PA: Highmark Foundation; 2011.

6. Center for Tobacco Policy Research at the George Warren Brown School of Social Work at Washington University in St. Louis. "Coalitions: State and Community Interventions." In: *Best Practices for Comprehensive Tobacco Control Programs User Guide*, Washington, DC: U.S. Department of Health and Human Services, Centers for Disease Control and Prevention; 2007.

7. *Developing Effective Coalitions: An Eight Step Guide,* Oakland CA: Prevention Institute; 2002. Available at http://www.preventioninstitute.org/ index.php?option=com_jlibrary&view=article&id=104&Itemid=127. Accessed Feb. 23, 2013

8. The Community Toolbox, "Choosing Strategies to Promote Community Health and Development: Section 5. Coalition Building I: Starting a Coalition; and Section 6. Coalition Building II: Maintaining a Coalition;" a service of the Work Group for Community Health and Development. Lawrence: University of Kansas; 2013. Available at http://ctb.ku.edu http://ctb.ku.edu/en/tablecontents/chapter_1010.aspx Accessed Feb. 23, 2013

9. *Highmark Healthy High 5: A Five-Year Initiative Report.* Pittsburgh, PA: Highmark Foundation; 2012. Available at http://www.highmarkfoundation.org/ publications.shtml. Accessed: Feb. 23, 2013

10. Smith P, Bell C. *Building Coalitions: Structure, University of Florida Extension, Institute of Food and Agricultural Sciences, FY504-P12, H12-A.* Columbus: The Ohio State University; 1992.

11. Cancer Prevention and Research Institute of Texas. *Coalition Building: 8 Easy Steps*; 2006. Available at http://www.texascancer.info/communitycoalitions.html. Accessed September 7, 2012.

12. Gladwell M. *The Tipping Point: How Little Things Can Make a Big Difference.* New York: Little, Brown and Company; 2000.

13. The Community Toolbox, a service of the Work Group for Community Health and Development. *Choosing Strategies to Promote Community Health and Development: Section 5. Coalition building I: Starting a coalition; and Section 6. Coalition building II: Maintaining a coalition.* University of Kansas; 2013. Available at http://ctb.ku.edu http://ctb.ku.edu/en/tablecontents/chapter_1010.aspx. Accessed Feb. 23, 2013

14. Parker EA, Eng E, et al. Coalition Building for Prevention: Lessons Learned from the North Carolina Community-Based Public Health Initiative. *J Public Health Mgmt Practice,* 1998; 4(2), 25–36.

15. Cupal S, Jonker N. *Creating Community Change: A Model Process for Enhancing the Health of a Community.* Flint, MI: Genessee County Health Department; 2008.

16. Wolff TJ. *Coalition Building: One Path to Empowered Communities.* Amherst, MA: AHEC/Community Partners; 1992.

17. Olweus D, Limber SP. The Olweus Bullying Prevention Program: Implementation and evaluation over two decades. In:SR Jimerson, SM Swearer, and DL Espelage, editors. *The International Handbook of School Bullying.* New York: Routledge; 2010.

11

Parents, Friends, and Bullying Prevention

James A. Bozigar, ACSW, LCSW

Objectives

1. To identify and understand the unique roles and responsibilities that parents, students, community members, and professionals play in the organization and execution of a school-based bullying prevention program.
2. To identify and understand how to strengthen school-based bullying prevention efforts through outreach and incorporation of various partners.
3. To identify and understand the procedures parents and school officials should take to resolve bullying situations, including cyberbullying.
4. To identify and understand how to prevent a bullying event from becoming a chronic condition and what can be done if it reaches that point.

In this chapter, the term *parent* refers to anyone who is responsible for the primary care of a child. This person may be a biological parent, a stepparent, guardian, grandparent, or other family caregiver. The goal of this chapter is to help educators and parents work together to prevent bullying and resolve bullying situations successfully. This chapter will also include a section detailing how school officials can interact with the community to broaden and enhance their bullying prevention efforts.

Parents are the child's first teachers. Loving a child entails teaching limits, respect for self and others, and being a contributing member of the family and community. Parents teach through the way they discipline their child. All too often, parents confuse discipline with punishment. Punishment is a negative consequence for a specific behavior, while discipline reflects a parent's overarching day-to-day interaction with their child. Effective discipline recognizes the child's positive behaviors, imparts supportive guidance, offers robust encouragement, and addresses negative behaviors through meaningful discussion and behavioral consequences. Discipline in both the home and school should be based on these principles.

The goal of all discipline is to teach a child self-control. The way a parent or educator responds and reacts to a child determines how well a child learns self-control. Like almost all relationships, the parent/child relationship and the educator/student relationship can be prime places for conflict. The parent and educator set limits and the child tries to extend those limits. How those conflicts play out and their ultimate resolutions determine how a child learns self-control. At the core of these interactions is the issue of power.

Power in a good parent/educator/child relationship is used in healthy ways. Power used in a parent/educator/child relationship to hurt, demean, shame, or harm is abuse. In a peer relationship, power used in this way is bullying.

In this chapter the first objective is to provide parents and educators with information that prevents and stops bullying behaviors in their child's school and virtual world. Cyberbullying will be addressed as an exceptional form of bullying that requires distinctive parental action and regard. The research cautions against parenting techniques that may lead some youth to engage in bullying behavior. The second objective is to give parents, as participating members of their child's school and community, information that expands bullying prevention into every area of their child's life. The third objective is to provide procedures that parents, working with school officials, can follow to best resolve bullying situations. By doing this, parents can create not only schools that are safe but also communities that are secure. Unfortunately, a bullying situation can become chronic. The fourth objective of the chapter is to provide information to parents and schools on resolving chronic bullying conditions.

BASICS OF BULLYING BEHAVIOR

In today's world, almost all school conflict is identified as bullying. There are many forms of conflict, but bullying is when someone or a group of individuals use power repeatedly and over time to purposefully harm someone or some group.[1] The harm can be physical, the destruction or stealing of property, name-calling, exclusion, gossip or rumor-mongering, shame, mocking, ignoring, belittling, humiliating, hazing, teasing, or sarcasm. Bullying can also be done electronically—cyberbullying. The operative word in all bullying situations is *power*. The person or the group doing the bullying has more power than the person or the group being targeted. The individual or the group being targeted typically has difficulty defending him or herself. Because the bullying behavior is generally repeated, it causes significant suffering and long-term harm.

Other forms of youth conflict are sometimes confused with bullying behavior. Youth may engage in "rough" play. This behavior is usually between youths who are friends. The purpose of this play is not harm, but sport. Youth can also engage in fighting. The power differential between the participants determines if the fighting is bullying. If one participant has more physical or social power, then the fighting may be bullying.[1]

Bullying behaviors have many negative effects for all youth, as cited in Chapter 5 on the health effects of bullying.

Intervention to prevent and intercede in bullying situations requires understanding of the power differential between the youth involved. With an understanding of this basic premise about bullying behavior, let us look at why certain strategies are not successful in stopping bullying behaviors.

Parenting and Bullying Behaviors

A number of researchers have attempted to identify which factors create the environment that leads to bullying behaviors in youth. Kutner's 1988[2] work concluded that the "roots of bullying rest more in the child's home than in the genes." Olweus[3] and Patterson et al.[4] found that parents of children who engage in bullying behaviors tended to punish their child's misbehavior more according to their own moods than in response to the child's misconduct. In other words, the child might receive a significant punishment for an insignificant misbehavior and an inconsequential consequence for a fundamental violation of behavior norms. Olweus also found that children who engaged in bullying behavior were subject to erratic parental attacks.

One study by Horne and colleagues[5,6] found that parents of children who engage in bullying behavior used significantly less praise, encouragement, and humor than parents whose children did not engage in bullying behaviors. The parents of the children who engaged in bullying behaviors also used more negative parenting techniques such as put-downs, criticism, and sarcasm than comparable parents whose children did not engage in bullying behaviors.

Eron's studies[7,8] of parents whose children engage in bullying and aggressive behaviors found that these parents were more likely to use harsh physical forms of punishment with violent emotional outbursts. These parents appear to be highly punitive, were liable to "blow up" at their children for seemingly minor infractions, ignored more serious negative behaviors, and had long periods where, even though their children were misbehaving, they provided no consequences.

Ferrington[9-11] found that youth who bully have parents who are usually more violent. His studies also reveal that bullying can be intergenerationally transmitted. Boys who were bullies at age 14 were likely to be fathers of children at age 32 who engaged in bullying behaviors at school. Wilczenski et al.[12] in her work found that parents of children who bully were very permissive, did not establish firm limits for acceptable behavior, and used vengeful disciplinary methods. These parenting techniques lead to youth having fewer reservations against using aggressive interactions with peers.

There is a paucity of research on parenting styles and children who are bully/victims. The few studies that have been completed indicate that these youth tend to have difficult relationships with their parents that are characterized by poor supervision, lack of warmth, and inconsistent discipline. According to Smith and Myron-Wilson,[13] bully/victims report both extreme overprotectiveness and neglect by their parents while Rigby[14] found that youth who are bully/victims report terrible family functioning. Bowers et al.[15,16] have found that bully/victims are less likely to have a father in the home than children who only engage in bullying behaviors.

Consistent discipline, appropriate punishment, and warm guidance by parents seem to prevent bullying behavior in youth. According to the studies of Baumrind[17] and Steinberg et al.[18] parents who use an authoritative approach to discipline, display acceptance of their child, and permit individual autonomy seem to promote psychological development that confers protections against engaging in bullying behaviors. By contrast, inconsistent, harsh, and unpredictable punishment linked to a lack of regard and interest in a child seems to create a family environment where bullying behaviors are likely to arise.

Research on family dynamics and parenting techniques are areas that will continue to give insight into how we might prevent bullying behaviors.

Other factors also influence bullying behavior. Prejudice, lack of supervision, adult modeling, and individual temperament are explanations for bullying behaviors.

Youth with aggressive, dominating temperaments may derive satisfaction from bullying others. They may feel the need to dominate and control. Environments where there is little structure or ineffective supervision, such as a school cafeteria or a school bus, are prime locations for bullying. If adults do not intervene when bullying occurs, youth will be encouraged to engage in bullying behaviors. For example, if a teacher is in the hall and hears one student call another student, "Fag!" and does not respond, the student calling the name is encouraged to continue this behavior.

Some youth are prejudiced. They may bully certain groups such as those with disabilities, members of specific ethnic groups, or people who are a particular race, religion, gender, or sexual orientation. Bullying behaviors can command attention and some youth use bullying to gain attention.

While people engage in bullying behavior for many reasons, including attention-getting or to feel powerful, the bottom line is that there are no good reasons for anyone to bully.

Ineffective Strategies for Bullying Prevention

Mediation is sometimes proposed as an intervention or prevention method for bullying. Peer and adult mediation as an intervention is based on a foundation of equality between the individuals involved in the conflict. In bullying, we know that the person or group targeted does not have equal status with the aggressor. Moreover, the aggressor will not only use the mediation process to his/her advantage, but also discount the competence of the individual doing the mediation. Mediation gives the person doing the bullying more power and control and further demeans the status of the person who has been targeted.

Conflict resolution, like mediation, is sometimes suggested as a way to address bullying. Again, even though an adult or student leader oversees the process, the person targeted does not have equal footing. A youth who engages in bullying will use the process to his or her advantage, discounting both the person targeted and the individual leading the conflict resolution process. Any outcome of this process will most likely be to the advantage of the bully. Conflict resolution does not stop bullying behaviors.

Anger management is sometimes suggested as a method to "help" the person doing the bullying. Some youth who engage in bullying might have problems with managing their anger, but anger management does not stop bullying behaviors. Individuals who engage in bullying lack empathy for those they target.

There are other intervention strategies such as Restorative Justice and Positive Behavioral Support, but the limited research on the outcomes in these programs prevents us from recommending them at this time.

Intervention methods like these are often suggested to combat bullying. But these methods fail to significantly address the prime factor that is the hallmark of bullying behavior— power. Bullying occurs because a person or a group has the power to bully. To be successful at preventing or intervening in stopping bullying behavior, a program or strategy has to recognize that imbalance.

Individuals who engage in abusive behaviors do not seem to understand basic boundaries of civility and respect for others. When a person or group engages in bullying behaviors, the lack of empathy for the person being targeted may lead to escalation and repetition of the bullying behaviors. In order for any school- or community-based bullying prevention program to succeed, the issue of imbalance of power in the bully/target relationship must be addressed.

COMMITMENT TO CHANGE: ESSENTIAL STEPS FOR SUCCESSFUL INTERVENTIONS TO STOP BULLYING

Although bullying is a specific act of individual violence, those acts take place within an environment. Wherever youth gather, there is the potential for bullying behaviors to occur. In this section we will describe the essentials of a program that is evidenced-based in creating the changes necessary to stop and prevent bullying behaviors. The role of parents in this program and the change that can take place will be explained.

In the School

The success of any school's bullying prevention program is dependent on the involvement of the administration, staff, students, parents, and community.

Parent involvement in a bullying prevention program begins by establishing parents as integral members at the formation of the bullying prevention team. The essential members of the bullying prevention team are administrators, teachers, staff, students, and community members. Parents should be part of this team at inception. At least two parents should be included on the team, depending on the size of the school and the community's needs. Students, the ones most directly affected by bullying behavior, should be members of middle and high school bullying prevention teams. The number of students should be based on the size of the student population and should represent each grade level. Students and parents bring valuable insight to the issues of bullying. Their role should not be superficial. They should have equal power and responsibility with the other members of the core team.

Some schools are reluctant to include parents and students for various reasons. Bullying prevention teams with parent and student members are more likely to bring success to the implementation of the school's bullying prevention program. Parents and students bring a face to the consequences of the bullying behaviors taking place in a school.

The real-life experiences that parents and students bring to the bullying prevention team make them the ideal contributors in designing a school's bullying prevention program. Parents and students play a noteworthy and instrumental role in planning classroom meetings, intervention strategies, kickoff events, and community meetings.

For example, in a bullying prevention training, as participants introduced themselves, a 12-year-old student reported that students were bullied every day when they disembarked from the buses. The school counselor asked, "How?" The student replied, "When kids get off the bus, the bullies grab the weaker kids and push them down the little hill opposite the sidewalk." The counselor replied, "I see that every day from my office. I always thought it was just kids playing around." The student replied, "Nope, it's the bullies pushing the smaller kids so that they're all covered with grass. The bullies really like it when there is snow, because then the kids they push get wet and dirty and are messed up all day!"

It is not always the students who do the bullying. At the end of the first day in one middle school training, a 14-year-old student nervously said, "We've been talking about kids bullying kids all day and I want you to know that the teachers do it, too. Last week in my biology class, one kid was answering a question and his voice cracked. Everyone laughed and then the teacher started calling him with a girl's name. That was bad enough, but it got worse. When we went to the next class, the teacher, standing at the door to the classroom announced that he had gotten a text from the biology teacher about the boy's voice cracking and then called the student by the same girl's name the biology teacher used. Then, when we got seated in the classroom, he said, 'Maybe you should be wearing a skirt!' to much laughter from the students. And he's continued to call him the girl's name ever since!" Including students in the planning and implementation of a school's bullying prevention program, educators will have access to their school's culture of bullying.

Through parent involvement, information on the school's bullying prevention efforts may be presented:

- At every PTA/PTO meeting.
- During the school's open house.
- At school events like concerts, plays, assemblies, holiday parties, etc.
- Before athletic events.
- At awards ceremonies.
- At events at community organizations.
- During designated bullying prevention events such as "No Name Calling Week," or Bullying Prevention Month.

A component of every bullying prevention program is a kickoff that starts a school's bullying prevention efforts for the school year. Parents can help plan the kickoff, which can include a variety of activities, such as designing and distributing T-shirts that will be worn on the days of the bullying prevention classroom meetings. Some schools have poster contests, slogan contests, or song contests to initiate the school's bullying prevention program. For older students, there can be a contest or collaboration to create a video, role-plays, or a skit to be performed at the kickoff. Parents and students may all play a role in creating these useful bullying prevention tools.

In one school, the parents on the core team took on the responsibility of planning the school's kickoff event. They collected food, donations, and gifts from area businesses to raffle off at the kickoff. In another school where parents planned the kickoff, they organized a rally, set up a field day for the students, and manned various activities for the students.

In the Community

In addition to parents and students, other members of the community should be part of the school's work on bullying prevention. Law enforcement officers, clergy, business owners, members of civic service clubs, and officers from other community resources such as YW/MCA can add to the dynamic of the core team. These members of the community can be essential partners in the expansion of the bullying prevention program into the community and assist in both prevention and intervention in bullying situations.

One school district partnered with local after-school programs to train administrators and child-care staff on bullying prevention and interventions in bullying situations. The school district established a mechanism for working cooperatively with after-school programs on specific bullying situations. The district worked with the local ministerial association to provide information on the school's bullying prevention program and arrange to share information with religious schoolteachers and religious school staff. Seneca Valley School District in Pennsylvania worked with area civic and business clubs to educate members about the school's anti-bullying program.

Many school districts include local law-enforcement officers on their core teams and in their bullying prevention training. One district has a very active community-policing program, and the officers participate in the school's kickoff events at the start of every school year. Another school district arranged for drug and alcohol counselors to be part of the school's bullying prevention training, while another arranged to include local librarians in their program. The librarians then stocked their libraries with resources and books on bullying prevention, leading to the libraries hosting some bullying prevention programs for the community. In one school district, the librarians involved in the district's bullying prevention program developed a special bullying prevention program using puppets to model how students can act together and individually to stop bullying behaviors.

In the Home

Considering the prevalence of bullying in schools, all parents should be prepared to address these behaviors with their children. Understanding the dynamics of bullying before beginning your discussion is important. Tell your child that you know that bullying exists. Describe how the use of power makes bullying different from other forms of conflict. Illustrate this by describing a bullying situation from your own childhood. Ask your child if he or she has seen any students bullying or if he has been bullied or engaged in bullying behavior. Listen to what your child tells you about bullying. Determine what information you need to share and what message you want your child to take away from your discussion. This chapter includes information about print and web resources that parents may use to explain and help their children respond to bullying behaviors.

Nixon and Davis[19] asked over 12,000 students what they thought were the most effective and least effective ways to respond to bullying behaviors. According to these students, some of the successful methods for responding to bullying include talking to an adult at home or at school or telling a friend about the bullying.

Some students have found that using humor is helpful by deflecting the bullying behavior and disarming the person doing the bullying. Others did some self-reflective cognitive reframing by reaffirming the fact that they were not responsible for the bullying.

In asking students what was not successful, Nixon and Davis[19] found that students learned that fighting back, seeking revenge, and ignoring the bullying were not helpful responses. Remembering that bullying is an issue of power, students discovered that telling the person to stop the bullying behavior and telling the person how they felt were unsuccessful in stopping the bullying behavior.[19]

PROCEDURES FOR RESOLVING BULLYING SITUATIONS: WHAT PARENTS CAN DO

As we have noted, students can play various roles in bullying situations. A student may be the target of bullying, be the aggressor, witness the bullying, or be both an aggressor and target. In this section we review these roles and suggest steps to guide parents through the intervention process. Working together with the school and community, parents can help their children deal with the difficult issues surrounding bullying.

Target of Bullying Behaviors

If your child has been the target of bullying, let him know that he did not deserve to be treated this way. The imbalance of power in the bullying dynamic may make it difficult for your child to defend himself. Let him know that you and the adults at school are there to protect him. Help him to understand that bullying is wrong and often requires adult intervention. He may fear that the bullying will become worse if it is reported. Listen to his concerns and fears. If he asks for confidentiality, reassure him that what he shares will only be used to help him. Do not promise confidentiality; it will tie your hands as you respond to the bullying situation. Do not blame him or suggest that he is responsible for the bullying behavior. Any child's report of bullying behavior should never be disclosed to the person accused of doing the bullying.

Keep a record (date, time, people involved, location, actions taken, etc.) of the bullying events and your interactions with the school (phone calls, letters, visits to the school, etc.) Obtain this information about the bullying:

1. Who is doing the bullying?
2. What are the bullying behaviors?
3. Where is the bullying taking place?
4. When is the bullying occurring?
5. How often does the bullying occur?
6. Who has witnessed the bullying?
7. Has your child spoken to anyone (peers or adults at school) about the bullying?

The next step is to work with the school. Contact the principal and inform him/her about what your child reported. Ask the principal to explain the school's bullying response policy and request a copy of it. What steps will the school take, and how will you be informed of the results? Who else on staff will be informed of the report, and what role would they play in stopping the bullying behaviors? Ask what you can do to support the school's efforts. Set a time to speak with the principal about his/her actions. Remind the principal that to prevent retaliation, information about the informant must be kept confidential.

Let your child know with whom you spoke and what the process will be to help stop the bullying behaviors. Help your child develop strategies to prevent and respond to future bullying.

Tell your child that if a bullying incident occurs, he is to tell an adult as soon as possible. Make sure he knows the name of the adult he informs. Follow up with a call to the principal and determine if anything was done about this incident.

If the bullying is chronic, meet with the principal, put your concerns and the information you have about the bullying into writing, and request a written response from the principal. In all cases, keep a record of your actions and the information you have from your child and from school.

Work with the school to make your child's educational environment as safe as possible.

Speak with other parents and work together to stop bullying by having speakers and school programs that help stop bullying and build caring among students. Stopping bullying is a systemwide effort. Every member of the community of learners is responsible for stopping it.

Engaging in Bullying Behaviors

If your child engages in bullying behaviors cooperate with the school on the consequences imposed. Speak with your child about the behavior and listen to his account of the event. Explain what the school has determined and the course of action it will take. If there seems to be a discrepancy between your child's and the school's account, arrange a meeting with the school to resolve the matter.

If you determine that the school has taken the correct action, let your child know that the behavior is wrong. Explain how bullying hurts the person who was targeted and the people who witnessed the bullying behaviors. Help your child to understand the reasons for his bullying behavior. Was he trying to impress someone? Was he seeking attention? Was he just being mean? Or was your child trying to accomplish something through the bullying behavior? For example, trying to be on a certain team on the playground, or part of a certain group in the cafeteria? If so, help your child examine how he might accomplish this goal without engaging in bullying behaviors.

Determine how you would like your child to make amends for engaging in bullying behavior. Impose a consequence at home for the bullying incident. Remind your child that the only person he can control is himself and that bullying happens when he loses control and crosses a boundary by breaking a rule. Discuss retribution against the person he has targeted. Let your child know that if he further bullies the person, he will incur more significant consequences. Encourage your child to show good judgment and maintain self-control. Tell your child that you know he can improve his behavior. Encourage this by acknowledging the good behavior he displays. Follow up by contacting the school. If there continues to be problems, meet with the school and consider additional support and interventions. Monitor your child's friends and always model the behavior you expect from your child.

Continue to speak with your child about bullying. Attend school events on the topic of bullying and contact your library for resources. We know that people who engage in bullying behaviors generally lack empathy for the people they target. Speak to your child about empathy and discuss the need to have empathy for others. Children's librarians often have books that address the issue of empathy. Read these books with your child. View movies that have characters that display empathy for others.

Some research seems to show that gratitude may have a positive impact on increasing a sense of empathy for others. Volunteering to help others is one way to demonstrate empathy.[15] Opportunities exist throughout the community. Doing these things together builds trust, as well as a better understanding of the needs of others while helping one to appreciate what one has. Stopping bullying behaviors early is necessary to prevent a child from developing a persistent pattern of behavior that is antisocial and destructive.

Witnesses to Bullying

As noted earlier in this chapter and in the chapter on bullying and child health, emerging research indicates that children who witness bullying behaviors can be adversely affected as well. If your child witnesses these behaviors it is important to discuss the bullying your child has observed. Find out the relationship of the people involved in the bullying situation. Help your child to understand the feelings he might have as a result of being a witness to a bullying event.

Listen and reflect the emotions your child shares. Help him to understand these emotions. Although we cannot see, hear, or touch them, emotions exist and exert strong influences on us. Help your child to appreciate that emotions come from what we think about something or someone. We can have many emotions at the same time. In fact, we can even have emotions that are opposite of each other. One may detest the person doing the bullying, but at the same time admire them because of their athletic ability or success in attracting friends. This is ambivalence. When a person has ambivalent feelings, it is often difficult to make a decision on how to react. In bullying situations, many children are caught in the dilemma of wanting to help the person targeted, but fearing that they might become a target. This ambivalence leads to inaction. The inaction gives the person doing the bullying permission to continue bullying. When your child witnesses bullying, you must help him to understand this dynamic. Let your child know that, at a minimum, he has told you, and that was good. Together you can determine the next step in stopping the bullying behaviors.

Help him to resolve any anxiety or ambivalence he has about his actions or the actions of others in the situation. Be firm that bullying behaviors are never acceptable. Understanding that your child is fearful of becoming a target of bullying behavior will help you give direction and comfort to your child. Discuss what actions he should take when the bullying happens again. Connect him to an adult in school he can go to if he witnesses bullying. Tell him that you have spoken to this adult and she will help him the next time he witnesses bullying. Help him to see that bullying is more than an individual act of aggression. Bullying affects everyone in the school. Provide information and engage in discussions on how he can make a difference in the school's culture. Work with the principal and your child's teacher on responding to bullying behavior. Participate in a class meeting and share your thoughts on responding to bullying. Encourage your child to model effective responses to stop bullying.

There is one condition on your child's response to bullying. Let your child know that he should not put himself in jeopardy or harm's way but should go to an adult if he is concerned that directly intervening will put him in danger. Remember the issue of power in bullying situations. The adults in your child's life should have the power to stop the bullying. A parent can practice with his child how to get to and tell an adult about the bullying.

Children Who Both Engage in Bullying Behavior and Are Targets of Bullying Behaviors

Some children are both targets of bullying behaviors and engage in bullying. This smaller group of children is known as provocative victims or bully/victims. This group of children constitutes roughly 10% to 20% of the students who engage in bullying behaviors. If your child is both a target and an aggressor, it is important for you to work with the school to monitor and support your child.

According to Olweus et al.,[20] children who engage in bullying and are also targets of bullying tend to show traits of both. On the one hand, they may have a submissive temperament, experience symptoms of depression, be uncomfortable and anxious in social situations, feel inferior and isolated from peers, and think that their peers dislike them.[20]

On the other hand, children who are both a target and a bully have some things in common with children who commit bullying. At times they display hostile, aggressive, and dominating behaviors. They may have learning disabilities, have problems with attention, be hyperactive and impulsive, and have the ability to "zero in" on children who are weak and defenseless. Boys are more likely to be either bullies or target/bullies. According to Olweus, boys outnumber girls in this category by a ratio of two or three to one.[20]

If your child both engages in bullying and is a target, it is important for you to work with the school on identifying your child's specific difficulties. Children who both engage in bullying behaviors and are the target of bullying behaviors may require an evaluation by a psychologist or mental health professional. Possible learning problems, hyperactivity, attention deficit disorder, depression, antisocial behavior, anxiety, and other behavioral problems must be identified and treated in order to resolve the victimization and bullying behaviors that is part of this child's life.

Recall the issue of power in bullying behaviors. Children who engage in bullying like to use their power to hurt others, whereas when we look at children who are bullies/targets, it appears that they do not seem driven by power in their bullying actions. Nor do they actively seek to be bullied. These children seem to have a temperament or personality that provokes negative responses from others. This set of responses seems to be true for both peers and adults in the child's life.

In the school, responding to a child who both engages in bullying behavior and is the target requires a unique approach.[21] Every school should have a policy on responding to bullying, with companion protocols detailing what actions and steps a school will take when bullying occurs. The protocol should include guidelines for responding to a child who both engages in bullying behavior and is the target of bullying. Although the number of children who are in this category is small, their impact on the school environment is significant.

All our work with children on ending bullying behaviors is an ongoing process. We must continue to discuss, model, set and enforce limits, provide guidance, and give positive acknowledgment to students as they work to stop bullying.

PARENTS AND CYBERBULLYING

The face of bullying behavior has changed dramatically with the advent of the digital age. In the last 20 years, bullying has become a 24/7 activity. For youth, living in the digital age is all they have known, while most adults have had to learn how to adapt to it. Most youths are digitally proficient while many adults still struggle to achieve technological competence.

Prensky[21] has coined the terms *digital native* and *digital immigrant*. The digital native is someone who was born into the digital age. The immigrant is someone who is adapting to it. Natives of the digital age have grown up using computers, cell phones, the Internet, instant messages, social networks, and all that the electronic age has to offer. They do not *use* technology; they *live* technology. By the time the typical person is 18 years old, that person has spent 20,000 hours watching TV, 10,000 hours playing video games, and less than 5,000 hours reading.[22]

Being an integral part of their lives, technology has become a means to bully. This new venue for bullying is cyberbullying. According to Hinduja and Patchin, cyberbullying is "willful and repeated harm inflicted through the use of computers, cell phones, and other electronic devices."[23] Like all bullying behaviors, it intends to harm a specific individual or group and is repeated. Cyberbullying has the capacity to significantly increase the harm intended against the target.

Cyberbullying can be devastating because technology is a major portion of most young people's lives. For this reason, it is important that parents be proactive when dealing with this type of bullying behavior. In this section we will examine what parents can do to provide some level of protection from cyberbullying to their children. We will then discuss what parents can do if their child is cyberbullied, engages in cyberbullying, or is a witness to it.

Preventative Actions for Cyberbullying

Most parents take proactive and preventative actions to protect their children from household dangers. Safety locks on cabinets, gates on stairwells, and outlet protectors are some of the things parents do when their children are young. As children grow, parents begin to think about other safety hazards in their child's life (e.g., when they should be able to cross the street on their own, ride a bike, or spend an overnight at a friend's home). In each of these situations, parents reflect on their child's level of maturity, ability to make sound decisions, and degree of independence.

Before a parent can let a child drive a car, the parent must know that the child is trustworthy. The parent must be able to trust the child with his own life and the lives of others, know that the child will obey the laws of the road, and be confident that the child can be trusted with a valuable piece of property. Before a child can be given access to technology, parents must be able to trust that their children will use the technology responsibly and safely. At what age should your children have a cell phone? When should they be able to use the Internet? When should they have video games, what type of video games, and what are the boundaries for using them? Parents should think about the child's use of technology as a privilege—one that requires trust.

Parents should consider these digital privileges as responsibilities that a child earns through demonstrating sound judgment and mature self-control. Parents should detail the expectations for using technology with their children. In addition, parents should detail consequences if their children abuse the use of technology. This should include the consequences if a child engages in bullying with it. Just as a parent would not permit a 2-year-old to chew gum, a parent needs to establish at what age children will be permitted to use a technology. Clear boundaries are as helpful to the child as to the parent. When children know their limits, it reduces the amount of conflict and strife in the home. Moreover, knowing the age that a child will be able to have a cell phone helps the parent prepare the child for this privilege.

As a child approaches the age when they can use a new technology, the parent should put a trial period in place. An example of this is creating an account on a social networking site or using an instant messaging site. When the child is permitted to create an account on a social networking site, the parent should be the one to create the account and the password. This way, when the child wants to be on the site the parent will be the one to log in. By doing this, the parent can monitor how the child is using the account, who else is on the site, and the child's activity. This process gives the child the opportunity to demonstrate responsible use of this technology. In this way, the parent learns that a child can be successful in using technology safely.

Demonstrating reason and wisdom in their use of technology, children can reassure their parents that they are competent digital natives.

If Your Child Is a Target of Cyberbullying

The most comforting thing a parent can give a child is a warm and accepting relationship in which the child feels valued and respected. A child who knows that he can go to his parent with any problem or worry has a priceless resource. Parents should be the "go-to" person in a child's life. Our work preparing a child for the use of technology will build a relationship of trust. That involves educating a child about cyberbullying. At the top of the list of things to do if a child is cyberbullied is to let the parent know about it.

In spite of prevention efforts and solid planning for the use of technology, a child may still be a target of cyberbullying. When your child comes to you to report being the target of cyberbullying, it is important to react in specific ways.

The parent must know the nature of the bullying incident and that the child is safe from further attacks. Determine the source of the bullying and block that individual's access to your child. Collect the evidence of the bullying. This includes text messages, postings on social websites, e-mails, voice messages, and anything else that may be relevant. All this evidence should have a date and the name of the person responsible. Do not destroy or delete any evidence of the bullying. Contact the school. The school's bullying prevention policy should include protocols on cyberbullying. The school is the institution that has the power to do something about the bullying. After contacting the school, contact your Internet service and the Internet service of the source of the bullying. Your provider has policies and procedures in place to respond to cyberbullying. If a physical threat has been made, contact the police.

As in all bullying situations, provide emotional comfort and support. Seek other resources if necessary and follow up to make sure the bullying has stopped and that there is no retaliation. If the bullying continues, meet with the principal, put your concerns and the information you have about the bullying into writing, and request a written response from the principal. *In all cases, keep a record of your actions and the information you have from your child, the school, and any other parties involved.*

Work with your school and other community agencies on educating students on the proper use of technology. Connect with state and national organizations that work to intervene and stop cyberbullying. Realize that your voice and actions, through the Internet, can reach a national audience and make a difference in your and your children's lives.

If Your Child Engages in Cyberbullying

Unfortunately, some parents will learn that their child has engaged in cyberbullying. In spite of a parent's proactive efforts and stern warning about engaging in bullying behavior with technology, some children may still cyberbully. If a parent has already discussed the consequences of engaging in cyberbullying, then those consequences should be applied. If not, then the parent should determine a consequence and support the school's consequence.

Contact the school and let them know about the incident. Cooperate with the school on the investigation. Cyberbullying often includes multiple individuals and events. Make sure all parties involved are contacted and alerted to what actions will be taken. Determine how your child is going to remedy the harm she has done. Speak with your child about apologizing.

Apology and forgiveness are two of the most important tools in human relationships. Apology has the power to undo hurt, shame, and guilt between individuals and groups. The quality of a relationship is not determined by the level of conflict, but by how conflict is resolved. Effective apology and forgiveness are two tools every healthy relationship requires.

Through apology, conflict can be resolved, grudges can end, and revenge can be prevented. Without apology there can be no forgiveness.

But at the same time, an apology is not complete without forgiveness. It is the action that begins the rebuilding of a damaged relationship. To forgive, one must move forward, absolve the hurt, and work to recreate a trusting relationship.

Forgiveness can occur with a healing apology that includes four basic components:

1. Acknowledgment of the wrongdoing.
2. An explanation for the hurtful behavior.
3. A genuine expression of sorrow and repentance.
4. An offer of reparation.

When an apology fails, one or sometimes all of these points are weak.

An apology heals a broken relationship because the person who has committed the hurt validates the rights and feelings of the person who has been offended. The person offering the apology restores dignity to the person hurt—the most significant attribute of a sincere apology. An apology requires courage, humility, and honesty.

Apology and forgiveness are hallmarks of mature, caring relationships. These are skills that must be learned and refined throughout life. When mastered and applied with sincerity, we experience the joy of sustainable healthy relationships.

To prevent a possible bullying, consider installing tracking and filtering software on the child's electronic devices. In all situations, schedule routine inspections of your child's online behavior, texting, phone contacts, and computer use. Work toward reestablishing trust. Remind your child that you want her to be responsible for herself, and that maturity brings the rewards of feeling good about yourself and your actions. Focus on how your child can overcome this lapse in judgment and learn from this error.

If Your Child Witnesses Cyberbullying

As with all bystanders of bullying, there is a fear that doing anything might lead to becoming a target. When parents prepare their child to use technology, one thing they should cover is how to respond to bullying they might witness. Reporting the bullying to an adult at home and school officials who can intervene is essential to stop the bullying. Bystanders must understand that most electronic bullying is something that adults are not going to see. The bystander plays a significant role in helping to stop bullying by telling an adult. Parents should advise their child to never forward a message, posting, joke, or photo that is hurtful or embarrassing to another child. If it is a threat, the child should document it. With the parent's guidance, the child can alert the Internet provider and file a complaint with the relevant website. If the threat is substantial, then the police must be informed. The parent should be involved in this process. Witnesses to cyberbullying may need to speak with you about their reaction and concerns. A parent might want to explore with his or her child how the child would react if she were the target. These discussions will help the child to see how serious cyberbullying is and the role a bystander plays in curbing this form of violence.

Cyberbullying is an evolving and dynamic part of the electronic age. The technology that makes mass communication so wonderful also makes it an unlimited source of pain. Parents, along with the school, must help their children learn to use technology with intelligence and discretion. Working as partners with the school and the community, technology can become a source for healthy growth and sustained learning, making our relationships richer and more valuable.

WHEN BULLYING IS CHRONIC

In some situations, bullying can become chronic. A child is targeted and the bullying continues even though the school may have intervened. In our work at HALT! Stop Bullying Now, we have worked with over 100 families where bullying has been chronic. When bullying becomes chronic, the parent must take action. In this chapter, we have already discussed what parents should do when their children are bullied. How to document bullying is described in detail. Please refer to that section. If the bullying is chronic, the parent and the child should detail the bullying events, including all contacts with the school. Be specific about dates, people involved, and what actions were taken. This document is important in working with the school on resolving the bullying behavior. Meet with the person in charge of bullying prevention at your school, and discuss how the school plans to address the matter. Ask to have this plan in writing. After the meeting, compose a summary document of the meeting and enclose it with a thank-you letter to the person who is working with you on stopping the bullying. In the letter, let the person know that you want a follow-up meeting to evaluate the plan's results.

If it becomes apparent that the plan is working, let the person at the school know. If the plan is not working, tell the contact person and ask for a written revision of the plan and information about what other actions the school will take. In all of these interactions, be cordial and always approach the school as a collaborator who wants the bullying to stop and for your child and all students in the school to be safe.

Chronic bullying exists for several reasons. The most rare, albeit glaring, one is a school culture that openly supports bullying behaviors. In other situations, the school culture may be passively supporting bullying behavior by only minimally intervening—a far more common occurrence. If the school's intervention with the person or the group doing the bullying is tepid, then the bullying behavior will continue. Remember that people engage in bullying behavior because they have the power to bully. People stop bullying when they know that there will be an adverse consequence for continuing the behavior or that someone with more power is present. Adults in the school and empowered bystanders can fill those roles. In most of the HALT! referrals, the school's initial response to the person doing the bullying was weak. This did not stop the bullying and gave the person doing the bullying license to continue the behavior. The schools needed to review their interventions and make sure that the initial response to the bullying behavior was significant in stopping the behavior.

How Should the School Respond to Reports of Bullying?

1. Identify *who* (bully, target, witnesses), *where,* and *when* the incident occurred, and any *prior incidents.* Contact the parents of the student who was bullied. Inform them of your actions and your plan. Apologize for the event. Reinforce the school's policy on bullying prevention and intervention. Contact the parents of the student who engaged in bullying behavior. Have the student inform his parents of his actions and the school's response. If necessary, schedule a meeting with the parents to review the school's plan and how the student will be monitored over the next week and the rest of the school year.

2. *Inform staff and colleagues* of the bullying behavior and identify the students involved. Review staff responsibilities, what they should be alert to, and how they should respond if an incident occurs.

3. *Separate the students* in class, at lunch, and on the playground, gym, playing fields, and bus. *Make sure that adults who supervise in these areas are briefed and know their responsibility to monitor the students involved.*

4. *Support the student who was the target* by connecting him or her with friends and supportive classmates, and encouraging him or her to report bullying to staff. Inform staff in the student's classes to help the student connect with peers. Consider changing classroom setting or seat assignments of the person who has committed the bullying if there is a potential problem.

5. *Inform student who engaged in bullying* that he or she should expect to be *disciplined* and *monitored,* and to *apologize* and make *reparations.* Inform staff in contact with this student to be alert to potential retaliation bullying. Meet with the student's parents.

6. *Follow up* with the targeted student and the student who did the bullying *within one week,* to ensure there were no more incidents. If this is the case, *reinforce the good behavior of the child who had engaged in bullying.* Inform the parent of your actions. Confirm that no bullying incidents have occurred.

7. Complete the school's bullying intervention report and *contact parents of both students.* Arrange a meeting with staff, parents, or students if necessary.

By following this format, the school has an improved chance to stop the bullying behavior and prevent it from happening again.

When the bullying is chronic, the school's response to the student who was targeted and his parents should be empathic and sincere. The school should apologize for the hurt the student and family experienced. The school should identify the reason for the lapse in the bullying prevention program and the corrective measures the school has taken to assure the student's safety.

How Should the Parents Respond?

The parent should follow up with the school when bullying has become chronic. Being involved with the school's bullying prevention program prior to an episode establishes a relationship that is based on mutual regard to prevent bullying. It is better that it is not linked to a crisis. The best approach to help a child deal with bullying is the proactive one. Working on the organization and implementation of the bullying prevention program, assisting in the school's kickoff events, participating in the classroom discussions, and being an active member of the community of learning gives a parent the chance to mold how the school will respond to bullying and contribute to its efforts to make the school safe for everyone.

This chapter has examined the role and responsibility of parents in the school and the community's effort to prevent and intervene in bullying behaviors. This work is not simple. To effectively prevent bullying, parents, school staff, community members, and students must work together to reduce and eradicate the power to bully that anyone has over others.

CONCLUSIONS

The goal of this chapter is to provide substantive information on the important roles that students, parents, community members, and professionals play in the planning and implementation of a robust bullying prevention program. Our experience reinforces the essential principles of every stakeholder's responsibility in decreasing the violence of bullying in our schools, communities, and homes.

Organizing, coordinating, and establishing these stakeholders into a cohesive and forceful unit to reduce bullying violence requires insightful and committed leadership. The people who spearhead this endeavor need both knowledge and skill. This chapter provides not only the core knowledge for this task but also insight into the more nuanced aspects of successfully accomplishing this work.

In order to achieve this, detailed procedures are included in the chapter. These procedures will enable school officials to resolve bullying problems and prevent them from turning into chronic situations. Should, however, a bullying situation become chronic, the chapter includes information to how to intervene.

Inherent in the violence of bullying are the specific roles that students willingly or unwillingly adopt. How and what parents can do to solve these situations is basic to reducing the violence of bullying and constitutes the core of reducing bullying behavior.

Each school has a culture. Bullying exists within that culture. How students, school staff, and parents respond to bullying determines the viability of bullying in that culture. This chapter has looked at the stakeholders in this culture and emphasized the fundamental ways they can work together to make inroads in reducing bullying and promoting a culture that guarantees each person's safety. Changing a school's culture requires dedicated, consistent, and compassionate thought and action. This chapter is a resource that can be used to accomplish this goal so that every student, staff member, and parent is safer because we all shoulder and know our responsibility for stopping the violence of bullying.

FREQUENTLY ASKED QUESTIONS

1. What are some common characteristics that researchers have found in the behavior of the parents of youth who bully?

Inconsistent, harsh, and unpredictable punishment linked to a lack of regard and interest in a child seems to create a family environment where bullying behaviors are likely to arise.

2. What other factors may influence someone to engage in bullying behaviors?

Other factors that influence bullying behavior include prejudice, lack of supervision, adult modeling, and individual temperament. Youth with aggressive, dominating temperaments may derive satisfaction from bullying others. Feeling the need to dominate and control, they receive pleasure from exerting their power over others, reaping the benefits of high status and social position. Environments where there is little structure or ineffective supervision, such as a school cafeteria or a school bus, are prime locations for bullying. If adults do not intervene when bullying occurs, youth will be encouraged to engage in bullying behaviors.

3. Why are anger management, conflict resolution, and mediation ineffective to stop bullying?

The reason for bullying is the misuse of power. These programs do not recognize this because they treat the participants as equals. This stance empowers the person doing the bullying and leads to further bullying behavior.

4. Describe why addressing the imbalance of power in relationships is a central tenet of successful bullying prevention?

Individuals who engage in abusive behaviors do not seem to understand basic boundaries of civility and respect for others. When a person or group engages in bullying behaviors, their lack of empathy for the person targeted may lead to escalation and repetition of the bullying behaviors. In order for any school- or community-based bullying prevention program to succeed, the issue of imbalance of power in the bully/target relationship must be addressed.

5. Why are parents and students essential members of a school's bullying prevention program?

Parents and students bring a face to the consequences of the bullying behaviors taking place in a school. Students are the school's eyes and ears to the bullying culture in the school. Parents provide collaboration with the home, improving the possibility of cooperation between parents and schools.

6. What information should a parent organize when reporting a bullying situation to the school?

1. Who is doing the bullying?
2. What are the bullying behaviors?

3.   Where is the bullying taking place?
4.   When is the bullying occurring?
5.   How often does the bullying occur?
6.   Who has witnessed the bullying?
7.   Has your child spoken to anyone (peers or adults at school) about the bullying?

7. What actions should parents take if their child is the target of chronic bullying?

If the bullying is chronic, the parent and the child should detail the bullying events including all contacts with the school. Be specific about dates, people involved, and what actions were taken. This document is important in working with the school on resolving the bullying behavior. Meet with the person in charge of bullying prevention at your school, and discuss how the school plans to address the matter. Ask to have this plan in writing. After the meeting, compose a summary document of the meeting and enclose it with a thank-you letter to the person who is working with you on stopping the bullying. In the letter, let the person know that you want a follow-up meeting to evaluate the plan's results. If it becomes apparent that the plan is working, let the person at the school know. If the plan is not working, tell the person and ask for a written revision of the plan and what other actions the school will take. In all of these interactions, be cordial and always approach the school as a collaborator who wants the bullying to stop and for your child and all students in the school to be safe.

8. What should a parent do to prevent his or her child from being a target or engaging in cyberbullying?

Before a child can be given access to technology, the parent must be able to trust that their child will use the technology responsibly and safely. Parents should think about the child's use of technology as a privilege—one that requires trust. Considering digital privileges as responsibilities that a child earns through demonstrating sound judgment and mature self-control helps a parent to set the limits for their use. Parents should detail the expectations for using technology with their children. In addition, the parent should detail consequences if the child abuses the use of technology. This should include the consequences if the child engages in bullying with it. Clear boundaries are as helpful to the child as to the parent. When the child knows the limit, it reduces the amount of conflict and strife in the home. Moreover, knowing the age that a child will have access to electronic devices helps the parent prepare the child for this privilege. As a child approaches the age when they can use a new technology, the parent should put a trial period in place. For example, create an account on a social networking site by setting up the password and access. Monitor for one year. If the child is trustworthy, then give the child the password, but continue to monitor activity. Demonstrating reason and wisdom in their use of technology, a child will reassure their parent that they are competent digital natives.

9. What steps should the school take to respond to reports of bullying?

1. Identify *who* (bully, target, witnesses), *where* and *when* the incident occurred, and any *prior incidents.* Contact the parents of the student who was bullied. Inform them of your actions and your plan. Apologize for the event. Reinforce the school's policy on bullying prevention and intervention. Contact the parents of the student who engaged in bullying behavior. Have the student inform his parents of his actions and the school's response. If necessary, schedule a meeting with the parents to review the school's plan and how the student will be monitored over the next week and the rest of the school year.

2. *Inform staff and colleagues* of the bullying behavior and identify the students involved. Review staff responsibilities, what they should be alert to, and how they should respond if an incident occurs.

3. *Separate the students* in class, at lunch, and on the playground, gym, playing fields, and bus. *Make sure that adults who supervise in these areas are briefed and know their responsibility to monitor the students involved.*

4. *Support the student who was the target* by connecting him or her with friends and supportive classmates, and encouraging him or her to report bullying to staff. Inform staff in student's classes to help the student connect with peers. Consider changing classroom setting or

seat assignments of the person who has committed the bullying if there is a potential problem.

5. *Inform student who engaged in bullying* that he or she should expect to be *disciplined* and *monitored*, and to *apologize* and make *reparations*. Inform staff in contact with this student to be alert to potential retaliation bullying. Meet with the student's parents.

6. *Follow up* with the targeted student and the student who did the bullying *within one week*, to ensure there were no more incidents. If this is the case, *reinforce the good behavior of the child who had engaged in bullying.* Inform the parents of your actions. Confirm that no bullying incidents have occurred.

7. Complete the school's bullying intervention report and *contact parents of both students.* Arrange a meeting with staff, parents, or students if necessary.

10. What is the most frequent reason for chronic bullying existing in a school?

When the school's response to bullying is tepid and the school climate supports bullying behaviors, even passively, chronic bullying thrives.

REFERENCES

1. Olweus D. *Bullying at School: What We Know and What We Can Do.* Oxford, UK; Cambridge, USA: Blackwell; 1993.

2. Kutner L. Bullies: Is a rough home life the root of playground evil? *Sacramento Bee.* August 6, 1988:1,3.

3. Olweus D. Familial and tempermental determinants of aggressive behavior in adolescent boys: A casual analysis. *Dev Psychol.* 1980; 16:6444–6660

4. Patterson GR, Reid JB, Dishion T. *Antisocial Boys.* Eugene, OR: Castalia; 1992.

5. Horne AM. Bullies, victims, and bystanders: The role of the family in reducing child and adolescent aggression. *Fam Psychologist.* 2006; 22:7–9.

6. Horne AM, Glaser B, Sayger TV. Bullies. *Counseling Human Dev.* 1994; 27:1–12.

7. Eron LD, Huesmann LR. The stability of aggressive behavior-even unto the third generation. In M Lewis, SM Miller, editors. *Handbook of Developmental Psychopathology*. New York: Plenum; 1990: 147–156.

8. Eron LD, Huesmann LR, Zelli A. The role of parental variables in the learning of aggression. In DJ Pepler, KH Rubin, editors. *The Development and Treatment of Childhood Aggression*. Hillsdale, NJ: Lawrence Erlbaum; 1991: 169–188.

9. Ferrington DP. Childhood aggression and adult violence: Early precursors and later life outcomes. In DJ Pepler, KH Rubin, editors. *The Development and Treatment of Childhood Aggression*. Hillsdale, NJ: Lawrence Erlbaum; 1991: 5–30.

10. Ferrington DP. Understanding and preventing bullying. In M. Tonry, editor. *Crime and Justice*, vol. 12. Chicago: University of Chicago Press; 1993: 381–458.

11. Ferrington DP. Antisocial personality from childhood to adulthood. *The Psychologist*. 1991; 4:389–394.

12. Wilczenski FL, Steegmann R, Braun M, et al. Children as victims and victimizers: Intervention to promote 'Fair Play.' *Sch Psychol Int*. 1997; 18:81–89.

13. Smith KP, Myron-Wilson R. Parenting and school bullying. *Clin Child Psychol Psychiatry*. 1998; 3:405–417.

14. Rigby K. Psychosocial functioning in families of Australian adolescent school children involved in bully/victim problems. *J Fam Therapy*. 1994; 16:173–187.

15. Bowers L, Smith PK, Binney V. Cohesion and power in the families of children involved in bullying problems at school. *J Fam Therapy*. 1992; 14:371–387.

16. Bowers L, Smith PK, Binney V. Perceived family relationships of bullies and victims in middle childhood. *J Soc Personal Relationships*. 1994; 11:215–232.

17. Baumrind D. Effects of authoritative parental control on child behavior. *Child Dev*. 1966; 37:887–907.

18. Steinberg L, Lamborn SD, Dornbusch SM, Darling N. Impact of parenting practices on adolescent achievement: Authoritative parenting, school involvement and encouragement to succeed. *Child Dev*. 1992; 63:1266–1281.

19. Nixon S, Davis C. *The Youth Voice Project*. State College: Pennsylvania State University, 2010. Available at http://www.youthvoiceproject.com/ YVPMarch2010.pdf.

20. Olweus D, et al. *Olweus Bullying Prevention Program Teachers Guide*. Center City, MN: Hazelden, 2010.

21. Prensky M. Digital natives, digital immigrants. *On the Horizon*. 2001; 9(5):1–2.

22. Adelman HS, Taylor L. Mental health in schools and public health. *Public Health Rep. 2006* May–Jun 2006; 121(3):294–298.

23. Hinduja S, Patchin JW. Bullying Beyond the Schoolyard: Preventing and Responding to Cyberbullying. Thousand Oaks, CA: Corwin Press; 2009.

12

Community Engagement in Bullying Prevention

Karla Good, MSW

Objectives

1. To gain an understanding of why community engagement is an important part of school-based bullying prevention efforts.
2. To be able to identify potential community partners.
3. To learn strategies for building and maintaining effective community partnerships.

Right now you might be thinking, "With everything I have to do in a day, you actually want me to engage the community in my bullying prevention efforts?" The answer is YES! Community partnerships with businesses, agencies, civic groups, faith-based organizations, and individuals can provide your school with valuable resources and support, allowing you to enhance and sustain your bullying prevention program and build community connections that benefit your school and community in a variety of ways. Furthermore, research supports the view that when schools, homes, and communities work together, schools can become more effective and caring places, resulting in improved academic performances, fewer discipline problems, and less violence.[1] Finally, it is important to remember that bullying isn't just a "school issue." Bullying doesn't end when the bell rings and the books are put away. Bullying can occur on playgrounds, at sports practices, dance classes, in neighborhoods, and countless other community gathering places. Basically, wherever young people congregate, bullying can occur.[2] Bullying is a community issue and a public health concern. Therefore, efforts to reduce and respond to bullying should include support and input from the larger community. Additionally, community engagement initiatives should aim to promote community awareness, increase community buy-in, and educate the larger community about the issue of bullying.

POTENTIAL COMMUNITY PARTNERS

In a time when funding for school-based initiatives is scarce, community partners can play a vital role in providing resources and support for your bullying prevention program. This support can take a variety forms and is limited only by your efforts and creativity. For example, community partners can potentially provide financial support in the form of monetary donations, or material support, such as posters and banners to promote your efforts throughout the community. They also can be a reservoir of human support in the form of volunteer hours and public relations support, such as partnering with local media outlets to promote your bullying prevention efforts.[2] Following is a list of potential community partners. Keep in mind that this is only a partial list and should be expanded based on program needs, as well as individual school contacts and connections within the community:

- Local businesses (restaurants, grocery stores, retailers, gas stations, movie theaters. Any business in your community is a potential partner. Brainstorm with your team to develop a comprehensive list...the possibilities are endless!).
- Community organizations and agencies (behavioral health agencies, healthcare providers, nonprofits, volunteer organizations).
- Universities and colleges.
- Local residents.
- Law enforcement.
- Faith-based organizations.
- Civic groups (Rotary Club, Kiwanis, Lions).
- Senior citizens' groups.
- Media (local news stations, radio, newspaper).
- Policy makers/local government officials.

Conversely, it is important to remember that these partnerships are not "one-way streets," and partnerships should be mutually beneficial to both parties. Your school is a vital member of the community and has many resources to offer your potential partners in return. These resources include, but are not limited to: the use of school facilities as meeting space for community groups; expertise and knowledge in the form of your teaching staff; access to staff, students, and family members; and increased visibility for businesses, agencies, and organizations within the community. These types of reciprocal relationships help to ensure that you are building lasting, sustainable partnerships that benefit both your school and the larger community.[2] For examples of reciprocal Community Partnerships, see Table 12.1.

Think broadly when identifying program needs and potential community partners. Identify both the short-term and long-term needs of your bullying prevention program. Do you need money to provide training and materials for your staff, volunteers to increase supervision in identified bullying "hotspots" within your school building, refreshments for a parent meeting or kick-off event, or help monitoring and evaluating your bullying prevention efforts? Finally, consider which businesses, agencies, or community groups might already have resources or programs in place to help address these needs.

STRATEGIES FOR EFFECTIVE COMMUNITY ENGAGEMENT

Once you have identified your needs and have developed a list of potential partners, it is time to formulate a strategy for effective community engagement:

- Designate specific school personnel to lead your community engagement initiative. This will ensure a coordinated approach with no duplicative efforts.
- Include students in your community efforts, especially in the secondary grades. This is an effective way to engage students in your bullying prevention program. Additionally, students will be able to identify community partners that are relevant in the eyes of young people.
- Be mindful that the businesses, agencies, and other community members that you are approaching are busy and their time is valuable. Be brief, concise, and appreciative when making contact.
- Remember that your potential partners are most likely being solicited by many other schools, agencies, and groups within the community. Let them know that you have resources to offer in return and are looking to build lasting partnerships with mutual benefits.

Table 12.1. Examples of Reciprocal Community Partnerships

Community Agency	Potential School Benefits	Potential Partner Benefits
1. Businesses	Donations to support BP efforts, mentoring opportunities for students.	Increased visibility in school and community, interaction with students/future employees.
2. Restaurants	Food/donations for BP related events (ie, kick-off event, parent meetings).	Publicity, potential to work with school in a paid capacity.
3. Community Organizations	Donations to BP efforts and presentations to students regarding issues relating to violence/bullying (cyberbullying, relational aggression, partner violence).	Increased visibility in school and community, interactions with students and staff.
4. Colleges/ Universities	Assistance with monitoring and evaluating BP efforts, volunteers to assist with a variety of BP activities (ie, kick-off events and classroom meetings).	Fulfillment of services learning requirements for current college students, access to future college students.
5. Local Residents	Potential BP planning committee members, playground, bus and cafeteria monitors, donations to support BP efforts, increased awareness in community.	Community input regarding issues relating to bullying, interaction with students and staff.
6. Law Enforcement	Presentation to students regarding variety of violence/bullying topics.	Development of positive relationships with students.
7. Faith-based Organizations	Donations to support BP efforts, dissemination of consistent information regarding effective BP strategies to larger community.	Increased visibility in school and community, interaction with students and staff.
8. Civic Groups (Rotary, Kiwanis, Lions etc)	Donations to support BP efforts, dissemination of consistent information regarding effective BP strategies to larger community.	Increased visibility in school and community, interaction with students and staff.
9. Senior Citizen's Groups	Playground, bus and cafeteria monitors (increased supervision).	Interaction with students and staff, access to school facility.
10. Media	Promotion of BP efforts (kick-off events etc), dissemination of consistent information regarding effective BP strategies to larger community.	Access to school/community related events.
11. Policy Makers/ Government Officials	Dissemination of consistent information regarding effective BP strategies, influence regarding funding issues relating to BP and other issues impacting schools.	Increase visibility in school and community.

*adapted from a chart developed by Kretzmann and McKnight.[6]

- A portion of your community engagement efforts should focus on education and creating community buy-in. This will ensure that a consistent message on bullying and bullying prevention is being disseminated throughout the larger community, and increases the likelihood that community members understand and support your efforts.
- Realize that you may meet some resistance within the community. Some might perceive your bullying prevention efforts to mean that bullying is a "huge" problem in your school, while others might not realize the seriousness of bullying behaviors and the negative long-term consequences that can result. Be patient and educate, educate, educate!
- Don't view community engagement as a "one and done" effort. This is an ongoing process and should be viewed as such. Continue to look for ways to maintain current partnerships, while actively pursuing and developing new ones.
- Strive to foster a sense of "we are in this together." Creating a safe environment for children in schools, communities, and homes is everyone's responsibility.
- Remember that it's all about the relationship! Consistent communication and personal contact is key. For example, although you may send an introductory letter explaining your bullying prevention efforts and program needs, it is essential to follow-up with a personal contact and maintain this type of interaction throughout the collaborative process.

It is important to remember that building strategic, effective, and sustainable partnerships is your goal. You are not merely asking community members to make a one-time donation to your school program. You are actively engaging them in your bullying prevention efforts in the hope of making your school and community safer places for all.

STRATEGIES FOR ENHANCING COMMUNITY PARTNERSHIPS

Once you have developed your partnerships and have garnered support and buy-in from the community, it is important to maintain and enhance these relationships. Here are a few strategies:

- Update community partners regarding program progress on a regular basis. This can be easily accomplished by sending email updates, newsletters, or convening regular meetings with all involved community partners.

- Find creative ways to acknowledge your partners' efforts and contributions. Send a thank-you letter, recognize them on your school website or newsletter, or invite them to a "partner appreciation" luncheon.
- Invite community partners to bullying prevention–related events. For example, if your school holds an annual kick-off event for your bullying prevention program, invite partners to attend. Additionally, consider including community members on your bullying prevention committee. By doing so, you can gain valuable insight into the perception of bullying in the larger community, increase community buy-in, strengthen already existing partnerships, and potentially create new relationships with additional community agencies/members.
- Ask your partners for input and feedback regarding your community engagement efforts. It is important that your partners see these relationships as effective and mutually beneficial.

By engaging in these simple strategies you will increase the likelihood that partners stay informed, feel connected and appreciated, and remain committed to the long-term success of your bullying prevention program. This allows not only for increased access to support and resources, improved buy-in, and community awareness regarding your efforts, but enhanced connection between school and community as well.

As stated earlier, research indicates that school–community engagement initiatives have potential benefits that extend well beyond bullying prevention.[7,10,11] Some of the positive outcomes that may be experienced as a result of consistent, comprehensive, and sustainable community engagement initiatives include improved academic achievement, fewer discipline problems, less violence, improved school climate, better attendance, increased student retention, and improved staff morale.[3–5]

Again, it is important to remember that school–community partnerships are not one-way streets, and that there are many benefits to the community as well. Potential community benefits include: access to resources such as space and equipment, access to staff, students and families, increased visibility for businesses, agencies and organizations within the community, increased community development, and safer communities and neighborhoods.[3–5]

It is clear that both schools and communities benefit from working together and establishing long-term, mutually beneficial partnerships. However, there is another important reason for establishing effective school–community collaborations. Although most bullying does occur on school grounds during school hours, it doesn't end there. Bullying incidents have the potential to occur wherever young people gather in the larger community. Bullying can take place at a sporting event, on a playground, in someone's backyard, or even by technological means, such as social networking sites or cell phones. Bullying is a complex problem that requires a comprehensive and multifaceted solution that includes school and community components. Additionally, it is important for students to see consistent messages in school and in the community regarding bullying prevention. This sends the message to students, and community members, that bullying isn't just a school issue, but is important to the entire community.[1] Community engagement is a key component of any bullying prevention program. Partnerships promote community buy-in and raise awareness, provide schools with necessary resources and support, and create a safer learning environment for students. The benefits also extend beyond the schoolyard, creating a connection between school and community in which the community is viewed as a partner in the safety and well-being of students and their families. By working together, educators and community members can make a difference in the lives of young people by providing them safer schools, communities, and neighborhoods.

Never doubt that a small group of thoughtful, committed citizens can change the world; indeed, it's the only thing that ever has.

—Margaret Mead

FREQUENTLY ASKED QUESTIONS

1. Why is it important to involve the community in school-based bullying prevention efforts?

It is important to involve the community in your bullying prevention efforts for a variety of reasons. First, community partnerships can provide your school with valuable resources and support, allowing you to enhance and sustain you bullying prevention program. Second, research supports the view that when schools, homes, and communities work together, schools can become more effective and caring places. Finally, it is important to remember that bullying isn't just a school issue. Bullying can occur wherever young people gather in the community, and therefore is a community issue, as well as a school issue.

2. Who are some potential community partners?

Potential community partners are only limited by your needs, efforts, and creativity:

- Local businesses (restaurants, grocery stores, retailers, gas stations, movie theaters).
- Community organizations (behavioral health agencies, healthcare providers, nonprofits, volunteer agencies).
- Universities and colleges.
- Local residents.
- Law enforcement.
- Faith-based organizations.
- Civic groups/associations (Rotary Club, Kiwanis, Lions).
- Senior citizens' groups.
- Media (local news stations, radio, newspaper).
- Policy makers/local government officials.

3. What types of resources can we offer potential community partners in return for their support?

Your school is a vital member of the community and has a variety of resources to offer potential community partners, in return for their support. These resources include, but are not limited to: the use of school facilities; expertise and knowledge in the form of your teaching staff; access to faculty, students, and families; and increased visibility for businesses, agencies, and organizations within the community.

4. What are some specific strategies for effective community engagement/involvement?

Involving the community in your bullying prevention efforts will take some planning and effort, but the potential rewards are well worth it. Some important points to consider follow:

- Designate specific personnel to lead community engagement initiatives. This will ensure a coordinated approach and maximize your engagement efforts.
- Include students in your community efforts, especially in the secondary grades. This is a great way to include students in your bullying prevention program, and students will be able to identify community partners that are relevant in the eye of young people.
- Be mindful that businesses, agencies, and other community members that you are approaching are busy and their time is valuable. Be brief, concise, and appreciative when making contact.
- Remember that your potential partners are likely solicited by many other schools, agencies, and community groups within the community. Let them know that you have resources to offer in return and are looking to build lasting partnerships with mutual benefits.
- Realize that you may meet some resistance within the community. Some may not realize the seriousness of the bullying behaviors. Focus some of your engagement efforts on community education so that there is a common understanding and message in both school and community.
- Community is not a "one and done" effort. Continue to look for ways to maintain partnerships, as well as pursuing and developing new ones.
- Strive to foster a send a sense of "we are in this together." Creating a safe environment for all children is everyone's responsibility.
- It's all about the relationship! Consistent communication is key.

5. Once we have established some community partnerships, are there steps we should take to enhance and maintain these relationships?

It is important to remember that your goal is to actively engage the community in your bullying prevention efforts. Therefore, maintaining these relationships is very important. You are not just asking for a one-time donation; you are building partnerships. Some ways to enhance and maintain these relationships include the following:

- Update partners regarding program progress on a regular basis.
- Publically acknowledge your partners' efforts and contributions.

- Invite community members to attend bullying prevention related events at the school. Additionally, include members of the community on your bullying prevention committee.
- Ask your community partners for input and feedback.

6. What are some of the potential benefits of community engagement?

There are many potential benefits associated with effective community engagement. These include access to needed resources to enhance and sustain your program and improved community relationships and understanding of the issue of bullying among community members. Additionally, research indicates that strong school and community partnerships, in any school-based initiative may lead to improved academic achievement, fewer discipline problems, less violence, improved school climate, and better attendance rates.

REFERENCES

1. Olweus D. *Olweus Bullying Prevention Program: Schoolwide Guide.* Hazelden; 2007.

2. Jehl J, Blank MJ, McCloud B. Ensuring a positive future for children and youth: Bridging the work of educators and community builders. In: Rockefeller Foundation Symposium, editor. *Leveraging Change: An Emerging Framework for Educational Equity.* New York: The Rockefeller Foundation; 2001.

3. Adelman HS, Taylor L. Mental health in schools and public health. *Public Health Rep.* May–June 2006; 121(3):294–298.

4. Blank MJ, Langford B. Strengthening partnerships: Community school assessment checklist. *Principal Leadership (High School Ed.)* 2001; 2(1):62–63.

5. Olweus D. *Bullying at School: What We Know and What We Can Do.* Oxford, UK; Cambridge, MA: Blackwell; 1993.

6. Kretzmann J, McKnight J. *Building communities from the inside out: A path toward finding and mobilizing a community's assets.* Evanston, IL: Center for Urban Affairs and Policy Research, Northwestern University; 1993.

13

Identifying Impact—Monitoring and Evaluating a Bullying Prevention Program

Allison Messina, MHPE

Objectives

1. To educate school personnel about why monitoring and evaluating a bullying prevention program is critical to its effectiveness.
2. To help school personnel understand why they should use the evaluation methods that already exist for their bullying prevention program and, if those methods don't exist, how to develop a basic survey so that they can effectively monitor and evaluate their program.
3. To explain to school personnel how to use collected data effectively and how to report the data to staff, parents, and community members.

IMPORTANCE OF EVALUATION

Evaluation activities are becoming an inseparable part of public health practice[1] and are an important tool to help ensure the success of any program or intervention. According to the Centers for Disease Control and Prevention (CDC), to achieve health improvement (the goal of any public health program), we must devote our skill—and our will—to evaluating the effects of public health actions."[2] An evaluation of your program will tell you how well it is working and why. The objectives of this chapter are to explain the importance of evaluating your school's bullying prevention program so that you can ensure that it is effective; to help you develop a survey tool if your program doesn't already have one and what measures you can use to track bullying behaviors; and to help you develop a plan to analyze your data and decide how to share them and with whom.

Implementing a bullying prevention program in a school setting is considered a public health program because its goal is to make the school a safer, better, healthier place for all students and staff. In order to determine whether the program is actually achieving that goal, it must be evaluated. Effective programs are instruments for improving social conditions,[3] and the key to knowing whether a program is effective is to evaluate it. In order to evaluate a program, one must establish early on evaluation strategies, ideally during the planning process. At this time, it is important that program implementers outline what the intended or desired outcomes (or goals) of the intervention will be. Next, specific and measurable objectives should be set to ensure that goals are met.

Evaluation is an ongoing process. It should be carried out concurrently and continuously,[4] not saved for the end of the program implementation. When a program is subject to regular evaluation, resources can be directed toward the most promising intervention activities[4] and results can be used to demonstrate the effectiveness of the program, identify ways to improve it, modify program planning, demonstrate accountability, and justify funding.[5]

Ideally, to maximize the school's financial investment, it is best to choose an evidence-based bullying prevention program, meaning one that has been thoroughly researched and proven effective (refer to Chapter 7). Choosing a program that has been shown to be effective is important because "scientifically sound strategies and approaches are essential for public health interventions to be successful in improving quality of life."[4] Using a program that has already been shown to be capable of producing the desired behavior changes—in this case, a reduction of bullying behaviors—is important to ensuring program success.

If your program satisfies these requirements, you are probably wondering, "Why do I need to further evaluate my bullying prevention program (or other any program that you introduce into your school setting)? It has already been evaluated by the experts, I already know it works, and we don't have the time, money, or staff to do one more thing." That thought process would be true, if you were implementing the program in exactly the same setting and in the same type of population as it was first developed and studied. However, different social, ethical, legal, and distributional factors may limit effectiveness in a particular setting.[6] So if your student population, or your school building, or your staff, are different in any way from the original program setting (which they most likely are), you won't know if the program is working the way it was intended unless you evaluate it. When done properly, coordinators can easily evaluate your program, especially if the program incorporates a built-in evaluation tool, such as a student survey that measures bullying behaviors. If your program has such tools, make sure they are part of your evaluation plan. Using already developed and validated tools requires minimal amounts of time and resources and will provide a wealth of useful information about the program and school climate. Some bullying prevention programs that use scannable student surveys, like the Olweus Bullying Prevention Program (OBPP), also generate a multipage report that summarizes the collected data. If your program has such a resource, it is important for the evaluation team to carefully review these reports and share them with program stakeholders in the school and community.

Peter Rossi et al.[3] define evaluation as "a social science activity directed at collecting, analyzing, interpreting, and communicating information about the workings and effectiveness of social programs. Evaluations are conducted for a variety of practical reasons: (1) to aid in decisions concerning whether programs should be continued, improved, expanded, or curtailed; (2) to assess the utility of new programs and initiatives; (3) to increase the effectiveness of program management and administration; and (4) to satisfy the accountability requirements of program sponsors."[3] Schools, of all places, should be comfortable with the idea of evaluation, as they are constantly evaluating the progress of their students. It follows, then, that any and all programs that a school implements must be evaluated, whether a bullying prevention program, an after-school student fitness program, a new math curriculum, and so on. With limited funding, schools can only afford to offer and allocate resources to programs that are effective at producing the desired changes in behavior. The role of any evaluation is simply "to provide answers about the program that will be useful and will actually be used."[3] Evaluation is essentially information gathering and interpretation that can be used to answer questions about a program's performance and effectiveness.[3]

GETTING STARTED

Now that your school knows why it needs to evaluate, let's talk about how. Evaluating your program is an important and necessary step, as important to its success as proper implementation and program fidelity. Without an evaluation strategy, it will be difficult to know if the program is reaching its target audience, if it is having a positive or negative impact on behaviors, or where programmatic changes may be needed. You must develop the evaluation strategy at the very start of the program, before any staff are trained or surveys given. It is important to establish early what you want the program to accomplish, and then set up evaluation strategies that can be employed, along the way to monitor and assess progress. The CDC has developed a framework that can help guide your evaluation (see Figure 13.1)[7] and we have outlined how these six steps can be applied to a bullying prevention program.

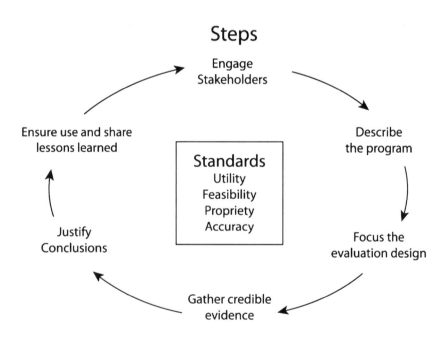

Figure 13.1. Framework for program evaluation.[7]

How This Framework Applies to a Bullying Prevention Program

- *Engage stakeholders.* Seek the input from those involved in the bullying prevention program implementation, those affected by the program (students, teachers, staff, parents), and others who would be interested in the program results.

- *Describe the program.* Why does the school need a bullying prevention program and what are the expected outcomes? What is needed to implement the program (resources, staff, activities, materials)?

- *Focus the evaluation design.* This will help identify what outcomes are most important to students, staff, and parents and allow for the efficient use of time and resources.

- *Gather credible evidence.* This will enable you to make stronger judgments about the program's effects and base recommendations on actual data.

- *Justify conclusions.* Link your recommendations to the data you've gathered.

- *Ensure use and share lessons learned.* Make sure to communicate your results to all interested stakeholders.

(For more detailed information about these steps visit http://www.cdc.gov/eval/steps/index.htm.)

Be specific when you are setting your objectives, and make them measurable. If you wait until after the implementation has ended, it will be too late. If your survey data show that the program didn't achieve its intended outcomes after it ends, at that point there is little you can do to fix things. Your money and manpower will be exhausted, and stakeholders (administrators, teachers, parents, students) will have lost faith in the program, possibly making them reluctant to support future programs. However, if you had surveyed the target populations throughout the program implementation, you could have used that data to determine what was working and what wasn't, and then worked to address and fix any identified problems.

To help with the evaluation process, the school can establish an evaluation team made up of one or several staff members familiar with the bullying prevention program. This team can oversee the data collection, analysis, interpretation, and dissemination. Possible team members could include a building administrator to ensure staff buy-in and compliance with survey administration, a teacher or aide who is familiar with statistics to help analyze and interpret the data, a student to help generate student support for the program, and even a parent representative to help disseminate the results to other parents and community groups.

DATA COLLECTION

After you've developed an evaluation plan and formed a team, the next step is actual data collection. Baseline data collection is important because you will use the data to benchmark your school's progress from year to year. Bullying is a widespread and pervasive epidemic that affects approximately one in three children in the United States, and there is no debate that any school would benefit from a properly implemented bullying prevention program. But each school's makeup is different, and each school may have different bullying prevention needs.

As a simplistic example, School A might have a serious problem with bullying in the stairways, while in School B bullying most often occurs in the classroom when the teacher is present. School A might have teachers who believe bullying is just "kids being kids" and School B's teachers might think that "bullying really isn't a problem at their school." However, you don't know what teachers and students are thinking, unless you survey and ask them. So before spending a lot of time or resources to address the bullying problems in your school, you need to first find out the specifics by collecting baseline student data. If you are School A, and you post additional aides at the playground to deter bullying, you may only see modest decreases in bullying behaviors because your school's larger problem is in the stairway and you have failed to identify and address it. Likewise, if you are School B, and you believe most bullying is happening at lunch time, and you separate grade levels or students you think are causing problems, your school won't see any major changes because you've failed to implement strategies to tackle classroom-based bullying.

Again, if you have chosen an evidence-based bullying prevention program, certain evaluation tools may already exist, so there is no need to reinvent the wheel. For example, the Olweus Bullying Prevention Program uses the Olweus Bullying Questionnaire (OBQ)[8] to collect information on students in grades 3–12. It contains 40 questions that measure bully/victim problems such as exposure to various physical, verbal, indirect, racial, or sexual forms of bullying and harassment, various forms of bullying, where the bullying occurs, pro-bully and pro-victim attitudes, and the extent to which the social environment (teachers, peers, parents) is informed about and reacts to the bullying. Schools implementing the OBPP administer the OBQ prior to the start of the program, and at the end of the first year to measure changes in bullying behaviors. It is recommended that they continue to administer the survey every few years.

Although this is just one example, most evidence-based bullying prevention programs should have validated survey tools to help collect baseline and post-implementation data.

Developing Your Own Survey

Using a validated survey tool (when one is available) is preferred because it has already been proven to measure what it is supposed to. If you develop your own survey, you risk missing out on important data that are necessary to assess your problem. For example, if you are trying to determine where bullying occurs in your school, make sure you give a variety of choices, and let respondents pick more than one answer (e.g., at recess, in the bathroom, in the cafeteria, the stairway). Also make sure that your sample size is large enough; without a large enough population, the data might not be reliable. If you only survey a few students per grade, or every other grade, there may be a lot of information that is missed, and student anonymity can't be guaranteed. For example, if in your school fifth graders are bullying in the hallway outside their classroom, but your survey doesn't contain any questions that ask students to indicate specific locations where bullying occurs, you won't capture this information and you won't know that there is a bullying problem in the fifth grade hallway that needs to be addressed. Likewise, if you only survey 15 students per grade, half of the respondents are girls, and your results show that one girl in eighth grade is being bullied because of her ethnicity, it could be very easy to identify which student she is. It's possible that students won't respond truthfully if they feel their responses could identify them.

However, if the program you've chosen doesn't have an existing survey tool or your school doesn't have the financial resources available to purchase one, it is possible to develop a simple survey to collect information about the current state of bullying in your building. In a document titled *A Guide to Conducting Your Own Youth Risk Behavior Survey (YRBS)*, the Centers for Disease Control and Prevention offers some helpful information for anyone who is interested in developing their own survey. Although the information is specific to the YRBS, it can easily be adapted by a school wishes to develop a bullying survey. This document lists questions that one should carefully consider when surveying a population.[9] Following are some question areas, along with things you should keep in mind when developing and administering your survey. This information is helpful whether you are creating one or using an existing survey.

1. Who will I survey?
   At a minimum you will need to collect information from the students. If your evaluation team has enough time and personnel, you may also want to consider surveying teachers, school support staff, and parents. (See page 264 in this chapter for more information about surveying additional groups.) Surveying multiple populations will give you the most complete picture of your school's bullying climate.

2. Whose permission must I get to conduct the survey?
   Do you need permission from the school board, or parents? Make sure you consult with your administration or school board to determine if your district has a policy regarding surveying of students. You may need to inform parents ahead of time that you are planning to conduct a survey of the students and provide them with some general information about the survey. Some schools require parents to sign a form granting the school permission to administer the survey, while some schools have a passive permission form in which a letter about the survey goes home to the parents. If parents do not wish their children to participate in the survey, then they have to sign the form and return it to school. If the school does not receive the form, then the parent consents to have his/her child take the survey.

3. How do I develop the questionnaire?
   Decide the most important questions to ask. At a minimum you should at least have a student survey that asks about the frequency of being bullied and bullying others. Be specific when developing your questions. It is also helpful to ask questions that delineate where the bullying is occurring. Is it in the bathroom? The stairwell? At recess? You can't address bullying situations if you don't know where they are happening. Make sure the language is at the same reading level as the youngest grade that is going to be taking the survey. It may also be helpful to pilot the survey to a small group of students to make sure students understand the questions and that the questions are measuring what you intended them to.

4. When should I conduct survey?
    You will need to conduct a baseline survey before the program starts and again after it's been in place for at least 6 months. If resources allow, it's helpful to survey students annually. After the first year, you may see an increase in baseline reported bullying now that students have been educated about what is and what isn't bullying and know how to define and report such behaviors. If surveying the entire building, it is a good idea that the survey is given to all grades at the same time on the same day. Classroom teachers can be used. It is important to have someone that the students are comfortable with giving the survey.

5. How will I analyze the data?
    If using an existing survey, it may include data processing and analyzing. If your school is developing its own survey, then there are several options. Many online survey tools (e.g., Survey Monkey) allow you to create surveys at low or no cost. These companies often provide basic data analysis tools to compare baseline data to post implementation data. If students take the survey online, there will be no need to manually enter the data. However, if you prefer that students take the survey by pencil and paper, then you will need to have someone manually load the results into the online survey.

If you need a more detailed analysis, you can look for help from your district's math department or from a local college or university. Community agencies could also serve as possible resources, or organizations that receive grant funding, as they often have to have an evaluation component to all their grants.

Developing your own survey is possible but it can be time consuming and might not be the best route for collecting baseline data. However, a survey developed by the school could be used to supplement an existing survey if there was a certain topic that needed to be explored further or an area of particular interest to the school or staff not addressed on an existing survey.

Using Other Data Sets to Assess Bullying in Your Building

If your program doesn't have validated survey tools or you don't want to develop your own, then what? There are many other sources of data you can use to assess bullying behaviors. The following are several alternative, existing data sets that can supplement your knowledge of bullying behaviors in your building.

Internal Discipline Logs

You can review internal existing discipline logs. If you choose to go this route, be careful to separate the discipline reports from the bullying reports. Remember, for an incident to be considered bullying, it has to be repeated, intentional aggressive behavior marked by an imbalance of power that occurs in the context of interpersonal relationships.[10] There is a difference between bullying and conflict, so be careful that what you are tracking is truly bullying. It is important to track the data from the first report through ongoing monitoring of the situation as it may still be occurring. Building administrators should also consider developing a consistent and standardized process for receiving and documenting bullying incidents that all buildings in the district utilize so that the data collection is standardized across the district.

Forms should allow for the identification of repeat offenders and repeat targets so that the faculty who "need to know" are aware and can respond appropriately. These forms should also include a section to identify what the follow-up has been to ensure that the targeted student is safe and what has been done to address the bullying on a schoolwide level. For example, if a review of the discipline forms shows that bullying incidents are frequently occurring outside the boys' restroom nearest the cafeteria, then the school should take steps to halt the behavior at this location by posting a monitor near this bathroom during lunchtime. If the forms show bullying occurs frequently on the stairwells, then the school can take action by making one set of steps "up" and the other set "down" so that students no longer can pass by each other. After several weeks or months, the discipline forms can be reviewed to determine what effect these actions have had.

Student Assistance Team Referrals

Another internal set of data available to schools is the school's student assistance program (SAP) team referrals. Program coordinators can review these referrals to determine if any of the cases are related to bullying, and if so, what follow-up has occurred with the students.

Tracking Transfers

Schools can also develop a tracking method to use when students transfer out of the district or building to determine if their leaving was related to bullying. Consider creating a brief survey to determine why these students are leaving. If it is a result of bullying, use the data to correct the deficiency that led to the student's departure. The reason may be something that is simple to fix, but the school can't fix the problem if they aren't aware of it. Addressing the identified problem may prevent other students from leaving as a result of bullying. In the best-case scenario, the school may actually be able to address the bullying-related problem and retain the student. For more information about the cost savings that result when students are retained in the district, see Chapter 14.

Indirect Measures

Indirect measures should be used in conjunction with a student survey since none are direct indicators of bullying. Data from the OBPP have indicated a correlation between student attendance and bullying rates.[11] In addition to using student surveys, the school can also look at absenteeism before and after implementation of a bullying prevention program. There are many factors other than bullying that contribute to absenteeism, so it can only serve as an indirect, but still important, measure of bullying.

If after a review of these data, or any of the data you look at, you notice a trend (e.g., there is a high level of absenteeism in seventh-grade girls, or an overall increase in the discipline reports for the tenth grade), you should take a closer look at that particular group of students to determine what else may be affecting the trend, either through surveying or interviewing students involved in bullying incidents.

Another valuable source of indirect information regarding bullying is the school nurse. Whenever possible, make sure to include the nurse on your building's bullying prevention team. Students who are trying to avoid a bully may repeatedly visit the nurse with "somatic" complaints, (e.g., headache, stomachache). Frequent visits of this nature could indicate a possible bullying situation. One way to capture this information is to have the school nurse report suspected bullying victims to a designated school official (principal, assistant principal, program coordinator). If it is determined that the student is being bullied, make sure that a procedure is in place to follow up with him or her.

Finally, you can review outside data sets to assess the school's bullying rates. If your school participates in a state youth survey, seek out these types of existing resources. For example, the Pennsylvania Youth Survey,[12] a survey taken by sixth, eighth, tenth, and twelfth grades to learn about their behavior, attitudes, and knowledge concerning alcohol, tobacco, other drugs, and violence, includes five questions related to bullying behaviors. When you refer to outside data sources, be aware of the questions that are asked and who completed them. If your school is an elementary school, review survey data from elementary students—don't base your program on statistics from a middle or high school population. Also be aware that there is often a delay of several months to a year from the time students take the survey until your school gets the results.

MOVING BEYOND THE STUDENT SURVEYS—WHO ELSE TO SURVEY AND WHY

Teachers

Once you have developed a plan to measure student responses of behavior, it's a good idea to survey other populations because teachers, support staff, and parents can help paint a complete picture of bullying in the building. This will allow you to better understand the impact of the bullying prevention program. Surveying these other populations can alert the school to problems that may be occurring in after-school programs, on sports teams, or at other school-sponsored events.

> How do I survey other groups outside of the school building? Simple, online surveys can be created using current survey tools such as Survey Monkey (www.surveymonkey.com) for little or no cost. These programs allow the user to create a variety of surveys, each with its own unique URL that can then be emailed to parents and teachers, or posted on the school website, or placed in the school newsletter. The software also typically provides a basic analysis of the data and several reporting formats so that you can easily share the results with the school and community.

Because it is often difficult to get parents and other school staff to complete a survey, school administrators should clearly communicate its importance. To increase response rates, they need to stress that responses will be kept confidential and not include identifying information, such as contact information, on the survey. Questions on these surveys should be similar in nature to those used on the student survey so that the teachers' perspectives can be compared to the students'. For example, the student survey may have a question that asks fifth graders how responsive their homeroom teacher is when he or she observes a bullying incident, and the results show that 65% of these students answer their teacher is "not very responsive." However, if the teacher survey has a question that asks "How responsive are you (as a homeroom teacher) when you observe a bullying incident?" and only 5% of the fifth-grade teachers respond "not very responsive," the surveys have identified a discrepancy between teachers and students that needs to be investigated more closely by the bullying prevention committee.

The teacher survey should also include questions about the program's implementation (also considered program fidelity) so that the bullying prevention committee is able to assess if any grade levels are not fully implementing program components, if there are areas in which teachers are struggling, or if there are any areas for which the staff need additional training. These questions can also help identify if there are any school system barriers that prevent teachers from properly implementing the program (such as no formal form for reporting bullying behaviors or not having enough adult staff available to supervise student lunch). Once the teacher survey data are collected and analyzed, they need to be shared with the building staff and stakeholders.

Parents

As all school personnel know, getting parents involved in school programs is a challenge, but nevertheless it is still important to include this group not only in your bullying prevention efforts but also in your evaluation strategy. There is emerging evidence highlighting the importance of collaboration between families and schools to more effectively prevent bullying and school violence.[13] Research supports the positive results that come from engaging parents, yet this aspect of education remains significantly limited across our nation.[14] Some parents may not even be aware that the school has a bullying prevention program, what the program involves, or what their role in the program should be. Without this information, parents aren't able to reinforce at home the bullying prevention message that their children learn at school. If children aren't getting consistent messages at home and at school regarding how to effectively handle bullying situations, the program will be less effective.

Parents' positive perception of the school's climate have been associated with teachers being able to effectively implement the school's bullying prevention programming and increases the likelihood that teachers will intervene when they witness a bullying situation.[15,16] Positive parent perception of school climate has also been associated with students' perceptions of safety and academic achievements.[17,18] Finally, research has indicated that parents are more likely to be involved in the school when they feel the school climate is safe and supportive and that the school is open and encourages their involvement.[13,19–21] If the school's bullying prevention program fails to engage parents, the school may be missing an important chance to strengthen its bullying prevention efforts and make the school safer for students.

The parent survey should be simple and straightforward. The survey should contain questions about whether or not their child has been bullied or has bullied others, as well as questions that ask parents their opinions as to how effectively the school responds to bullying situations or how well teachers intervene. Again, the questions can be similar to those on the teacher survey and should not include any identifying information. It would also be helpful to insert a paragraph or two at the start of the survey or send home a cover letter as another way to educate parents about the bullying prevention program. To help increase participation rates, schools may consider giving incentives to grades that have at least 50% or more of parents completing the survey (e.g., 15 extra minutes of recess for a week for grades with a response rate of 50%, or a homework-free day). To make the survey even easier for parents to complete, the school can make the computer lab available during parent–teacher conferences or back-to-school night. The school could also have paper copies on hand during these events. Make sure to have a collection box for parent surveys in a convenient space. Once all paper copies are collected, the school can manually enter the data into the same online survey database.

School health promotion and disease prevention programs are most effective when they are developmentally appropriate and when they take into account the relationships among the student, family, school, community, and society.[22] These additional surveys are so important because they provide a more complete look at how bullying is perceived by different groups as well as the school's overall bullying prevention program. These data sets, when used with student surveys, give the bullying prevention committee the most complete picture of problems within the school so they can work to address issues that are most prevalent without spending time or resources in areas that do not need further attention. Surveying the adults will show whether or not they are not supporting the bullying prevention program tenets; if they aren't, the likelihood of the program being effective is diminished.

IMPLEMENTING WITH FIDELITY

No matter which evidence-based bullying prevention program you chose, make sure the program meets the needs of your school and staff and ensure that all staff members from the top down are committed to program fidelity. Program fidelity is an important component of your bullying prevention program, and it refers to whether or not the program was implemented as it was intended. As mentioned previously, the school's teacher survey should include questions that measure program fidelity, and the fidelity questions should be developed from your bullying prevention program's materials. For example, if your program requires staff to meet monthly to discuss bullying-related issues or requires teachers to intervene every time they witness bullying behaviors, these types of questions should be on the survey.

Fidelity data are important because they can uncover issues before they completely derail the bullying prevention program. Fidelity data also allow the school to protect the financial investment it has made in the program. If the program fails because of a problem that could have been identified through the evaluation process and then remedied, then the school has essentially missed its opportunity to provide effective programming to its students and wasted resources. Furthermore, staff may be less eager to implement other programs in the future, and administrators will be less willing to allocate resources to prevention programs because they may view your program as unsuccessful, even if it wasn't the program that failed but its implementation.

The manner in which a program is implemented can have an enormous impact on its effectiveness—even the best programs are effective only when implemented with high quality and fidelity to the program's design.[23] You can only be sure that your program will produce the intended results if it is implemented as designed with minimal to no changes. The fewer changes that are made to a program, the more likely it will have the desired effect on participants.[24] If it becomes necessary to make program adaptations, consider contacting the program's developers to see if others have made those changes, and if so, what the outcomes were. Below is a list of adaptations that could be problematic to your program's implementation.

Risky or unacceptable program adaptations[24]

- Reducing the number or length of sessions or how long participants are involved.
- Lowering the level of participant engagement.
- Eliminating key messages or skills learned.
- Removing topics.
- Changing the theoretical approach.
- Using staff or volunteers who are not adequately trained or qualified.
- Using fewer staff members than recommended.

As mentioned earlier, measuring program fidelity needs to be part of your evaluation. If you aren't seeing the desired changes in bullying behaviors, it is important to determine whether or not the staff is implementing the program as it was intended. If they aren't, program coordinators should assess which program areas the staff have changed or stopped implementing, and why.

INTERPRETING AND REPORTING THE DATA

Once you've collected the baseline data from the various groups, the next step is to analyze and report them. In an effort to keep the evaluation manageable, it will be necessary to review the data periodically. It is also important to look at the different perspectives together to get a complete picture about your program.[25] Doing so will allow you to say, with some accuracy, whether or not your program has achieved what it intended.[25] Reviewing the data as information accumulates has several advantages: it helps you identify themes, it makes the analysis process less intimidating versus waiting until all of the data have been collected, and most importantly, it enables you to use the results to improve your program.[25]

If the survey and evaluation strategies have been properly developed, they will address areas of program performance most at issue for key stakeholders and will provide meaningful information about program performance.[3] Once a population is surveyed, the data must be reviewed and disseminated. The data produced can and should be used to inform behaviors. By reviewing the collected data, program coordinators can determine if the program is working as intended, and if it isn't, where changes need to be made. Sometimes this may involve working with the original trainer to address fidelity issues, conducting mini-trainings on certain topic areas for portions of the staff or new staff members, or figuring out a way to increase staff and parent buy-in. The important point to remember is that unless you survey and review your data, it is very difficult to know how the program is performing and what potential problems there are. Without knowing the problems, it is impossible to fix them.

SHARING THE DATA

The last steps in an evaluation are to not only use what has been learned through the evaluation but also to share the lessons learned with stakeholders.[1] It is important to know what to share and when to share it. The ultimate purpose of a program evaluation is to use the information to improve the program and maintain support for your program. The purpose identified early in the evaluation process should guide the use of and reporting of the evaluation results.[5]

Formal evaluation reports can provide key information to stakeholders and be a valuable public relations tool.[25] By sharing the program's good results, program administrators will gain support for their bullying prevention efforts. The data can demonstrate that important work has been done to ensure that the school building is a safe environment for all. Engaging stakeholders and informing them of the program's successes and challenges will help ensure their buy-in of the program and their continued support of it in subsequent years.

The formal evaluation report that is shared with stakeholders should be presented simply and concisely and should include a mix of quantitative (survey results) and qualitative (stories, interviews, quotes, etc.) data. Here are some key points to consider:

- The objectives of the program and the targeted audiences.
- What data were collected, why, and how.
- The evaluation results in terms of the program's goals and objectives.
- The plan for using the evaluation to improve and sustain the program.[25]

There are many potential audiences who would be interested in the school's bullying prevention program. In addition to informing school staff, students, and parents about the results, consider sharing them, or a portion of them, with city council, state legislators, other schools in the area, police departments, healthcare providers, and even workplaces. Many of these groups could serve as potential partners in future prevention programs or as additional sources of funding. For example, local businesses might be interested in supporting your school's bullying prevention efforts by providing students with T-shirts. Students could design anti-bullying artwork for the shirts, which could be worn by the entire student body during special school events or on days to show their support of the anti-bullying efforts.

Why Do I Need to Share my Results?[9]

Don't miss an opportunity to share any good news about your program with others, including local media. Programs that have the support of multiple outside groups and agencies may make them easier to sustain.

Parents: Parents may be more inclined to support anti-bullying policies, programs, and activities if they are informed about the prevalence, consequences, and costs associated with bullying, both mental and physical.

Teachers: Teachers will benefit from having more information about the prevalence of bullying behaviors among their students and from knowing where the hot spots occur. They will be better able to increase supervision of these areas when they know where they are.

Students: Students may want to be involved in designing and implementing relevant policies and programs to address reduce bullying behaviors.

Administrators and school board members: Administrators and school board members can use the data to guide development of school policies.

Agencies and organizations working with youth: These agencies and organizations may be interested in using survey results to improve their own programs and activities.

CONCLUSION

Keeping the bullying prevention program or any initiative that the school implements on track through an evaluation process is a simple, cost-effective way to ensure the program's effectiveness. No plan to implement a bullying prevention program in the school can be complete without an evaluation strategy. The method in which you choose to evaluate your program doesn't need to be complex, costly, or time consuming, but it does need to be: (1) well-thought out and planned prior to program implementation, (2) comprehensive in that multiple audiences should be surveyed (students, teachers, other adults), and (3) ongoing. Choose staff in your building that are knowledgeable about the program and have a basic understanding of data analysis and statistics to help with your evaluation efforts.

Because changes constantly happen within the school, it's important to survey your identified populations at baseline and ideally once a year, or at least every two years. This will allow you to document positive changes in student and teacher behaviors, identify program weakness, develop plans to address deficiencies, and share real data and information about the program with the students, families, communities and stakeholders to maintain support for your program and increase awareness outside of your school building. If your school is going to invest time, manpower, and financial resources into a bullying prevention program, an effective evaluation strategy will help the school ensure that its investment will succeed and that the school will be a better place for its students.

FREQUENTLY ASKED QUESTIONS

1. What will an evaluation of my program tell me?

A program evaluation will tell you how well your program is working and why. The data collected through your evaluation process can alert you to areas that may need additional attention as well as which program areas are successful. Evaluations are conducted for a variety of practical reasons: to aid in decisions concerning whether programs should be continued, improved, expanded, or curtailed; to assess the utility of new programs and initiatives; to increase the effectiveness of program management and administration; and to satisfy the accountability requirements of program sponsors."[3]

2. Why do I need to evaluate my bullying prevention program if it is an evidence-based program?

The key to knowing whether or not a program is effective is to evaluate it. Although your school may have chosen an evidence-based program, your school population is probably different than the original population on whom the program was tested. When done properly, evaluating your program can easily be done by its coordinators, especially if the program incorporates a built in evaluation tool, such as a student survey that measures bullying behaviors.

3. What is the first step in evaluating my bullying prevention program?

After the school has established measurable objectives and goals for its bullying prevention program, program coordinators should develop a strategy to measure these objectives. This should be done prior to program implementation. Baseline data should be collected via a survey of students to assess the current rates of bullying in the building (students who have been bullied, and students who have bullied others), where the bullying is occurring, and teachers' responsiveness to bullying incidents. Program coordinators will need to consider if their bullying prevention program already has existing survey tools, or if they will need to develop a survey themselves.

4. If I don't want to survey the students in my building, how else can I assess bullying behaviors?

There are several indirect measures that a school can use for assessment, including review of disciple logs, Student Assistant Program team referrals, an exit interview when students leave the district to determine if it was related to bullying, attendance rates and nurse visits pre- versus post-program implementation, or outside data sets.

5. Should I survey other populations?

If your school has the time and resources it is a good idea to survey additional populations because teachers, support staff, and parents can help paint a complete picture of bullying in the building. This will allow you to better understand the effect the bullying prevention program is having in the schools. By surveying these other populations, you can also alert the school to problems that may be occurring in after-school programs, on sports teams, or other school-sponsored events.

6. How often should I survey?

Students should be surveyed prior to program implementation and then again after at least 6 months of program implementation. If resources exist, it is ideal to survey annually for 3 to 5 years to determine if the program has taken root and produced the desired changes in behaviors. Teachers should be surveyed on the same schedule, and parents once a year.

7. Why is it important to measure program fidelity?

Program fidelity is an important component of your bullying prevention program. It refers to whether or not the program was implemented properly, as it was intended. Fidelity data are important because the information can uncover issues before they completely derail the bullying prevention program. Program fidelity also allows the school to protect the financial investment it has made in the program. If the program fails because of a problem that could have been identified through the evaluation process and then remedied, then the school has essentially missed its opportunity to provide effective programming to its students and has wasted resources.

8. Who can I use to help with the data analysis and interpretation?

If possible, try to include on your evaluation team a staff member who is familiar with basic data analysis and statistics. It could be a teacher from the math department or a building administrator. If you need more detailed analysis, you can look for help from a local college or university. Community agencies could also serve as possible resources, or organizations that receive grant funds, because they often have to have an evaluation component to all their grants.

9. Who should the data be shared with?

It is important to share the results of your evaluation with multiple groups, including, district leaders, teachers, support staff, parents, students, community members, and the media. The purpose of a program evaluation is to use the information to improve the program and to maintain support for your program. Formal evaluation reports can provide key information to stakeholders and be a valuable public relations tool.[25] The data can demonstrate that important work has been done to ensure that the school building is a safe environment for all. Engaging stakeholders and informing them of the program's successes and challenges will help ensure their buy-in of the program and their continued support of it in subsequent years.

REFERENCES

1. Milstein BW, S. A Framework featuring steps and standards for program evaluation. *Health Promot. Practi.* 2000: 221–228.

2. Centers for Disease Control and Prevention. Framework for Program Evaluation in Public Health. *Morbidity and Mortality Weekly Report.* 1999; 48(RR11):1–40.

3. Rossi PH, Lipsey MW, Freeman HE, Howard E. *Evaluation: A Systematic Approach.* 7th ed. Thousand Oaks, CA: Sage; 2004.

4. Turnock BJ. *Public Health: What It Is and How It Works.* 2nd ed. Gaithersburg, MD: Aspen Publishers; 2001.

5. Centers for Disease Control and Prevention. *Introduction to Program Evaluation for Public Health Programs: Evaluating Appropriate Antibiotic Use Programs.* 2006. Available at: http://www.cdc.gov/getsmart/program-planner/downloads/Manual_04062006.pdf. Accessed:

6. Teutsch S. A framework for assessing the effectiveness of disease and injury prevention. *Morbitity and Mortality Weekly Report.* 1992; 41.

7. Center for Disease Control and Prevention. A Framework for Program Evaluation. 2013. Available at http://www.cdc.gov/eval/framework/. Accessed

8. Olweus D. *The Revised Olweus Bully/Victim Questionnaire.* Mimeo. Bergen, Norway: Research Center for Health Promotion (HEMIL Center), University of Bergen. 1996.

9. Centers for Disease Control and Prevention. *A guide to conducting your own youth risk behavioral survey.* 2012. Available at http://www.cdc.gov/healthyyouth/yrbs/pdf/yrbs_conducting_your_own.pdf.

10. Olweus D. *Bullying at School: What We Know and What We Can Do.* Oxford, UK; Cambridge, USA: Blackwell; 1993.

11. www.olweus.org. Accessed May 23, 2012. (2007). Introducing the Olweus Bullying Prevention Program. In D. Olweus, & S. P. Limber, Olweus Bullying Prevention Program Teacher Guide (p. 4). Center City: Hazelden.

12. Pennsylvania Commission on Crime & Delinquency. *2009 PennsylvaniaYouth Survey: Statewide Report*; 2009.

13. Waasdorp TE, Bradshaw CP, Duong J. The link between parents' perceptions of the school and their responses to school bullying: Variation by child characteristics and the forms of victimization. *J Educ Psychol.* 2011; 103(2):324–335.

14. Falcetta E. *Bullying Prevention: Ways for Parents and Educators to Work Together.* 2012; www.ld.org. Accessed May 23, 2012.

15. Beets MW, Flay BR, Vuchinich S, et al. Allred C. School climate and teachers' beliefs and attitudes associated with implementation of the positive action program: a diffusion of innovations model. *Prevention Science: The Official Journal of the Society for Prevention Research.* Dec 2008; 9(4):264–275.

16. Kallestad J, Olweus D. Predicting teachers' and schools' implementation of the Olweus Bullying Prevention Program: A multi-level study. *Prev Treatment.* 2003; 6(1):3–21.

17. Appleton J. Student engagement with school: Critical conceptual and methodological issues of the construct. *Psychol Schools.* 2008:369–386.

18. Glew G, Rivara F, Feudtner C. Bullying: children hurting children. *Pediatr Rev.* 2000; 21(10854313):183–189.

19. DePlanty J, Coulter-Kern R, Duchane KA. Perceptions of parent involvement in academic achievement. *J Educ Res.* Jan. 1, 2007; 100(6):361–368.

20. Griffith J. The relation of school structure and social environment to parent involvement in elementary schools. *Elementary Sch J.* 1998; 98(1):53–83.

21. Sheldon SB, Epstein JL. Improving student behavior and school discipline with family and community involvement. *Educ Urban Soc.* November 1, 2002; 35(1):4–26.

22. Inman DD, van Bakergem KM, Larosa AC, Garr DR. Evidence-based health promotion programs for schools and communities. *Am J Prev Med.* Feb 2011; 40(2):207–219.

23. Office of the Surgeon General, National Center for Injury Prevention and Control, National Institute of Mental Health, Center for Mental Health Services. Prevention and Intervention. *Youth Violence: A Report of the Surgeon General.* Rockville, MD: Office of the Surgeon General; 2001.

24. O'Connor C, Small S, Cooney SM. *Program Fidelity and Adaptation: Meeting Local Needs Without Compromising Program Effectiveness.* 2007. Available at http:// whatworks.uwex.edu/attachment/whatworks_04.pdf. Accessed:

25. Bond S, Boyd S, Rapp K, et al. Making sense of the evidence-interpreting and reporting your data. *Taking Stock: A Practical Guide to Evaluating Your Own Programs.* Chapel Hill, NC: Horizon Research, Inc.; 1997:39–42.

14

Economic Evaluation of Bullying Prevention Implementation

Carla Zema, PhD

Objectives

1. To understand the importance of economic evaluations of a bullying prevention initiative.
2. To understand the value of conducting a cost–benefit or cost-effectiveness analysis as an economic evaluation for a bullying prevention initiative.
3. To conduct a cost–benefit or cost-effectiveness analysis of a bullying prevention initiative.
4. To understand how to design cost–benefit or cost-effectiveness analyses to meet the needs of specific stakeholders of a bullying prevention initiative.

One of the great mistakes is to judge policies and programs by their intentions rather than their results.[1a]

—Milton Friedman

In the previous chapter, Messina discussed the critical importance of monitoring and evaluating bullying prevention programs. Bullying prevention is a laudable goal, and few would argue against its merits. However, as economist Milton Friedman notes, policies and programs should not be judged by their good intentions but, rather, by their results. Bullying prevention programs that are not evidenced-based or are implemented poorly have the potential to cause more harm than good by eroding school climate and decreasing student, teacher, and staff retention.

Similarly, economic evaluations are just as important when trying to determine program effectiveness. Friedman, a Nobel laureate in economics, includes economic evaluation when describing policy and program "results." Economic evaluations should be used in conjunction with evaluations of effectiveness and can be used prospectively for decision making (e.g., Should we adopt this program?), concurrently for program monitoring (e.g., How is the implementation going? Do we need to make any modifications or adjustments?), and retrospectively for evaluation (e.g., What were the results of our program implementation?).

COST–BENEFIT ANALYSIS AND COST-EFFECTIVENESS ANALYSIS

When considering whether to adopt a program based on effectiveness and cost, there are four possible results. Figure 14.1 illustrates these four results, obtained by measuring effectiveness with cost when comparing two alternatives, such as a new program compared to the status quo or comparing two different program options. A new program that is both less effective and more costly is easy to reject; likewise, a program that is more effective and less costly is an easy decision to adopt. Unfortunately, adopting a new program generally comes with some implementation cost. These costs can be monetary, but also include time and

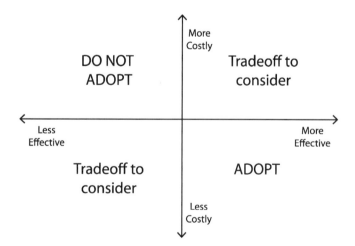

Figure 14.1. Comparing program effectiveness and cost

other resources. More detail on costs will be presented later in this chapter. What is important to understand at this point is that economic evaluations can help inform decisions by adding an essential aspect for consideration.

Cost-effectiveness analysis (CEA) and cost–benefit analysis (CBA) are two common methods for comparing options when resources are limited. Initially developed in the military, these approaches were applied in healthcare in the mid-1960s[1] and, more recently, to program evaluation—although application to social programs has not reached maturity.[2] CEA is used to relate the cost of a program to its measure of effectiveness, such as a key outcome or benefit. Results of a CEA are typically expressed as a cost-effectiveness ratio obtained by dividing total costs by the unit measure of effectiveness:

$$\text{Cost-effectiveness ratio} = \frac{\text{Total costs}}{\text{Measure of effectiveness}}$$

An example from bullying prevention could be the total costs divided by the number of students that are prevented from experiencing bullying, or cost per students saved from experiencing bullying. This ratio is also often expressed in marginal or incremental terms, referred to as the incremental cost-effectiveness ratio (ICER), meaning a per-unit measure. In the example, instead of cost per students saved, the ICER would be cost per student saved from experiencing bullying. CEAs are helpful when comparing programs with similar outcomes. Comparing the ICER for each option gives a clear indication of the most cost-effective option. On the other hand, measures of effectiveness may be a bit awkward to interpret. CEAs can also be difficult to use if a program is intended to achieve more than one benefit.

CBA is similar to CEA, except it goes a step further by valuing the benefits of the program. Therefore, costs are weighed against the benefits monetarily; thus, results of a CBA are expressed as net benefits.

$$\text{Net benefits} = \text{Total benefits} - \text{Total costs}$$

If total costs exceed total benefits then results are referred to as net costs. Another way to summarize results of a CBA is a cost–benefit ratio, which is calculated by dividing the total benefits by the total costs.

$$\text{Cost} - \text{benefit ratio} = \frac{\text{Total benefits}}{\text{Total costs}}$$

Table 14.1. Characteristics of Cost-Effectiveness and Cost–Benefit Analyses

	Cost-Effectiveness Analysis (CEA)	Cost–Benefit Analysis (CBA)
Description	Measure of total cost per measure of effectiveness	Measure of net benefit
Basic calculation	$CER = \dfrac{\text{Total costs}}{\text{Measure of effectiveness}}$	Net benefit = Total benefit − Total costs Ratio = Total benefits/Total costs
Result	Cost per measure of effectiveness (or incremental/marginal cost per unit measure of effectiveness)	Net benefit valued in dollars
Advantages	• Easy to compare programs with similar outcomes • Useful if outcomes are difficult to value	• Results are in dollars making interpretation easy • Useful when considering only one program and/or when programs have different outcomes
Disadvantages	• Measure of effectiveness can be awkward to interpret • Difficult to use if more than one benefit	• Can be difficult to value benefits

Cost–benefit ratios are greater than one if total benefits exceed total costs and less than one if total benefits are less than total costs. One advantage of CBAs is that net benefits/costs are easy to interpret by stakeholders. CBAs are useful when considering one program or programs with different outcomes. However, benefits can be difficult to value. For example, what is the dollar value of preventing a student from experiencing bullying? Table 14.1 summarizes the characteristics of CEAs and CBAs.

PROCESS FOR CONDUCTING ANALYSIS

Regardless of whether you choose to conduct a CEA or a CBA (or perhaps even both), the overall process for conducting the analyses is the same:

1. Define the framework for the analysis.
2. Determine the perspective of the analysis.
3. Decide on the time frame for the analysis.
4. Define the population.
5. Identify and measure the costs and benefits.
6. Value the benefits (for a CBA).

7. Discount (depending on time frame).
8. Calculate results.
9. Conduct a sensitivity analysis.
10. Use results for decision making.

Some believe that conducting a CEA, and especially a CBA, requires a high level of methodological and specialized expertise.[3] Although the methods for some CEA and CBA models can be complex and highly technical, simple models can and should be used by any evaluation team, regardless of formal training. CEAs and CBAs can be conducted by any and for any interested stakeholder. Simple models for which data are readily available can be developed and analyzed rather quickly. The framework for the CBA or CEA model will determine the audience for the results.

This chapter will walk you through the steps of using these methodologies for bullying prevention programs as an example. CBA and CEA models can be used by many stakeholders of bullying prevention initiatives, depending on the framework for the analysis. Schools may want to use the results to justify implementing a bullying prevention initiative to both internal (e.g., administration, teachers, staff) and external (e.g., parents, students, community) stakeholders. Community organizations may use results to justify partnering with schools on bullying prevention to improve the overall culture of the community. Healthcare organizations can use results to justify investment in community efforts, such as bullying prevention, that reduce healthcare utilization and improve health outcomes. Finally, evaluators can use results to complement other evaluation data sources such as program effectiveness. CBA and CEA models are versatile and have a myriad of uses and value to stakeholders.

Define the Framework for the Analysis

You will first need to establish the framework for the analysis. There are several steps that are necessary to accomplish this, beginning with defining the question this analysis will answer. This can sometimes be the most difficult part of the process—not due to technical difficulty but rather due to honing in on the set up for the analysis. Additionally, the overall process steps are not necessarily linear and sequential. You may find that after you have defined your framework that you will need to modify it based on options that become apparent in the next several steps of the overall process. Ultimately, this becomes an iterative process.

The initial step is to define your overall objective for the analysis. In other words, what is the question that you would like this analysis to answer? You may start with a very broad question such as, "Is bullying prevention cost-effective?" This is a perfectly acceptable start to developing your framework. Most likely, you will find that question will get refined significantly as you go through the next several steps in the overall process. In the end, the actual question that you may end up answering is, "Is implementing a bullying prevention program over three years in a high school cost-effective to a school district?" It makes no difference whether this level of detail is considered at this point in the process or refined as you go through the next several steps. If you take the latter approach, just make sure to go back and refine your objective so that stakeholders will clearly understand what this analysis addresses.

CEAs and CBAs can be used for a variety of purposes and have application beyond economic evaluations based on accounting principles. They can certainly be used to evaluate the economic impact of the program. Additionally, CEAs and CBAs can be used to extrapolate findings to predict the economic impact in the future and/or with a different population. For example, you may have data from a pilot program and want to know what the impact would be on the entire population, or you may be considering expanding your existing program. These analyses are also invaluable for examining outcomes for which there are not direct data available. Data from various sources, such as published literature, can be brought together in a CEA/CBA to address a question that cannot be answered from the direct program data. The framework design will be key to how and whether these data can be used to meet the overall objective.

Is there more than one option to be considered? Comparisons may be made between more than one program or even different options of the same program. Understanding what you will be comparing is an important step in defining your framework. This will also lead to the next question—how will your results be defined? In other words, how is effectiveness measured? For bullying prevention, this may be the number of students that are prevented from experiencing bullying either as the bully or the victim. Depending on the perspective of the analysis, which will be addressed in more detail in the next section, this could also be a downstream outcome such as preventing health-related consequences of bullying, preventing students from transferring schools or dropping out due to bullying, or improving school performance. Defining how effectiveness will be measured is critical to the overall analysis. Like your overall objective, this definition may change as you refine your framework through the next several steps of the overall process.

Another important aspect is to define the status quo. What does the school climate look like if none of the options were implemented? This is critical to determining the costs and benefits that will be included in the analysis. Understanding the status quo will also help define contributing factors that may influence the outcomes. Social programs, including bullying prevention programs, address complex and multi-faceted issues. One of the most difficult aspects of this analysis will be determining which factor(s) will be *directly* affected by the intervention. Defining the status quo will be necessary for sorting through these complexities.

As mentioned previously, these analyses can be conducted prospectively, retrospectively, or even concurrently. The timing of the analysis is often associated with data sources in that timing can influence the availability and completeness of data that can be used in the analysis. For example, an analysis that is conducted concurrently with the implementation of the bullying prevention program may not have data available on the overall effectiveness of the program. Handling missing data will be discussed in greater detail later, but refining the framework is one way of dealing with missing data. If using results from the current implementation is important to your audience then you may have to opt for retrospective analysis rather than a concurrent one.

Of course, you will also need to decide whether to conduct a CEA or a CBA. Consider the advantages and disadvantages of each approach as well as whom the audience is for your results.

Determine the Perspective of the Analysis

Determining the perspective of the analysis may seem obvious, but it is not a trivial step in the process. Some experts believe that CEAs and CBAs should be conducted from the societal perspective.[4] The societal perspective measures the impact of the program on society as a whole. While this is a critical perspective, the societal perspective can sometimes be too broad for some decision-makers. For example, a school district that is trying to decide whether to implement a program may not find the societal perspective as informative as an analysis examining the costs and benefits that directly influence them. Moreover, analyses from the societal perspective are typically prospective extrapolations that often require more advanced modeling, such as Markov models or Monte Carlo simulations, where individuals cycle through various stages throughout a lifetime. This is not to suggest that societal models are not important, but rather a recommendation to consider the specific audience for the results.

Defining the perspective of the analysis is essential to understanding what costs and benefits to include. One way to help determine the appropriate perspective for the analysis is to consider what will be done with the results. Are the results intended to determine whether a school should implement a bullying prevention program? Perhaps the results are needed to justify why a healthcare provider, system, or insurer might want to invest in a community-wide implementation of a program. Considering how the results will be used specifically will most likely lead you to the appropriate perspective for the analysis.

Decide on the Time Frame for the Analysis

The analysis must also have a clearly defined time frame. Time frames for analyses can range from extremely short to as long as a lifetime. Consider what time frame might be most appropriate for your analysis. Does the program you are evaluating have a specific time frame for implementation? How long does it take for results to be seen? For example, the Olweus Bullying Prevention Program (OBPP) has a specific implementation time frame of three years. The first year for baseline measurement and training, meaning the program does not reach students until the second year of implementation. The timing of implementation and the expectation of results influenced the time frame for the analysis as well as how costs and benefits were accounted for in the analysis.

Similar to determining the perspective of the analysis, consider how the results will be used. Is there a time frame that is meaningful to the primary audience for the results? CEAs/CBAs are commonly used for prescription medicines. The intent of these analyses is to provide payers with information to inform decision making on whether to include specific pharmaceuticals on their formularies, which affects coverage by health insurance. A study of how payers use CEA/CBA information was conducted in which formulary decision makers were given two published CEA studies for the same condition that compared the same treatment options.[5] One of the studies presented an analysis using a simulation of stroke patients over a lifetime,[6] while the other used a one-year time frame.[7] In terms of analysis time frame, formulary decision makers did not feel that a lifetime time frame was helpful to their decision making and preferred a shorter time frame of 1–3 years. Knowing what time frame your audience finds valuable is important to obtaining results that will be most useful for them.

Define the Population

The analysis will also need a clearly defined population. Who will be included in the analysis? For an analysis of bullying prevention, the obvious answer is that the study population will be students. However, there are many considerations to clearly define the study population:

- From particular schools or school districts? A certain geography (e.g., state, county)?
- What level or grades?
- Public, private, and/or charter schools?
- All buildings or only buildings with a minimum number of students?

Suppose a state was interested in evaluating the cost-effectiveness of implementing bullying prevention programs at the middle school level for all public schools. Although this population description seems detailed enough and answers the questions just posed, there are still some additional considerations. Will middle schools that cover grades 6–8 and schools that cover grades 7–9 be included? Most education experts would agree that both these schools should most likely be included. What about schools that are grades K–8 or 6–12? How will they be included? You may decide to exclude them, or only include the students in the relevant grades. Many of these decisions may be dependent on the state's plans for whether to implement a bullying prevention program in those schools. Be prepared to address specific questions when defining the population for the analysis.

Identify and Measure the Costs and Benefits

Identifying appropriate costs and benefits to include depends on the framework, perspective, timeline, and population of the analysis. Costs and benefits that are incurred above and beyond the status quo should be included. Costs and benefits fall into three categories: (1) direct, (2) indirect, and (3) intangible. Direct costs and benefits are the easiest to identify and represent the costs closely related to the program itself. Examples of direct costs include materials, personnel, and facilities. Indirect costs and benefits represent spillover or unintended consequences as a result of the program. An example of an indirect benefit of a bullying prevention program could be higher teacher retention due to the improved school climate that results from reductions in bullying. Finally, intangible costs and benefits are those that are difficult to quantify and value. Improved school climate would be an example of an intangible benefit of bullying prevention.

Be careful to include only actual or real costs and benefits that are beyond the status quo, and not transfers. A *transfer* represents a cost or benefit that is simply redistributed. For example, if it is necessary to hire a staff coordinator for the implementation of a bullying prevention program, the salary of the new coordinator is a direct cost of implementation. If an existing staff member is identified as the program coordinator with some of that individual's responsibilities being shifted to a different staff member, there is not a direct cost to the school but, rather, a transfer of tasks between existing staff members. Using that same example, suppose a new staff member was necessary not for the program coordination but to assume some of the responsibilities that were transferred from the existing staff member that assumed the role of program coordinator. The salary of the new hire would be included as a cost because this salary was the result of the program being implemented. If the program were not implemented (i.e., status quo) then the new salary would not be necessary even if the salary is being used to cover responsibilities not associated with the program being evaluated.

Perspective is important to define what costs and benefits are included. Consider a bullying prevention program in which a healthcare insurer is contemplating co-sponsoring the implementation of the program and would share the cost of implementation with the school district. A CBA from the perspective of the school district would look very different from the CBA from the perspective of the healthcare insurer. For simplicity, assume that the financial responsibility of the program implementation was equally divided. The direct costs of program implementation would be the same for both the school district and the insurer. The benefits, however, would be very different.

Benefits to the school could include better teacher, staff, and student retention; increased school performance; improved school climate; decreased school violence; and increased attendance. None of these benefit the insurer, which might instead benefit from decreased utilization from the health-related consequences of bullying, such as depression, anxiety, headache, abdominal pain, and alcohol and drug abuse. The parameters of the analysis framework must be maintained throughout the analysis.

One of the benefits of CEAs/CBAs is that they often can be used to extrapolate information when a direct study has not been done. Consider again the example of the CBA from a health insurer's perspective examining the health-related consequence of bullying. To date, a longitudinal study of students tracking the experiences with bullying and their healthcare experiences and utilization has not been conducted. However, a CBA can use a cross-sectional study of the health-related consequences of bullying, combined with studies of utilization and treatment rates of conditions and symptoms that represent the health-related consequences of bullying, to extrapolate and estimate reductions in utilization related to the health-related consequences of bullying that would come with reductions in students experiencing bullying. The framework of the analysis is critical to defining the costs and benefits in ways that are measurable with available data.

Inevitably, there may be data and information that are needed for the analysis that will not be available or do not exist. One way of addressing this is to determine whether the framework of the analysis can be adjusted to account for information that is not available. Another method would be to calculate the data that are needed from the existing, available data. Perhaps there is not a particular variable available, but two other existing variables can be used to calculate the necessary information. However, it is not uncommon for the data to be unavailable and impossible to calculate from existing information. In such instances, reasonable estimates may have to be made for inclusion in the analysis. Of course, this is the least-preferred method.

Another situation that is commonly encountered is having multiple values available for variables in the analysis. This may be the result of variation in the variable, or data coming from different sources. At least for the primary analysis, only one value can be used for each of the variables included in the analysis. The values that are chosen for the primary analysis are commonly referred to as the *base case*. (More detail will follow in a later section on conducting sensitivity analyses after the primary analysis.) The base case serves as the foundation for the primary analysis. One common method for dealing with multiple values available is to use the mean or median of the data in the base case. Perhaps data are coming from multiple published articles, but one article seems to be more widely accepted than the other. This may lead you to select that value over another, based on general acceptance by experts in the field. Use good judgment and consider what the stakeholder audience will support.

Costs and benefits may need to be further broken down by one-time versus ongoing occurrence. This is especially critical for multiyear analyses. Some costs are start-up or baseline and only occur one time while other costs occur regularly on an ongoing basis as the program is maintained over time. Be sure to account for these types of costs and benefits appropriately in the analysis.

Value the Benefits for a Cost-Benefit Analysis

Although CBA findings can often be more intuitive to interpret, the difficulty comes in valuing benefits for inclusion in the analysis. In many cases, especially in program evaluation, the benefits are not necessarily easy to value. One method of valuing benefits is to consider the downstream financial impact of the benefit. For example, one benefit to schools of reducing bullying is decreases in the student dropout rate. The monetary value of a student from dropping out to a school is the loss of state revenue that is received on a per-student basis. While measuring the value of preventing a student from dropping out this way ignores the intangible benefits, the financial impact to the school is clearly quantified.

Benefits are not always gains but may be represented by costs avoided. Prevention is often difficult to value because its true benefit is preventing a future cost or negative consequence from happening. The previous example is an illustration of this concept in that schools that prevent students from dropping out do not necessarily gain revenue. Rather, they prevent the loss of revenue. Cost avoidance is an important benefit to consider.

One common way to value benefits is to assign the market value of the benefit. This is also referred to as *shadow pricing*. This method is often used with the difficult task of measuring the value of time. Time is often valued by considering the income that could be earned if the time were spent working. In addition to measuring time, products and services are often valued by the price of the product or service if purchased.

One of the main criticisms of CBAs is that the methods used to value benefits lead to results that are not realistic or do not fairly represent the true benefits. Consider whether the framework for the analysis will lead to such criticisms. It may be possible to adjust the framework to make the analysis more realistic in the eyes of the stakeholders. Ultimately, consideration for how results will be accepted by the primary stakeholders should be an important driver of how the analysis is framed and conducted.

Discount (Depending on the Time Frame)

For long-term evaluations, costs and benefits should be discounted. Discounting is a process by which the future value is reduced compared with the value today. This is necessary because the same amount of money today would be worth less in the future due to inflation and opportunity costs, or the value of the next best alternative. The amount by which the future value is reduced is referred to as the discount rate. There is no consensus on the standardized discount rate that should be used for CEAs/CBAs.[4] While many evaluations of social programs use a 4% discount rate, a range of 3%–5% is typically used in medicine while the Consumer Price Index (CPI) is used in some financial sectors. The current value of future money is referred to as the net present value (NPV). Consider $2,000 today. The NPV of that $2,000 a decade from now (assuming a discount rate of 5%) would be just over $1,200. Therefore, if you had to choose between $1,500 today or $2,000 10 years from now, you would choose the $1,500 today because it is worth more than the $2,000 will be in the future.

Discounting adds complexity to your analysis and is not as critical unless you are conducting a long-term evaluation. In fact, some recommendations on which discount rate to use vary based on the time frame of the analysis, with longer-term projects using a higher discount rate.[8] There are a variety of NPV calculators available online, and Microsoft Excel has an NPV function.

Calculate Results

Generally with simple models, calculations mean basic math. Computer spreadsheet software, such as Microsoft Excel, makes calculations simple and transparent. As with many of the steps in the overall process, calculation of the results does not necessarily have to wait until this point in the process. It is strongly recommended that you use a spreadsheet as you go along. Consequently, calculations are done throughout the process so that when you are finished with the previous steps, you may actually not need to do any further calculations, or you may simply need to calculate the final cost-effectiveness ratio or net benefit/cost. Refer to Table 14.1 for the formulas to calculate both CE ratio and net benefit/cost. Spreadsheets have simplified tremendously what used to be a time-intensive part of the overall process.

Transparency is critically important to these analyses to ensure that stakeholders clearly understand the methods that were used. It is not uncommon for stakeholders to refer to such analyses as a *black box* when methods are unclear, thus motivating mistrust of the results. Descriptions and reporting of the results should be able to be replicated if desired by the reader. Share the calculations spreadsheet with the reporting of findings to at least a few reviewers to ensure that the results are clear and transparent.

One tip to increasing transparency pertains to how the spreadsheet is set up. Each cost and benefit should have a unique cell in the spreadsheet, as should any multipliers, such as quantities, rates, and percentages. Calculations can then be conducted using the cells directly with the results in a new cell. Data that appear only in functions are difficult to see and follow. Another benefit to this approach is that variables can be easily changed by simply changing the value in a cell. Results will then be automatically recalculated. This approach is tremendously helpful for the next step in the process—sensitivity analysis.

Conduct a Sensitivity Analysis

Throughout the process, you probably have had to make assumptions, estimate values due to missing data, and/or decide on using an average value or value that is one of a range of values. Sensitivity analyses give you the opportunity to explore the variation in your results that are obtained if you were to modify the input variables. In fact, the sensitivity analysis may be the most valuable result of the overall CEA/CBA to some stakeholders.[3] Two types of sensitivity analyses can be conducted: (1) partial sensitivity analysis and (2) extreme-case sensitivity analysis. Both approaches offer useful, but different, information.

Partial Sensitivity Analysis

With partial sensitivity analysis, one input variable is varied at a time, holding everything else constant. Results with this variation can be compared to the results obtained from the base case used in the primary analysis. The following types of variables make great selections for the sensitivity analysis:

- Variables representing assumptions that were made for the analysis.
- Variables that have a range of possible values.
- Variables that were estimated due to missing or unavailable data.
- Variables that have uncertainty.

The variable chosen is varied either to a specific value (e.g., the low end of the range of possible values) or a predetermined percentage (e.g., decreased by 10%). The change in results is recorded, and then the variable is varied in the other direction (e.g., the high end of the range of possible values or increased by 10%). The sensitivity analysis provides a range of possible results. Partial sensitivity analyses can be conducted on multiple variables provided that the variable that was just changed is restored to its original value before another variable is varied to ensure that only one variable is changing at a time. Results from sensitivity analyses are typically presented graphically in what is commonly referred to as a *tornado diagram,* with each row representing a variable that was used in the partial sensitivity analysis. Figure 14.2 shows an example of a tornado diagram.

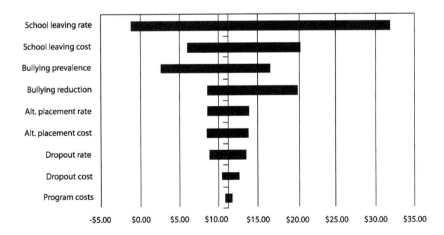

Figure 14.2. Tornado diagram example of net benefit per student

Suppose you are conducting a CBA of a pilot implementation in three elementary schools to determine the cost–benefit ratio of expanding the program to all elementary schools in the county. Using data from the pilot implementation, the three schools reduced the percentage of bullying by 20%, 35%, and 38%, respectively. You decided to use the average of the three rates, 31%, for the base case in the primary analysis. The result of the overall analysis showed a net benefit of $11.24 per student if the bullying prevention program were expanded to all elementary schools. A good choice for a partial sensitivity analysis would be to vary the bullying reduction rate from a low value of 20% to a high value of 38% based on the actual variation seen in the pilot program.

Extreme-case Sensitivity Analysis

The extreme-case sensitivity analysis is very similar to the partial sensitivity analysis in terms of the choice of variables to vary as well as selection of the magnitude of the variation. However, instead of only varying one variable at a time as with partial sensitivity analyses, all variables that have been selected for the sensitivity analysis are changed at the same time—once in a "best-case" scenario and then in a "worst-case" scenario. Variations are not necessarily in the same direction but, rather, the direction that produces the best/worst outcomes, respectively. For example, in the best-case scenario, program costs would be minimized while bullying reduction rates would be maximized—the opposite occurs in calculating the worst-case scenario. On the one hand, if the results are tolerable even under the worst-case scenario, then it makes sense to move forward. On the other hand, you might pause or even decide against the program if the results are questionable even under the best-case scenario.

Each approach offers different information, and one is not necessarily better than the other. Consider the expectations of the audience for the results. Will the results from one approach provide more compelling information for decision making? In some cases, extreme-case sensitivity analyses are especially useful when there is a high degree of uncertainty. It may even be beneficial to conduct both types of sensitivity analyses.

Use Results for Decision Making

Now that you have the results of your analysis as well as the results of the sensitivity analysis, you can use the results to inform your decision making. CEAs/CBAs can be designed to meet the needs of different stakeholders and offer unique information that can be used to complement other available information so that decisions can be evidence-based.

CONCLUSION

CEAs/CBAs are not a silver bullet and do not provide a definitive answer. Moreover, this chapter is not a comprehensive guide to conducting CEAs/CBAs, but is intended to offer guidance on conducting simple analyses. However, these types of analyses provide important information that can be used with other evaluations to inform decision making. The reality is that resources are limited. Therefore, educated decisions must be made to ensure the most efficient and effective use of those limited resources, and CEAs/CBAs are valuable tools for program evaluation.

FREQUENTLY ASKED QUESTIONS

1. Why is conducting an economic evaluation of a bullying prevention program so important?

Bullying prevention is a laudable goal, and few would argue against its merits. However, policies and programs should not be judged by their good intentions but by their results. Economic evaluations should be used in conjunction with evaluations of effectiveness. Unfortunately, adopting a new program generally comes with some implementation cost. With limited resources, decision makers must determine whether the benefits of a program outweigh the costs of implementation.

2. What is the value conducting a cost–benefit analysis (CBA) or cost-effectiveness analysis (CEA) as an economic analysis for a bullying prevention initiative?

Cost-effectiveness analysis (CEA) and cost–benefit analysis (CBA) are two common methods for comparing options when resources are limited. The overall costs of a program are weighed against the benefits achieved by the program. CBAs and CEAs are unique in that costs and benefits that are not typically included in economic evaluations using accounting principles are often included; thus, a more comprehensive economic evaluation is conducted of the program.

3. How can a cost–benefit analysis (CBA) or cost-effectiveness analysis (CEA) be used?

There are many uses for a CBA/CEA. A CBA/CEA can be conducted before implementation to help inform the decision of whether to adopt a particular program. Conducted after program implementation, a CBA/CEA can evaluate the cost–benefit or cost-effectiveness of an existing program. Additionally, CEAs and CBAs can be used to extrapolate findings to predict the economic impact in the future and/or with a different population. For example, you might have data from a pilot program and want to know what the impact would be on the entire population, or you might be considering expanding your existing program. These analyses are also invaluable for examining outcomes for which there are not direct data available.

4. What is the difference between a cost–benefit analysis (CBA) and a cost-effectiveness analysis (CEA)?

CEA is a technique that is used to relate the cost of a program to its measure of effectiveness, such as a key outcome or benefit. Results of a CEA are typically expressed as a cost-effectiveness ratio obtained by dividing total costs by the unit measure of effectiveness. CBA is similar to CEA, except it goes a step further by valuing the benefits of the program. Therefore, costs are weighed against the benefits monetarily; thus, results of a CBA are expressed as net benefits.

5. Who should conduct a cost–benefit analysis (CBA) or cost-effectiveness analysis (CEA)?

Some believe that conducting a CEA, and especially a CBA, requires a high level of methodological and specialized expertise. Although the methods for some CEA and CBA models can be complex and highly technical, simple models can and should be used by any evaluation team regardless of formal training. CEAs and CBAs can be conducted by any and for any interested stakeholder. Simple models for which data are readily available can be developed and analyzed rather quickly. Therefore, simple CBAs and CEAs can really be calculated by any stakeholder that can access the necessary information about the program.

6. What are the steps in conducting a cost–benefit analysis (CBA) or cost-effectiveness analysis (CEA)?

Regardless of whether you choose to conduct a CEA or a CBA (or perhaps even both), the overall process for conducting the analyses are the same.

1. Define the framework for the analysis.
2. Determine the perspective of the analysis.
3. Decide on the time frame for the analysis.
4. Define the population.
5. Identify and measure the costs and benefits.
6. Value the benefits (for a CBA).
7. Discount (depending on time frame).
8. Calculate results.
9. Conduct a sensitivity analysis.
10. Use results for decision making.

7. How can a cost–benefit analysis (CBA) or cost-effectiveness analysis (CEA) be designed to meet the needs of specific stakeholders of a bullying prevention program?

CBA and CEA models can be used by many stakeholders of bullying prevention initiatives depending on the framework for the analysis. Schools may want to use the results to justify implementing a bullying prevention initiative to both internal (e.g., administration, teachers, staff) and external (e.g., parents, students, community) stakeholders. Community organizations may use results to justify partnering with schools on bullying prevention to improve the overall culture of the community. Healthcare organizations can use results to justify investment in community efforts, such as bullying prevention, that reduce healthcare utilization and improve health outcomes. Finally, evaluators can use results to complement other evaluation data sources such as program effectiveness.

8. Are the steps for conducting a cost–benefit analysis (CBA) or cost-effectiveness analysis (CEA) sequential?

The overall process steps are not necessarily linear and sequential. For example, you may find that after you have defined your framework that you will need to modify it based on options that become apparent in the next several steps of the overall process. Ultimately, this becomes an iterative process.

9. How many options can be considered in a cost–benefit analysis (CBA) or cost-effectiveness analysis (CEA)?

Comparisons may be made between more than one program or even different options of the same program. One of your comparisons may also be the option of not implementing any program. Understanding what you will be comparing is an important step in defining your framework.

10. I have many different stakeholders of my bullying prevention program. How do I decide what perspective to use for the cost–benefit analysis (CBA) or cost-effectiveness analysis (CEA) model?

Determining the perspective of the analysis can sometimes seem obvious, but it is not a trivial step in the process. The societal perspective measures the impact of the program on society as a whole. While this is a critical perspective, the societal perspective can sometimes be too broad for some decision makers. This is not to suggest that societal models are not important, but rather a recommendation to consider the specific audience for the results. Considering how the results will be used specifically will most likely lead you to the appropriate perspective for the analysis.

11. Which students should be included in a cost–benefit analysis (CBA) or cost-effectiveness analysis (CEA)?

The population of your CBA/CEA will obviously be students, but there are several considerations that must be made when determining which students to include. You will need to consider whether the following should be included/excluded:

1. Particular schools/school districts
2. A certain geography
3. Certain levels (e.g., elementary school vs. middle school) or specific grades?
4. Public, private, and/or charter schools
5. All buildings or just some buildings.

Be prepared to address specific questions when defining the population for the analysis.

12. Is special software needed to conduct a cost–benefit analysis (CBA) or cost-effectiveness analysis (CEA)?

Generally with simple models, calculations mean basic math. Computer spreadsheet software, such as Microsoft Excel, makes calculations simple and transparent.

REFERENCES

1. Primer on cost-effectiveness analysis. *Eff Clin Pract.* 2000;3:253–255. Available at http://www.acponline.org/clinical_information/journals_publications/ecp/sepoct00/primer.pdf. Accessed June 15, 2012.

1a. Heffner R. The Open Mind. 1975. Available at www.thirteen.org/openmind/public-affairs/living-within-our-means/494/. Accessed August 14, 2013.

2. Karoly LA. Valuing benefits in benefit-cost studies of social programs. RAND. 2008. Available at http://www.rand.org/pubs/technical_reports/TR643.html. Accessed June 15, 2012.

3. Kee JE. At what price? benefit-cost analysis and cost-effectiveness analysis in program evaluation. *The Evaluation Exchange.* 1999; 5(2/3):4–5.

4. Tuan MT. Measuring and/or estimating social value creation: insights into eight integrated cost approaches. Bill & Melinda Gates Foundation. 2008. Available at: http://www.gatesfoundation.org/learning/pages/december-2008-measuring-estimating-social-value-creation-report-summary.aspx. Accessed June 17, 2012.

5. Zema CZ, Rybowski LS. Real world application of comparative effectiveness: meeting the needs of formulary decision-makers. Poster presentation at the 2010 Annual Meeting of the International Society of Pharmacoeconomic and Outcomes Research; Atlanta, GA.

6. Matchar DB, Samsa GP, Liu S. Cost-effectiveness of antiplatelet agents in secondary stroke prevention: the limits of certainty. *Value in Health.* 2005; 8(5):572–580.

7. Malinina D, Zema C, Sander S, Serebruany V. Cost-effectiveness of antiplatelet therapy for secondary stroke prevention. *Expert Rev Pharmacoecon Outcomes Res.* 2007; 7(4):357–363.

8. Cellini SR, Kee JE. Chapter 21. Cost-effectiveness and cost-benefit analysis. *Handbook of Practical Program Evaluation.* 3rd ed. In: Wholey JS, Hatry HP, Newcomer KE, editors. San Francisco, CA: Jossey-Bass, 2010:493–530.

15

Call to Action for Schools and Legislators

David Keller Trevaskis

Objectives

1. Explain the motivation behind bullying prevention laws (responding to the events that causes a concern for inappropriate responses to anecdotal experiences, attempts to limit liability, responses to federal action).
2. Outline the federal legal foundation (Title VI, Title IX, and the ADA) and then discuss how state laws apply.
3. Showcase problems for bullying laws (LGBT bias and concerns about creating new areas of litigation and liability).
4. Present a model state law.

INTRODUCTION

As *bullycide* has become an accepted term of art[i] in public discourse about bullying prevention, many who care about young people in schools have looked to the law for answers. Parents, educators, students, law and justice

---

[i]From a first use in 2001 (http://wordspy.com/words/bullycide.asp), as of June 2012 there were over 148,000 results in a simple Google search of the term *bullycide*. Although the term minimizes the complexity of adolescent suicide, it captures the pain of loss for those who lose someone who has been subjected to bullying. Accessed June 15, 2012.

professionals, and legislators have worked to both use existing laws and craft new laws to protect children targeted for bullying.

Much bullying behavior involves actions that could be viewed as crimes under existing laws in every state in the country,[ii] but the focus of this chapter will not be the criminalization of bullying. The American Psychological Association Zero's Tolerance Task Force defines *zero tolerance* as "a philosophy or policy that mandates the application of predetermined consequences, most often severe and punitive in nature, that are intended to be applied regardless of the gravity of behavior, mitigating circumstances, or situational context."[1] However, zero-tolerance school disciplinary policies and criminal prosecution of bullying fail to stop bullying from happening and do little more than feed a "school-to-prison pipeline."[2,iii] Criminally prosecuting a person who bullies another may provide specific deterrence, but no research exists that suggests a wider deterrent effect. There is more hope in following restorative, not punitive, justice principles.[3,4,iv] Civil laws that broadly affect schools and support bullying prevention efforts will be the focus of this chapter, which will explore existing law and court interpretations of existing law and conclude with suggestions for model state legislation.

[ii] A cursory review of Pennsylvania law indicated that bullying behavior could meet the standards of the following crimes:

- Assault.
- Terroristic threats.
- Harassment, harassment by communication or address, stalking.
- Possession of child pornography.
- Distribution of child pornography.
- Sexual abuse of children.
- Sexual exploitation of children.
- Unlawful contact/communication with a minor.
- Ethnic intimidation (hate crime).

[iii] Article defines "school to prison pipeline" as a "growing pattern of tracking students out of educational institutions, primarily via "zero tolerance" policies, and, directly and/or indirectly, into the juvenile and adult criminal justice systems."

[iv] Article defines restorative justice as "a process whereby parties with a stake in a specific offence [sic] collectively resolve how to deal with the aftermath of the offence and its implication for the future."

THE LAWS OF BULLYING

As of June 2012, 49 states have specific anti-bullying laws (for details, see www.stopbullying.gov/laws/index.html and www.bullypolice.org). Only Montana fails to have an anti-bullying law. Although there are no specific federal anti-bullying laws, there are a number of federal statutes that may be applied to certain bullying situations.[5] Among the civil rights laws used in anti-bullying efforts are Title VI of the Civil Rights Act of 1964, which prohibits discrimination on the basis of race, color, and national origin; Title IX of the Education Amendments of 1972, which prohibits discrimination on the basis of sex; and Section 504 of the Rehabilitation Act of 1973 and the Americans with Disabilities Act of 1990, which prohibits discrimination on the basis of disability. Simply creating a new statute or following the existing laws, however, will not prevent bullying from happening, and anti-bullying laws cannot guarantee that incidents of bullying will be handled effectively.

Under most anti-bullying laws, schools need only have anti-bullying policies in place, respond to bullying situations of which teachers and administrators are aware, and report bullying incidents to the appropriate government agency or official. Doing enough to meet the requirements of the law, however, might not be doing enough to protect children from the damaging consequences of bullying. Even in the few states that have far more stringent anti-bullying requirements, successful bullying prevention efforts do not rely on the law but on the partnership of educators, parents, students, and the community at large. Clearly, educators have professional and moral standards that direct them to do more than the law dictates.

Although bullying has probably been an issue for schools since schools were first formed, significant attention to bullying came after the April 20, 1999, shootings at Columbine High School in Colorado. Many early media accounts of the Columbine tragedy reported that the shootings were retaliation for bullying against the perpetrators, although Cullen provides a detailed account of the tragedy, the media coverage, and the flawed narrative that the Columbine attack was in retaliation for bullying.[6] Such media attention often results in legislation being drafted in an almost knee-jerk fashion, and in that spirit, anti-bullying laws did follow Columbine.[7]

Skip a little more than a decade ahead in time and you can see the same media-driven pattern occur, as the suicide of Tyler Clementi helped push through significant revisions to New Jersey's anti-bullying law.[8] Clementi, a

Rutgers University student, took his own life in 2010 after his roommate used a webcam and social media to bully him. The criminal trial and conviction of Clementi's roommate, Dharun Ravi, resulted in him serving 20 days of a 30-day sentence.[9,10] Developments in technology that are highlighted in the Clementi matter add a new element to efforts to craft laws that can protect students who are bullied, as the reach of those who would target others is now seemingly unlimited.

The U.S. Department of Health and Human Services (HHS) defines cyberbullying as "bullying that takes place using electronic technology. Examples of cyberbullying include mean text messages or emails, rumors sent by email or posted on social networking sites, and embarrassing pictures, videos, websites, or fake profiles."[11] This is the area where the law seems most at a crossroads as courts try to apply legal concepts created before technological advances raised implications unimagined by the jurists of earlier times.[12] (In the case of social media, such "earlier times" might be yesterday!)

Tyler Clementi's death galvanized the Obama administration's anti-bullying efforts. On October 22, 2010, President Obama spoke about the importance of bullying prevention and safe school climate.[13] Importantly, the Obama administration clarified that Title IX, the federal law that prohibits discrimination on the basis of sex and by extension gender stereotyping by recipients of funds from the United States Department of Education (DOE), may offer protection to lesbian, gay, bisexual, and transgender (LGBT) students who are victims of bullying, even though LGBT students do not receive specific federal protection by nature of their LGBT status. In addition, LGBT students are often not specifically protected under state anti-bullying laws. This is covered more fully in Chapter 6.

THE APPLICABILITY OF ANTI-DISCRIMINATION LAWS TO BULLYING BEHAVIOR

Anti-discrimination laws have recently been expanded and clarified to cover bullying.

On October 26, 2010, the DOE's Office for Civil Rights (OCR) issued a *Dear Colleague Letter* that clarified the relationship between bullying and discriminatory harassment under the civil rights laws enforced by OCR, including Title VI (race, color, and national origin), Title IX (sex), and Section

504 and Title II of the ADA (disability).[14] It is important to note, however, that these laws do not apply to bullying that does not rise to the level of harassment based on race, color, national origin, sex, including gender stereotyping, or disability. The *Dear Colleague Letter* explained how student misconduct that falls under an anti-bullying policy may also trigger responsibilities under one or more of the anti-discrimination statutes enforced by OCR. Specifically, the *Dear Colleague Letter* discussed harassment based on race and national origin, sex and gender stereotyping, and disability, and illustrated how a school should respond in each case. It also reminded schools that failure to recognize discriminatory harassment when addressing student misconduct may lead to inadequate or inappropriate responses that fail to remedy violations of students' civil rights.[14,v]

The *Dear Colleague Letter* also explained the extent of a school's obligations under these anti-discrimination statutes. According to the DOE, once a school knows or reasonably should know of possible student-on-student harassment, it must take immediate and appropriate action to investigate or otherwise determine what occurred. If harassment has occurred, a school must take prompt and effective steps reasonably calculated to end the harassment, eliminate any hostile environment, and prevent its recurrence. These duties are the school's responsibility even if the misconduct is also covered by an anti-bullying policy or law and regardless of whether the victim makes a complaint, asks the school to take action, or identifies the harassment as a form of discrimination.

REPORT FROM THE GOVERNMENT ACCOUNTABILITY OFFICE

The anti-bullying push at the federal level continued in June 2012 with the issuance of a report by the Government Accountability Office (GAO) on school bullying titled *Legal Protections for Vulnerable Youth Need to Be More Fully Assessed*.[15] In its highlight summary on the report, the GAO reflected on a number of state statutes, school district policies, and applicable federal law, finding "that the nature and extent of protections available to students who are bullied depend on the laws and policies where they live or go to school."[15] The report summary notes:

---

[v]The *Dear Colleague Letter* also noted that colleges and universities have the same obligations under the antidiscrimination statutes as elementary and secondary schools.

We also found that while federal and state civil rights laws may offer some protections against bullying in certain circumstances, vulnerable groups may not always be covered. Federal civil rights laws can be used to provide protections against bullying in certain circumstances, but some vulnerable groups are not covered and therefore have no recourse at the federal level. For example, federal agencies lack jurisdiction under civil rights statutes to pursue discrimination cases based solely on socioeconomic status or sexual orientation. Some state civil rights laws provide protections to victims of bullying that go beyond federal law, but federal complainants whose cases are dismissed for lack of jurisdiction are not always informed by Education about the possibility of pursuing claims at the state level.

Finally, regarding federal coordination efforts to combat bullying, we found that a variety of efforts are under way, but that a full assessment of legal remedies has not been completed. Specifically, Education, HHS, and Justice have established coordinated efforts to carry out research and disseminate information on bullying. For example, The Federal Partners in Bullying Prevention Steering Committee serves as a forum for federal agencies to develop and share information with each other and the public, and (http://www.stopbullying.gov) consolidates the content of different federal sites into one location to provide free materials for the public. In addition to these efforts, Education has issued information about how federal civil rights laws can be used to address bullying of protected classes of youths and is conducting a comprehensive study of state bullying laws and how selected school districts are implementing them. However, no similar information is being gathered on state civil rights laws and procedures that could be helpful in assessing the adequacy of legal protections for victims of school bullying.[15]

DAVIS V. MONROE COUNTY BOARD OF EDUCATION

Federal anti-bullying efforts can be traced back to the U.S. Supreme Court's 1999 decision in the case of *Davis v. Monroe County Board of Education*.[16] In that case, a female fifth-grade student at Hubbard Elementary School in Monroe County, Georgia, named LaShonda Davis was repeatedly sexually harassed by a male classmate, "G.F." The incidents of reported sexual harassment began in December 1992 when G.F. attempted to touch LaShonda's breasts and genital areas while making vulgar statements. LaShonda reported the incident to her teacher, but the school did not initiate any action to prevent future occurrences of the behavior. The behavior continued on two separate days in January 1993 when G.F. committed similar offensive actions against LaShonda. LaShonda reported both incidents to her teacher and to her mother. When her mother reported the incidents to LaShonda's teacher, she was told that the principal had been informed of the incidents. No disciplinary action, however, was taken against G.F.

G.F. similarly harassed LaShonda on two occasions in February 1993. The first February incident happened in physical education class when G.F. again acted in a sexually suggestive manner toward LaShonda. She reported the incident to her physical education teacher, but the school did not take any action against G.F. A week later, another classroom teacher, Mrs. Pippin, observed G.F. engaged in similar behavior and again no disciplinary action was taken. In March 1993, G.F. harassed LaShonda in physical education class once again and the incident was once more reported to the physical education teacher and to Mrs. Pippin. Although the principal was told of the incident, no disciplinary action was taken. G.F. rubbed his body against LaShonda in a sexually suggestive manner again in April 1993 and LaShonda reported the incident to her classroom teacher, and like the previous times, no disciplinary sanctions were taken against G.F.

During the time that G.F. was harassing LaShonda, he was also harassing other female classmates. A number of the girls, including LaShonda, asked to speak to the principal about G.F.'s conduct. However, their teacher denied the request, saying that the principal would call them if he needed to do so. When LaShonda's mother talked to the principal about the continuing incidents, the principal told her, "I guess I'll just have to threaten him a little harder." The principal also told Mrs. Davis that LaShonda was the only student complaining about G.F.'s behavior. In May 1993, the local police charged G.F. with sexual battery for the repeated incidents of misconduct against LaShonda. (This case underscores the limitations of criminal prosecution of bullying behavior since LaShonda suffered months of abuse before police intervened.) G.F. pleaded guilty. Although the harassing behavior stopped, LaShonda's grades plummeted,

| A PUBLIC HEALTH APPROACH TO BULLYING PREVENTION

she was no longer able to concentrate on her studies, and her father found a
suicide note that LaShonda had written to a friend.

In 1994, Mrs. Davis filed a civil suit in United States District Court. The suit
alleged that the school board had violated Title IX by not taking action to stop
the student-on-student sexual harassment. Specifically, the suit alleged that the
school district's deliberate indifference created an intimidating, hostile,
offensive, and abusive school environment in violation of the law. The
complaint sought compensatory and punitive damages, attorney's fees, and
injunctive relief. The question that the Supreme Court grappled with was not
whether the behavior of G.F. against LaShonda was offensive, but whether
federal anti-discrimination law provided her a remedy. In a 5–4 decision,
Justice Sandra Day O'Connor enunciated a standard that allowed for liability
under Title IX when schools act with deliberate indifference to gender-based
harassment that is severe enough to prevent victims from enjoying educational
opportunities. Prior to the Court's decision, traditional tort remedies would
apply only against G.F., and it is unlikely that the resources of a fifth-grade
student would provide much relief to a victim.

T.K. V. NEW YORK CITY DEPARTMENT OF EDUCATION

There are a number of areas in which courts are expanding existing law to
provide remedies for the victims of bullying behavior. The 2011 United States
District Court decision in *T.K. v. New York City Department of Education*[17]
provides an excellent summary of the applicability of anti-discrimination laws
to bullying of special needs students when the bullying behavior may lead to
the denial of a free appropriate public education. In that opinion, Senior Judge
Jack B. Weinstein reviewed how various circuit courts have handled such
claims and enunciated the following standards of review:

- When responding to bullying incidents that might affect the opportunities of a special education student to obtain an appropriate education, a
  school must take prompt and appropriate action.
- It must investigate if the harassment is reported to have occurred.
- If harassment is found to have occurred, the school must take
  appropriate steps to prevent it in the future.

These duties of a school exist even if the misconduct is covered by its anti-
bullying policy, and regardless of whether the student has complained, asked

the school to take action, or identified the harassment as a form of discrimination (pp. 46–47).[17]

FIRST AMENDMENT CONSIDERATIONS

One of the primary concerns in crafting anti-bullying legislation is the extent to which such legislation might interfere with students' First Amendment[vi] free speech rights. In the school context, however, these concerns are greatly diminished, as the Supreme Court has considerably limited the free speech rights of students over the course of the last several decades. The opinions have established that student speech rights must be weighed against the significant interests of administrators in maintaining an orderly learning environment, with considerable discretion given to schools.

SHORTFALLS IN ANTI-BULLYING LAWS

The failure of many existing anti-bullying laws to address off-campus speech not only limits the ability of school officials to deal with traditional bullying, but leaves schools at an extreme disadvantage in attempting to handle cyberbullying. The Internet provides a medium through which bullies have access to victims without the need for a classroom, cafeteria, or schoolyard. The fact that many bullying laws do not address cyberbullying is disconcerting; but even those that do are often powerless to regulate it if those laws do not extend to off-campus speech.

There are other, nonconstitutional concerns regarding state laws' treatment of cyberbullying as well. Notably, while many states criminalize cyberbullying, the effectiveness of criminalization relative to education programs as a deterrent is in question. Another problem, shared by traditional bullying legislation, is a lack of clarity in the definition of *bullying* and *cyberbullying*—something that not only leads to trouble with enforcement but also exposes the

---

[vi]"Congress shall make no law respecting an establishment of religion, or prohibiting the free exercise thereof; or abridging the freedom of speech, or of the press; or the right of the people peaceably to assemble, and to petition the Government for a redress of grievances…"*U.S Const. amend. I.* The key language for cyberbullying legal analysis is "Congress shall make no law… abridging the freedom of speech."

308 A PUBLIC HEALTH APPROACH TO BULLYING PREVENTION

laws to the prospect of being ruled facially invalid under the constitutional overbreadth and vagueness doctrines.

Another large concern is the fact that the discretion granted to school administrations that may allow for the regulation of bullying speech is a double-edged sword. The fact that school officials are legally able to impose regulations on students does not mandate action on the part of the schools. Thus, there is no mechanism to ensure that school officials are properly addressing the broad range of bullying behaviors and activities. This discretion is also open to abuse, allowing school officials to restrict what may be constitutionally protected speech, which could occur without malice as a result of the ambiguity surrounding the definition of bullying.

LEGAL REMEDIES FOR BULLYING

The relevant traditional channels for private relief in tort law include defamation, intentional infliction of emotional distress, and harassment lawsuits. There are a variety of concerns with these channels. Notably, they often require that a private individual hoping to bring suit has ample resources at his or her disposal in order to adequately litigate and that the tortfeasor has the solvency to make litigation valuable. Further, private suits are often likely to be defeated by First Amendment claims on the part of the defendant, and certain torts—notably, defamation—are strictly defined in such a way that does not align well with bullying scenarios. Finally, encouraging individuals to seek relief through tort law potentially runs the risk of excessive litigation and frivolous lawsuits resulting.

Concerns about administrative discretion have, as bullying laws have developed, given way to concerns that those laws' reporting requirements are inadequate. In many cases it is only required that more severe cases of bullying be reported. Further, the laws may, at times, discourage the reporting of bullying, as reporting may portray schools in a negative light. Alternative proposals have involved criminalizing nonfeasance on the part of teachers and school officials or providing qualified immunity to those who report incidents.

New Jersey's law may well serve as the foundation for a model state law. Arguably the most far reaching and comprehensive anti-bullying legislation in the country is found in New Jersey. In 2011 the state passed the Anti-Bullying Bill of Rights Act, which not only provides a clear definition of bullying but also mandates and provides guidelines for an institutionalized system for addressing bullying in schools, focused both on prevention and remedial concerns.[18]

This law is argued to more substantively address concerns that teachers and schools may only minimally comply with anti-bullying requirements by putting into place a more comprehensive system to tackle the issue. While some might prefer alterations—it does not, for example, address cyberbullying directly and does not provide for criminal sanctions—it serves to address concerns that anti-bullying laws are largely allowing for minimal compliance on the part of schools without properly seeking to root out the underlying problems. The law effectively creates a set of institutions through which concerns about bullying are pervasive.

WHAT SHOULD BE INCLUDED IN ANTI-BULLYING POLICY OR LAW?

Based on the previous historical and legal overview of the benefits, restrictions, and gaps in antibullying policy and laws, what are essential components to be included? Below is a list of elements that should be included in effective antibullying policy and law:

1. Create a definition of bullying that encompasses concepts of harassment, intimidation, and cyberbullying that interferes with the orderly operation of the school or the rights of the students and/or creates a hostile school environment.
2. Include incidents of bullying that occur off schoolgrounds in policy especially related to cyberbullying and incidence of retaliation for asserting or alleging an act of bullying.
3. Consider the use of a group of stakeholders including school administrators, staff, students, families, and members of the community to assist with the policy/law development.
4. Clearly identify sanctions to be implemented for bullying behaviors, including levels of intervention that might include notification of law enforcement.
5. Communicate bullying policy, sanctions, and expectations of behavior comprehensively to students, parents, teachers, community members, and so on. Require communication to student and parents who have reported bullying regarding a plan of action in a timely fashion.

6. Provide remediation for current or ongoing bullying situations, including identified school and/or community resources for counseling, mental health, or other health services as needed.
7. Develop a procedure for reporting and tracking bullying incidents as reported by students, teachers, and families, and ensure confidentiality in reporting as well as protection from retaliation. Provide clear documentation evidence of the incident, response, resolution, and follow-up.
8. Provide for schools to deliver annual reports related to the number of reported bullying incidents, and responsive actions taken with appropriate privacy protections to ensure student confidentiality.
9. Provide training and ongoing continuing education for teachers and administrators regarding issues related to bullying, effective interventions, and prevention (www.stopbullying.gov/laws/key-components/index.html).

CONCLUSION

As long as circuit courts across the country continue to read broadly the power of the state to regulate student speech, the door is open to expansive anti-bullying legislation that reaches beyond schoolgrounds. States—especially those within the circuits that have explicitly supported more considerable restrictions of student speech—should take advantage of those speech limitations in order to expand their regulation of bullying. Although the constitutional boundaries of bullying regulation are amorphous, states have an opportunity to address bullying and cyberbullying in a comprehensive, yet fair, manner.

FREQUENTLY ASKED QUESTIONS

1. Where can I find bullying laws for my own state?

State by state reports can be found at http://www.stopbullying.gov/.

2. What about the grades given at http://www.bullypolice.org/?

The grades are helpful shorthand but this site, as opposed to the government-controlled site, reflects the biases of the folks involved in maintaining it. Know their biases and use their grades as a shorthand for how good—or bad—state policies are.

3. Which state has the best anti-bullying law?

Best is a subjective term. New Jersey has a very strong law but the danger there is that even schools that respond well to bullying situations might still fail to meet their obligation under the law. BullyPoliceUSA gives NJ an A++.

4. Why shouldn't bullying behavior be criminalized?

Some bullying behavior crosses over into criminal action, but criminalizing behavior doesn't change that behavior—note that crime doesn't go down just because we put people in prison. The key is to work to change behavior, of everyone from the child who bullies to the bystander who needs to act.

5. What can citizens do if their state does not have an effective law on bullying?

Get involved and let your representatives know that you think action is needed!

6. Should we have a federal anti-bullying law?

Pennsylvania's Senator Robert Casey has advocated for such a law in recent congressional terms. Federal case law and current educational policy is protective of many students who are bullied if they fit into protected classes under the law.

7. What aren't LGBT children protected from bullying under the law?

LGBT children are protected under certain local and state statutes and the current interpretation of Title IX by the Obama administration calls for protection, but until all who work with children protect all children, there will still be gaps in this area.

8. Should we be using the law to control behavior that is just part of growing up?

Bullying is not part of growing up, but the concern for government control exists among many who would not want children bullied. We are a nation of laws and, as such, we turn to the law to try to create policies that reflect our values. Protecting children is a core American value.

9. Do we need special laws for cyberbullying?

Laws specifically covering cyberbullying have the benefit of reinforcing our values in new areas of technology. However, the technology is changing so fast that many of the laws are outdated as they are passed.

10. Is any law banning cyberbullying considered unconstitutional because it violates free speech?

The Supreme Court has not considered how to apply its school speech cases to cyberbullying. There will be defense arguments of protected speech but speech has often been limited in school settings to maintain order, prevent encouragement of drug use and where the school is presenting curriculum. Lower Courts have split on this issue.

REFERENCES

1. American Psychological Association Zero Tolerance Task Force. Are zero tolerance policies effective in the schools? An evidentiary review and recommendations. *Am. Psychol.* 2008; 852(63):9.

2. Heitzig NA. Education or incarceration: Zero tolerance policies and the school to prison pipeline. *Forum on Pub. Policy.* 2009; 1. Available at www.forumonpublicpolicy.com/summer09/archivesummer09/heitzeg.pdf. Accessed June 15, 2013.

3. Bazemore G, Walgrave L. Restorative juvenile justice: In search of fundamentals and an outline for systemic reform. *Restorative Juvenile Justice: Repairing the Harm of Youth Crime.* 1999: 45, 48.

4. Christensen LM. *Sticks, Stones, and Schoolyard Bullies: Restorative Justice, Mediation and a New Approach to Conflict Resolution in our Schools.* 2009; 9 Nev. L.J. 545. Available at http://works.bepress.com/leah_christensen/7. Accessed June 16, 2013.

5. U.S. Department of Health and Human Services. *Policies and Laws.* Stop Bullying. Available at http://www.stopbullying.gov/laws/index.html. Accessed July 6, 2012.

6. Cullen D. *Columbine.* New York: Twelve, Hatchette Book Group; 2009.

7. Colorado's anti-bullying legislative declaration was approved May 1, 2001. Bully Police USA. *Colorado.* Available at http://www.bullypolice.org/co_law.html. Accessed July 6, 2012.

8. Hu W. Bullying law puts New Jersey schools on spot. *New York Times* (August 31, 2011). Available at https://www.nytimes.com/2011/08/31/nyregion/bullying-law-puts-new-jersey-schools-on-spot.html?_r=1&pagewanted=all. Accessed July 6, 2012.

9. Parker I. Story of a suicide. *The New Yorker* (Feb. 6, 2012). Available at http://www.newyorker.com/reporting/2012/02/06/120206fa_fact_parker. Accessed July 6, 2013.

10. Ng, C. *Ex-Rutgers Student Dharun Ravi Released from Jail.* ABC News (June 19, 2012). Available at http://abcnews.go.com/US/rutgers-student-dharun-ravi-released-jail/story?id=16602245#.T_FYY9VVmU4. Accessed July 6, 2013.

11. U.S. Department of Health and Human Services. *Cyberbullying.* Stop Bullying. Available at http://www.stopbullying.gov/cyberbullying/index.html. Accessed July 6, 2012.

12. Cyberbullying Research Center. *News.* Cyberbullying Research Center. Available at http://www.cyberbullying.us/index.php. Accessed July 6, 2013.

13. Associated Press. *President Obama Releases Anti-Bullying Message.* October 22, 2010. Available at http://www.youtube.com/watch?v=IYOeQsLszvU. Accessed July 6 2013.

14. U.S. Department of Education, Office of Civil Rights. *Dear Colleague Letter.* October 26, 2010. Available at http://www2.ed.gov/about/offices/list/ocr/letters/colleague-201010.pdf. Accessed July 6, 2013.

15. U.S. Government Accountability Office. *Legal Protections for Vulnerable Youth Need to Be More Fully Assessed.* June 8, 2012. Available at http://gao.gov/products/GAO-12-785T. Accessed July 6, 2012.

16. *Davis v. Monroe County Bd. of Ed.*, 526 U.S. 629 (1999). Available at http://supreme.justia.com/cases/federal/us/526/629/case.html. Accessed July 6, 2013.

17. *T.K. v. New York City Department of Education,* 779 F.Supp.2d 289 (E.D.N.Y, 2011). Available at http://paperdame.0catch.com/lawstuff/04-25-11%20T%20K%20v%20New%20York.pdf. Accessed July 6, 2013.

18. N.J.S.A. Harassment, intimidation, and bullying: prohibited conduct. New Jersey Statutes Annotated. 18A:37-14. August 6, 2007.

16

Program Sustainability

Charvonne N. Holliday, MPH

Objectives

1. To illustrate planning strategies to sustain school-based programming.
2. To relate the importance of maintain program fidelity and evaluation.
3. To address barriers related to sustainability, including program sustainability when funding is low; sustaining program training; and dealing with changes in administration.
4. To briefly outline necessary steps/components in implementing an evidence-based bullying prevention program successfully.

APPROACHES TO OVERALL CHANGE AND SUSTAINABILITY

Introduction

Many times school-based programs are implemented with little planning and regard to the future.[1,2] In essence, school personnel are often left scrambling for programmatic funding, spending a copious amount of staff time sorting through request for proposals (RFPs) and writing grants. In preparing grant documents, a common requirement is to indicate some form of program planning to justify the request of money; nonetheless, planning for program maintenance is generally an afterthought. With budget cuts and economic hardship, the main focus within your school may be to sustain the upcoming school year, let alone brainstorm about years to come. In an effort to provide the most relevant and up-to-date activity to enhance the experiences of students, grant money is sought to support existing needs or to fund pilot projects.

The overarching idea among individuals of any discipline is that program continuation is achieved with a continuous stream of funding. When an evidence-based program that is most fitting for the school environment is discovered, the hope is to maintain the structure that has been invested in by feeding money into "the situation." This is not to say that we, school administrators or public health professionals, are negligent in our strategic planning, but the premise of this chapter is to shed light on a perspective of sustainability: exercising appropriate program planning and nurturing what has been implemented. Through proper evaluation and fidelity to a particular evidence-based program, we can begin to tailor a suitable program and maintain the effects of the program long-term.[3] In short, with proper planning, monitoring, and routine maintenance, an evidence-based program has the ability to flourish without a continuous funding stream. Related to the issue of sustainability are these questions: What would happen to the students and your school if program funding ended abruptly? Was the funding received used in the most effective manner? Is a program that will not be sustained worth your time and effort?

Over the years we have seen a greater increase in the translation of school-related research into school-based bullying prevention activity.[4-6] These evidence-based implementations, including programs like the Olweus Bullying Prevention Program (OBPP), have enhanced our schools.[6,7] The question is, how can we see continued success subsequent to program implementation?

Program sustainability is the maintenance of an organization's ability to continue a specific program, considering the process from the standpoint of ethics and efficacy such that the beneficial programming is perpetuated.[2,8,9] Sustainability is a process that takes into account the overall outcomes of evidence-based programming to determine the overall impact of the program.[2] As recipients of grant funding, we are stewards of that investment and should feel obligated to ensure that the money is spent in the most efficient manner. In terms of ethical considerations and accountability, foundations and other grant makers are interested in knowing that their investments will be worthwhile.[8] Thus, in order to sustain the investments at hand, as well as maintain a noble reputation among funders, planning, including a preliminary plan for evaluation, is vital. Despite the fact that sustainability is an organization's capacity to continue on with the implementation or outcomes of a program, in order to build this capacity, sustainability must be discussed during the planning process.[2]

Even before beginning to implement an evidence-based program, an ideal end point is identified. The only way to maintain the endpoint or desired health outcomes is to plan an intervention that is reasonable and effective, appropriately reaches the target populations, and is able to be sustained.[10] Although program sustainability may be thought of as the endpoint of intervention, sustainability should be a constant focus during the planning phases, as well as throughout program implementation.[2]

Capacity building is another factor to consider in sustaining or institutionalizing a successful evidence-based program.[11] Capacity building is an individual's or community's development of a skill or set of skills such that the individual or group may continue to impact positive change consistent with the specific program.[10] This process is also known as *routinization*,[9] in wherein programmatic activities become routine after being implemented. Nonetheless, for activities to become routine and positive health outcomes to prevail, capacity, or the ability to carry out the program must be gained.[9–11]

Program Sustainability in a School-based Setting

As an educator, you probably can appreciate the process of learning as well as the benefits of reinforcement. In regards to program sustainability, although the preliminary work of implementing a program may be challenging and time-consuming, we must keep in the back of our mind that behavior is moldable. In the public health field, we believe that there are early adopters of a particular behavior and those who lag behind.[12] Those who respond to programmatic activity are more likely to serve as role models for the laggards or late adopters. In time the desired behavior will begin to appear. This process is known as the diffusion of innovation.[12] So, in terms of bullying prevention within the school, with sustainable implementation, eventually your school will transform into a more prosocial environment and the target population will develop the ability to exercise the program ideology.[6] The OBPP[5] requires two years of program implementation. Based on our results, we have seen an increase in reports of bullying during the first year, which is thought to be attributed to an increase in awareness of bullying behavior. However, during the second year of implementation and in subsequent years, our data show that student reports of being bullied, as well as student reports of witnessing bullying of other students, declined.[13,14] Additionally, students report that their teachers are more likely to intervene in an incidence of bullying subsequent to program implementation.[13,14]

In building this capacity in a school, the administrator must buy into the ideology and be involved in the dissemination of the program. Consistent with the diffusion of innovation theory just mentioned[12] and the administrative structure of school districts, bullying prevention may take a top-down approach, meaning the school administrator must advocate on behalf of the program as well as set expectations for his or her school faculty and staff who should be included in the program planning and decision-making process.

Without receiving approval from the school administrator, educators may be reluctant to implement an additional program into their daily activities. However, by including faculty members in the pre-implementation phase and providing encouragement and setting expectations, individuals who do not believe in the program initially may begin to value it. Eventually, these individuals will be on board, so to speak, as they begin to see the results of the program. Although program implementation may ultimately be the school board's decision, the administrator has direct contact with school personnel and witnesses the day-to-day interactions of their students and teachers.

Based on common theory, we realize that the act of adapting a particular culture or set of ideas within an institution may result in the diffusion of innovation ideology.[12] The OBPP is known to promote a prosocial school environment by changing the expectations of not only students but also school administrators, educators, cafeteria workers, bus drivers, and other personnel involved in daily school activities. In implementing this overall change, individuals become aware of what is expected in terms of behavior, but there is always turnover. With students leaving and more enrolling, as well as turnover among teachers, it is important that we maintain the overall culture such that these new individuals become acclimated to the expectations of the school environment without necessarily restarting program implementation.

So that programmatic efforts are not in vain, proper planning is required primarily in an effort to continuously sustain the evidence-based program. With appropriate planning and implementing your evidence-based program with fidelity, the results of the program will begin to be evident in your environment.

To provide an example of behavior change in very simplistic terms, I compared pedestrian laws in the United States versus Scandinavian countries. In the United States, it is acceptable for a pedestrian to walk out in the crosswalk with the idea that drivers will yield. It is not uncommon to see an American enter into the crosswalk before receiving the walk sign. However, an American who travels to Finland, for example, will quickly realize that it is inappropriate to enter the crosswalk without receiving the walk sign. This realization will most likely happen in one of two ways: the pedestrian will follow behind the city natives or have an encounter with a speedy vehicle after walking into the street. Similarly, within the school system, a new student or teacher may contribute to or tolerate a bullying incident, but, based on subsequent consequences, will soon realize that their respective behavior does not fit the mold of their environment. Therefore, this individual will begin to conform and also serve as a model for incoming students and educators.

Despite transitions among the student population, educators, and perhaps administrators, the climate of your school indicating intolerance for bullying behavior will be apparent to individuals transitioning into the school. In essence, a sustained bullying prevention program will only need to be maintained rather than receive continuous implementation as new people enter the system. Such maintenance may be achieved through school kickoff events, reminding students of the bullying prevention ideology, or yearly teacher in-service trainings.

Program sustainability can be compared to the maintenance of a car. For instance, undergoing an oil change every 3,000 miles increases the likelihood that your car will function longer. Conversely, negligence to routine upkeep will end up costing more money in the long run as the car runs into a continuous stream of problems. Additionally, maintaining the oil does not mean that one will never have costly repairs as the car ages, but the overall function of the car will be more manageable and less burdensome. To reiterate, in-depth planning, evaluation, and fidelity to the evidence-based program of choice is key. The take-home message here is that even after program implementation has ended, students begin to adapt the OBPP ideology that is demonstrated by fewer reports of bullying despite the program's end.

PLANNING STRATEGIES: EVALUATION AND FIDELITY

The lack of program planning is equivalent to teaching an entire course without a syllabus or lesson plan ideas. Some believe that one cannot get to where they need to be unless they know where they are going. But, another perspective is that one may reach their desired destination but with much backpedaling and many wrong turns. The literature documents program planning as an important part of programmatic activity.[12,15]

The Logic Model

The primary tool to programmatic planning is the logic model.[3,16] A logic model is composed of five main categories that are arranged sequentially, taking into account what is planned based on available resources and what the hypothetical or desired outcomes will be (Figure 16.1).[16]

The first phase of the logic model is to list all of the resources available to implement the program. This category includes financial input, staff members, and other resources that have been made available.

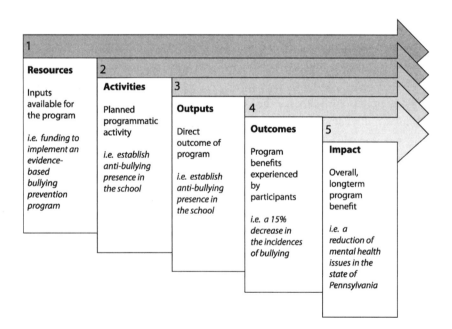

Resources

Inputs available for the program

i.e. funding to implement an evidence-based bullying prevention program

Activities

Planned programmatic activity

i.e. establish anti-bullying presence in the school

Outputs

Direct outcome of program

i.e. establish anti-bullying presence in the school

Outcomes

Program benefits experienced by participants

i.e. a 15% decrease in the incidences of bullying

Impact

Overall, longterm program benefit

i.e. a reduction of mental health issues in the state of Pennsylvania

Figure 16.1. Logic model framework

Second, planned activities, an overview of actions that will be executed during the program, are listed. In terms of OBPP, example activities that should be listed include classroom activities, coordinating committee meetings, a kick-off event, surveying, as well as other activities that adhere to the evidence-based program. The first two categories can be manipulated during the planning process. The next three categories are listings of what is intended. In essence, the logic model will aid in the visualization of the planning design, as well as what is desired in terms of programmatic activity, including how the program will be implemented, markers to gauge what has been completed, and outcomes.

The third section of the logic model, output, is for a listing and explanation of the intended activities; the magnitude in which the planned activity will be implemented. For instance, an activity of OBPP is to host classroom meetings. Therefore, an output would be to host weekly classroom meetings and perhaps list a total of classroom meetings that are expected to be held throughout the school year. Another example output may be the listing of the percentage of students that you wish to survey during a particular school year. Finally, the output of the program should be measurable and listed as short-term and medium-term outcomes.

Fourth, the primary outcome of the OBPP is to reduce the incidences of bullying, which many would consider to be an intermediate outcome. This prevalence rate may exist on a continuum. More specifically, perhaps a short-term outcome would be to see a very small decrease in bullying behavior, but have a medium-term outcome in which the expectation would be to see a much greater decrease in bullying behavior, consistent with other data gathered by schools implementing the evidence-based program you have selected. As already mentioned, outcomes should be measurable and are important parts of program evaluation since they can be used to convey the benefits of the program.

The fifth category is impacts, which sometimes may be incorporated into the outcomes category. The impact category is often referred to as "pie in the sky," as the impact results are often not seen or able to be documented until the passing of many years. An example of an impact of OBPP would be a decrease in the number of felony convictions by the age of 24 among students who bullied their peers.[17,18] Although a longitudinal study would have to be conducted in your school population to determine the number of felony convictions among bullies by the age of 24,[17,18] research supports that this statistic is plausible. Therefore, in theory, we believe that by implementing OBPP with fidelity, the students receiving the program will benefit over the long run.

Although not directly incorporated into sequential flow of the logic model, other considerations also included in the planning process are assumptions. These assumptions are generally thought of prior to the overall planning process and provide a foundation for why the program is needed and the theory to support the associated logic or perceived effectiveness of the program. Since OBPP is an evidence-based program, an assumption that may be included are the data reported by other schools that are similar to your school type, for instance. An example of another assumption would be that hosting schoolwide rules helps decrease undesired behaviors among students.

In drafting this logic model, one is able to visualize the relationship between what is available, what is planned, and what may be brought about based on the first category. In addition to being a planning tool, a logic model also serves as a visual roadmap, allowing for a more convenient way to chart program successes based on the predetermined outcomes.

Ultimately, the logic model becomes the blueprint to your program, including all the specificities as well as common principles. This document will hold throughout the duration of the program, serving as a template during the planning process and providing direction throughout program implementation and evaluation. The outcome and impact categories not only represent your expectations of the program but are also used to gauge your successes and failures in implementing it. For instance, perhaps your school did not see the decrease in bullying behavior that was expected. In reviewing your logic model, perhaps you notice that only 15 classroom meetings were held throughout the school year when programmatically, a classroom meeting should have been held each week. In enhancing your program for long-term sustainability, the frequency of classroom meetings should be increased to keep fidelity to the program and to improve overall results.

The PRECEDE-PROCEED Model

The logic model complements or is a supplement to the PRECEDE-PROCEED model, which was mentioned earlier in the text. Although the PRECEDE-PROCEED model is more of a comprehensive planning tool,[19] including social, epidemiological, environmental, and political diagnoses or assessments, the logic model can serve as a roadmap. In initiating the planning process, the PRECEDE-PROCEED model incorporates the underlying issues associated with the stated problem.[19]

In a step-by-step planning process, these underlying barriers, opportunities, and predispositions are considered in developing an appropriate program plan based on the target audience. Urban schools may see more instances of bullying as children from urban environments are more likely to witness violence resulting in children who adapt aggression as a survival tool[20,21] or, perhaps your students come from an impoverished environment in which their parents lack formal education. Before program implementation, as the administrator, you would want to plan for these challenges by first understanding the environment in which students reside and then educating the teachers about varying cultures.

Underlying Factors of Program Sustainability

In achieving program sustainability, it is important to consider the aspects that feed into the situation. Initially, a public health and ecological approach is used to determine how interlocking aspects are affected by one another. More specifically, in the school setting, a child's behavior is impacted not only by the school environment but also by the physical and social environments this child faces while at home.[15,22] In addition to this, family norms and values and

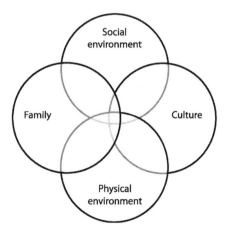

Figure 16.2. An ecological perspective to school-based bullying prevention

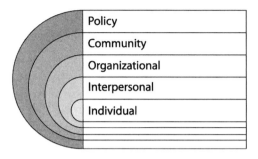

Figure 16.3. Socioecological framework

overall culture must be considered (Figure 16.2). In implementing a school-based bullying prevention program, there are underlying factors that must be considered in order to tailor the program to a particular school environment (Figure 16.3). For instance, based on research, it has been found that in more urban settings, students tend to be more physical and less inclined to report incidents of bullying when compared to their more suburban or rural counterparts.[20,21] Moreover, cultural norms and experiences such as domestic violence may influence the students' reception of the prevention program.[22,23] Thus, in order to implement a successful and sustainable program, such factors must be included in the overall planning process (Figure 16.3).[24]

In addition to planning for sustainability, ultimately, we are interested in the overall benefit of the program, the ability for program activities to continue, the continuation of practices or policies established as a result of the program, and maintenance of partnerships. An additional component of program sustainability is the reliability of the program to be replicated or adapted in any setting.[2]

BARRIERS TO PROGRAM SUSTAINABILITY

We fall short in establishing sustainable programs by placing all of our focus on the implementation stage. Implementation and planning for the actual program are certainly important components of any program, yet we must also be aware of the underlying factors that exist. In Chapter 1 of this book, the PRECEDE-PROCEED model used by public health professionals is referenced in greater detail. The overall premise of PRECEDE-PROCEED model is to assess social, epidemiological, environmental, and behavioral impacts on a problem.[19,24] In this case, the community could be the students, teachers, administrators, or a mixture of these categories. By assessing the needs as well as the wants of this community, we begin to plan for the actual implementation.

Also considered in the first half of this model is any administrative- and policy-related opportunities or challenges that might be involved in program implementation. In taking a snapshot of these particular elements, the implementation can actually be adapted, effectively, to suit the particular school. More specifically, research supports that schools situated in an urban setting tend to have different behavioral and environmental factors when compared to students enrolled in a more suburban or rural school. This issue sheds light on the significance of tailoring the selected program. Evidence-based programs are just that—evidence-based. However, this does not mean that the resulting model is a perfect fit for every environment. Therefore, the program can be sustainable without being effective first.

With the increase of evidence-based programs being implemented in our schools, it is important to understand influences that may hinder long-term sustainability and implementation with fidelity.[25] Based on a review of the literature by Han and Weiss,[25] factors related to the school as well as the teaching staff are associated with implementation and sustainability of school programming. In particular, buy-in by school administration, self-efficacy and program beliefs among teaching staff, as well as professional burnout should be considered.

As already mentioned, support from school administration is vital in promoting evidence-based programming. Without knowledge of the program benefits, requesting participation of program educators and monitoring program implementation, the sustainability of the program will be hindered. Furthermore, self-efficacy, capacity building, and belief in the effectiveness of the program on behalf of the teaching staff are also needed to adhere to the program guidelines in an effort to promote program maintenance.[25] Research indicates that when educators believe in a program and feel that is working, program goals were more positively achieved. More positive outcomes are achieved when the self-efficacy of educators is higher as these individuals invest more time into the program.[25] (Chapter 9 has more information on the roles of administrators and educators when implementing an evidence-based bullying prevention program.)

In addition, educators are faced with an abundance of responsibilities throughout the school day, including preparing for standardized testing, parenting their students, and addressing additional requirements and programming. Due to professional burnout, educators become less inclined to focus on programmatic activity.[25] Based on a study conducted by Cheek, Bradley, Parr, and Lan,[26] nearly 65% of all educators display symptoms of stress, while 30% clearly show signs of burnout. Overwhelming symptoms of stress and burnout result in detachment from their students, an increase in absenteeism, and decreases in morale and effort. Studies show that 50% of all educators will leave the profession after teaching for only five years. Educators who are burned out are less invested in program implementation and are more likely to have negative and perhaps damaging attitude toward the new program.[27]

In addition to administrative buy-in, when implementing a new program, it is important to educate and consult with your staff before deciding on a particular approach; this ties in with the beginning stages of the PRECEDE-PROCEED model, with the first step requiring input from the community. On the school level, the community can be faculty and staff, parents and students, and other stakeholders. During this first step the problem is stated. Yet, if the community—in this case, teachers—does not perceive bullying to be an issue, it might be less inclined to implement the program. Furthermore, if teachers are not aware of the effectiveness of a program, what the program entails, or how much time and energy they will invest, they are also less likely to be on board with program implementation.[25] Thus, teacher training and motivation to implement the program along with ongoing implementation will eventually result in changes in student behavior and sustained program results.[25]

TAKE-HOME POINTS

1. Select an evidence-based bullying prevention program that is a good fit for your school.
2. Take a public-health approach in planning for the implementation of your program prior to actual implementation. The PRECEDE-PROCEED model is a planning tool that takes into account social,

epidemiological, educational, and administrative benefits and challenges prior to program development and implementation. The second half of the model includes the evaluation of the overall program process, impact, and long-term outcomes.

3. A logic model may serve as a supplement to the PRECEDE-PROCEED model, although this planning process may stand alone. While the PRECEDE-PROCEED model provides more foundation and is a step-by-step guide to program planning, the logic model also takes into account available resources and activities, actual program outputs, as well as short-term, intermediate, and long-term outcomes.

4. In addition to program planning, program evaluation is a vital step in the execution of your evidence-based bullying prevention program. Via the program evaluation process, you can discern whether your program is being implemented with fidelity and determine the overall benefit of your program implementation. With this analysis, you are able to make appropriate changes to the implementation of your bullying prevention program in order to see greater benefits, which will hopefully lead to a sustained program. For more step-by-step guidance regarding program implementation, please see Chapter 13.

5. Program sustainability is a process rather than an endpoint. During your planning process, be sure to plan for sustainability. How will you sustain the positive outcomes and associated activities of your program with reduced or nonexistent funding?

6. An evidence-based program, when evaluated and implemented with fidelity, has the potential to alter your school environment, long term. Program continuation or institutionalization can be achieved with small-scale maintenance.

7. Administrative buy-in and educating your staff about the benefits of the evidence-based program will result in a more sustained effort.

FREQUENTLY ASKED QUESTIONS

1. What is program sustainability?

Program sustainability is the maintenance of an organization's ability to continue a specific program, taking into account ethics and efficacy so that the beneficial programming is perpetuated. Sustainability is a process that takes into account the overall outcomes of evidence-based programming to determine the overall impact of the program.

2. How much funding do I need to sustain my program?

While funding is an important aspect, funding alone will not sustain your program. Rather, the use of an evidence-based program, fidelity to that program, and planning are key. In short, with proper planning, monitoring, and routine maintenance, an evidence-based program has the ability to flourish at a reduced cost.

3. At what point should I begin thinking about program sustainability?

Although sometimes an afterthought, programs are most effective when program sustainability is included in the initial planning stages. You should be thinking about how your program will be sustained as you are planning the initial phases of the program, such as how the intervention will be implemented.

4. What strategies should I use in planning my program?

The primary tool to programmatic planning is the logic model. A logic model is composed of five main categories that are arranged sequentially, taking into account what is planned based on available resources and what the hypothetical or desired outcomes will be. The logic model complements or is a supplement to the PRECEDE-PROCEED model, which is more of a comprehensive planning tool that incorporates social, epidemiological, environmental, and political diagnoses or assessments. However, before developing one or both of these models, establish a committee that is representative of your school. These committee members are vital in the planning phase.

5. How can I build capacity among the faculty members at my school?

Capacity building is an individual's or community's development of a skill or set of skills that allow positive change consistent with the specific program to continue. In order to build capacity among the faculty members at your school, these individuals must be knowledgeable of the components of your evidence-based program and undergo the training process suggested by it. Preliminary training as well as refresher seminars will help to enhance your school's ability to implement the program with fidelity.

6. How can I enhance the sustainability of my program?

Administrative buy-in and educating your staff about the benefits of the evidence-based program will result in a more sustained effort. Also, through proper evaluation, planning, and fidelity to the program you will be better able to maintain the effects of your program over the long term.

7. What are challenges to program sustainability?

Teacher burnout or resistance to the program, lack of administrative buy-in, poor planning, infidelity to the evidence-based program, or perhaps an evidence-based program that is not a good fit or properly adapted for your school are factors that may hinder the sustainability of your program.

8. What role do faculty members play in program sustainability?

Self-efficacy, capacity building, and belief in the effectiveness of the program on behalf of the teaching staff are needed to adhere to the program guidelines in an effort to promote program maintenance. Research indicates that when educators believe in a program and feel that is working, program goals were more positively achieved.

9. What role does evaluation play in sustaining my program?

In addition to program planning, program evaluation is a vital step in the execution of your evidence-based bullying prevention program. Via the program evaluation process, you can discern whether or not your program is being implemented with fidelity and determine the overall benefit of your program implementation. With this analysis, you are able to make appropriate changes to the implementation of your bullying prevention program in order to see greater benefits, which will hopefully lead to a sustained program.

10. How do I approach program sustainability from a public health perspective?

In approaching school-based bullying prevention from a public health perspective, first, assess capacity and underlying factors that contribute to the issues you would like to address. The PRECEDE-PROCEED model is a planning tool that takes into account social, epidemiological, educational, and administrative benefits and challenges prior to program development and implementation. The second half of the model includes the evaluation of the overall program process, impact, and long-term outcomes. A logic model can also be used to aid your planning process. Furthermore, it is important to select an evidence-based bullying prevention program that is a good fit for your school. In addition to program planning and selecting an evidence-based program that is a good fit, program evaluation is a vital step in the execution of your evidence-based bullying prevention program.

REFERENCES

1. Greenberg MT. Current and future challenges in school-based prevention: the researcher perspective. *Prevention Science: Official J Soc Prevention Res.* Mar 2004; 5(1):5–13.

2. Scheirer MA, Dearing JW. An agenda for research on the sustainability of public health programs. *Am J Public Health.* Nov 2011; 101(11):2059–2067.

3. Rossi PH, Lipsey MW, Freeman HE, Howard E. *Evaluation: A Systematic Approach.* 7th ed. Thousand Oaks, CA: Sage; 2004.

4. Bowllan NM. Implementation and evaluation of a comprehensive, school-wide bullying prevention program in an urban/suburban middle school. *J Sch Health.* Apr 2011; 81(4):167–173.

5. Olweus D. *Bullying at School: What We Know and What We Can Do.* Oxford, UK; Cambridge, USA: Blackwell; 1993.

6. Fekkes M, Pijpers FI, Verloove-Vanhorick SP. Effects of antibullying school program on bullying and health complaints. *Arch Pediatr Adolesc Med.* Jun 2006; 160(6): 638–644.

7. Nansel TR, Overpeck M, Pilla RS, et al. Bullying behaviors among US youth: Prevalence and association with psychosocial adjustment. *JAMA*. Apr 25 2001; 285(16):2094–2100.

8. Shediac-Rizkallah MC, Bone LR. Planning for the sustainability of community-based health programs: conceptual frameworks and future directions for research, practice and policy. *Health Educ Res*. Mar 1998; 13(1):87–108.

9. Pluye P, Potvin L, Denis J-L, Pelletier J, Mannoni C. Program sustainability begins with the first events. *Evaluation Prog Planning*. 2005; 28(2):123–137.

10. Hawe P, Noort M, King L, Jordens C. Multiplying health gains: The critical role of capacity-building within health promotion programs. *Health Policy*. Jan 1997; 39(1):29–42.

11. Israel B, Eng E, Schulz A, et al. *Methods in Community-Based Participatory Research for Health*. San Francisco: Jossey-Bass; 2005.

12. Issel LM. *Health Program Planning and Evaluation: A Practical, Systematic Approach for Community Health*. 2nd ed. Sudbury, MA: Jones and Bartlett; 2009.

13. Masiello M, Schroeder D, Barto S, et al. *Bullying Prevention: A Statewide Collaborative That Works*. Pittsburgh, PA: Highmark Foundation; 2009.

14. Schroeder BA, Messina A, Schroeder D, et al. The implementation of a statewide bullying prevention program: Preliminary findings from the field and the importance of coalitions. *Health Promot Pract*. 2012; 13:489–495.

15. McKenzie JF, Neiger BL, Thackeray R. *Planning, Implementing, and Evaluating Health Promotion Programs: A Primer*. 5th ed. San Francisco: Pearson/Benjamin Cummings; 2009.

16. *Logic Model Development Guide*. 2004. Available at http://www.wkkf.org/knowledge-center/resources/2006/02/wk-kellogg-foundation-logic-model-development-guide.aspx. Accessed June 27, 2013.

17. Olweus D. Bully/victim problems at school: Facts and intervention. *Eur J Psychol Educ*. 1997; 12:495–510.

18. Band SR, Harpold JA School Violence: Lessons Learned. *FBI Law Enforcement Bulletin*. 1999; 68(9):9–16.

19. Green LW, Kreuter MW. *Health Promotion Planning: An Educational and Ecological Approach*. 3rd ed. Mountain View, CA: Mayfield Pub. Co.; 1999.

20. Bowes L, Arseneault L, Maughan B, et al. School, neighborhood, and family factors are associated with children's bullying involvement: a nationally representative longitudinal study. *J Am Acad Child Adolesc Psychiatry*. May 2009; 48(5):545–553.

21. Yonas MA, O'Campo P, Burke JG, Gielen AC. Neighborhood-level factors and youth violence: Giving voice to the perceptions of prominent neighborhood individuals. *Health Educ Behav*. August 1, 2007; 34(4):669–685.

22. Baldry A. Bullying in schools and exposure to domestic violence. *Child Abuse Negl*. July 2003; 27(7):713–732.

23. Bauer NS, Herrenkohl TI, Lozano P, et al. Childhood bullying involvement and exposure to intimate partner violence. *Pediatrics*. Aug 2006; 118(2):E235–E242.

24. Best A, Stokols D, Green LW, et al. An integrative framework for community partnering to translate theory into effective health promotion strategy. *AJHP*. Nov–Dec 2003; 18(2):168–176.

25. Han SS, Weiss B. Sustainability of teacher implementation of school-based mental health programs. *J Abnorm Child Psycholo*. Dec 2005; 33(6):665–679.

26. Cheek JR, Bradley LJ, Parr G, Lan W. Using music therapy techniques to treat teacher burnout. *J Mental Health Counceling*. 2003; 25(3):204–217.

27. Evers WJ, Brouwers A, Tomic W. Burnout and self-efficacy: A study on teachers' beliefs when implementing an innovative educational system in the Netherlands. *Br J Educ Psychol*. Jun 2002; 72(Pt 2):227–243.

Appendix A

Bullying Intervention

Know your school's bullying prevention policy and procedures for intervening in bullying situations. Being knowledgeable and prepared will make interventions go more smoothly and quickly.

Bullying is not meant for adult eyes or ears. Youth who engage in bullying effectively conceal this behavior from adults. For this reason, adults must become familiar with how bullying is transacted by closely observing youth's behavior in those areas where bullying is likely.

Through the Olweus Bullying Prevention Survey, school personnel will learn about the locations and bullying behaviors committed at a school. This information will help to increase the possibility of intervening when bullying occurs. Educators on alert for bullying will look at the interactions between students, monitoring both tone and content of student relationships. In positive interactions, all the students involved should be interacting in an upbeat and cheerful manner. If there is angst, sorrow, or fear involved in the interactions, bullying may be occurring. Educators may rely on their professional intuition if they suspect bullying behavior. If this is the case, here are some suggestions on how to intervene:

1. Approach the situation, stating in a firm tone that the observed behavior must stop. Do not ask any questions. Asking a question will give the student engaging in bullying behavior the opportunity to deny or defend the behavior. State what the observed behavior was and that it looked like bullying.

2. Make sure that the targeted student is safe. If physical bullying has occurred, you may consider sending the student to the nurse or the office for care. Engage other adults in the bullying situation if it seems volatile or involves a number of students. Apologize for the bullying behavior occurring, saying something like this: "I'm sorry this has happened.

Bullying is not tolerated at our school. This shouldn't have happened." Help the targeted student return to his typical activities as soon as possible, but let the student know you will be in touch before the end of the day.

3. Speak to the student who bullied. Be firm and prepared for denial and/or excuses for the behavior. If more than one student is involved, separate the students from each other out of eyesight and hearing. Ask for assistance or take the students to the office, if necessary. State how the behavior was bullying and why it was wrong. Do not become involved in extended discussion. You may consider having the student write down what was done and why it was bullying. If you are knowledgeable about the school's discipline for the particular bullying act, state what the consequence will be and impose it.

4. Engage the students who are bystanders in the incident. If the student bystanders were supporting the bullying, consider consequences or other interventions. Build empathy for the student who was targeted by explaining why the bullying was hurtful. Correct any thinking errors about the bullying behavior such as, "She deserved it." or "We were only teasing." Let the bystanders know how they can intervene when bullying occurs and what they can do to support other targeted students. If the bystanders were trying to intervene, recognize their courage and actions. Reinforce positive behaviors. Help the bystanders return to their typical routines.

5. After imposing the consequence for those involved in the bullying, let them know that you will follow up by the end of the day and will check on them over the next several days. Encourage positive behaviors. Let the student(s) know that they can do better and that they can play a positive leadership role in the school.

6. Follow up with the student who was targeted and the student(s) engaged in the bullying behaviors. Follow the school's protocols for documenting the intervention. This includes contact with administration, parents, and other school personnel.

Strategies to consider for students who are bullied:

A. Be supportive, try to reduce fear, and verify self-worth by explaining that the student is not responsible for being bullied.

B. Reduce self-blame through education about bullying and cruel behavior.
C. Demonstrate compassion and empathy.
D. Connect the student to supportive peers and help the student build friendships.
E. Consider conducting friendship groups and clubs.
F. Engage parents in your efforts to help the student.

Strategies to consider for students who engage in bullying behaviors:

A. Be direct and matter-of-fact when discussing the bullying behavior with the student.
B. Give brief and clear descriptions of unacceptable behaviors.
C. Identify the emotions of the person who was bullied.
D. Consider atonement for the bullying behavior.
E. Help the student use their leadership skills in positive ways.
F. Engage parents in your efforts to help the student.

Appendix B

Suggestions for Further Reading

Baldry AC, Farrington DP. Parenting influences on bullying and victimization. *Legal and Criminological Psychology*, 1998; 3:237–254.

Baldry AC, Farrington DP. Bullies and delinquents: Personal characteristics and parental styles. *Journal of Community and Applied Social Psychology*, 2000; 10:17–31.

Berdondini L, Smith PK. Cohesion and power in the families of children involved in bully/victim problems at school: An Italian replication. *Journal of Family Therapy*, 1997; 18:117–162.

Blank MJ, Langford B. Strengthening Partnerships: Community School Assessment Checklist. Principal Leadership (High School Ed.) vol. 2 no. 1 (Sept. 2001) pp. 62–63.

Olweus D. *Bullying at School: What We Know and What We Can Do*, 1993. Blackwell Publishing.

Emmons RA, McCullough ME. Counting blessings versus burdens: An experimental investigation of gratitude and subjective well being in daily life. *Journal of Personality and Social Psychology*, 2003; 84:377–389.

Garnefsti N, Okma, S. Addiction-risk and aggression/criminal behavior in adolescence: Influence of family, school and peers. *Journal of Adolescence*, 1996; 19:503–512.

Georgiou SN. Bullying and victimization at school: The role of mothers. *British Journal of Educational Psychology*, 2008; 78:109–125.

Hazler RJ, Carney JV, Green S, Powell R, Scott-Jolly L. Areas of expert agreement on identification of school bullies and victims. *School Psychology International*, 1997; 18:5–14.

Jehl J, Blank M, McCloud B. Ensuring a positive future for children and youth: Building the work of educators and community builders. Washington, DC: Institute for Educational Leadership. Retrieved July 18, 2005. Available at www.rockfound.org/Documents/444/Martin_Blank_paper.pdf.

Loeber R., Hay, D. Key issues in the development of aggression and violence from childhood to early adulthood. *Annual Review of Psychology,* 1997; 48:371–410.

Lowenstein LF. 'Who is the bully?' *Bulletin of the British Psychological Society*, 1978; 31:147–149.

Nansel TR, Overpeck M, Pilla RS, et al. Bullying behaviors among US youth: Prevalence and association with psychosocial adjustment. *JAMA: The Journal of the American Medical Association.* 2001; 285(16):2094–2100.

Nix RL, Pinderhughes EE, Dodge KA, Bates JE, Pettit GS, McFadyen-Ketchum SA. The relation between mother's hostile attribution tendencies and children's externalizing behavior problems: The mediating role of mothers' harsh discipline practices. *Child Development;* 70:896–909.

Olweus D. *Aggression in the Schools: Bullies and Whipping Boys*, 1978. Washington, NY: Hemisphere Pub. Corp.; distributed solely by Halsted Press.

Olweus D. Aggressors and their victims: Bullying at school. In N. Frude and H. Gault (Eds.). *Disruptive Behavior in Schools*, 1984, pp. 57–76. Chichester: Wiley.

Olweus D. Bully/victim problems among school children: Basic facts and effects of a school based intervention program. In D. J. Pepler and K. H. Rubin

(Eds.) *The Development and Treatment of Childhood Aggression*, 1991, pp. 411–448. Hildsdale, NJ: Lawrence Erlbaum.

Smith PK. The silent nightmare: Bullying and victimization in school peer groups. *The Psychologist*, 1991; 4:243–248.

Smith KP, Bowers L, Binney V, Cowie H. Relationships of children involved in bully/victim problems in school. In S. Duck (Ed.) *Learning About Relationships*, 1993, pp. 184–212. London: Sage.

Snyder J, Cramer A, Afrank J, Patterson GR. The contributions of ineffective discipline and parental hostile attributions of child misbehavior to the development of conduct problems at home and school. *Developmental Psychology*, 2005; 41:30–41.

About the Authors

Dr. Matthew G. Masiello, MPH, FAAP is Director of the Center for Health Promotion and Disease Prevention (CHPDP), at the Windber Research Institute (WRI), in Windber, Pennsylvania. He also serves as a U.S. Network Coordinator for the International Health Promoting Hospital Network (HPH). From 2010 to 2012 he served on the Governance Board of HPH. Over the past 15 years, from his initial days in Pittsburgh, Dr. Masiello has led his respective teams in the support, development, and implementation of a multitude of evidence-based, health promotion initiatives. These programs now extend throughout Pennsylvania, nationally as well as internationally. They include child bullying prevention, clinical health promotion initiatives, childhood obesity and injury prevention initiatives, medical home development, worksite wellness programs, community need assessments, program evaluation services, coordinated school health council, and public health undergraduate curriculum development. Dr. Masiello has had the opportunity to present his work nationally and internationally through peer review journals, reports, and national presentations. In 2012, along with other similar recognition over the years, he was awarded the Pennsylvania Public Health Association Keystone Award for Distinguished Service in Public Health. Dr. Masiello earned his bachelor's degree from Marist College, and his medical degree from the Universidad Autonoma de Guadalajara, Mexico. His pediatric medical training was at Bridgeport Hospital and Yale University and his pediatric critical care fellowship took place at Harvard University, Boston Children's Hospital. His master's degree in public health was earned at the George Washington University School of Public Health and Health Services. He has held faculty positions at St. Vincent College and St. Francis University. He is a practicing pediatrician and has assisted in various national and international humanitarian projects.

Diana Schroeder, MSN, RN has worked in school-based prevention since 1995. She is a pediatric clinical specialist and currently serves as the Director of Bullying Prevention Initiatives at the Center for Health Promotion and Disease Prevention at Windber Research Institute. In 2001, she became a Certified Olweus Bullying Prevention Program trainer and has over 10 years of experience in working with schools in implementing bullying prevention programming. She also holds a faculty position as program coordinator for the University of Pittsburgh-Johnstown bachelor's of nursing program. Her pediatric/community health focus has included injury prevention, obesity prevention, worksite wellness, and coordinated school health initiatives. Diana has been a member of the Westmont Hilltop School Board for 10 years and currently serves as its president.

CONTRIBUTING AUTHORS

Shiryl Barto, MEd
Manager, Bullying Prevention Initiatives
Center for Health Promotion and Disease Prevention—Windber Research Institute
Windber, PA

James A. Bozigar, ACSW, LCSW, MSW
Allegheny County Safe Schools Coordinator
Allegheny Intermediate Unit
Pittsburgh, PA

Heather Cecil, PhD
Evaluation Coordinator
Center for Schools and Communities
Camp Hill, PA

Jonathan Cohen, PhD
President
National School Climate Center: Educating Minds and Hearts Because the Three Rs Are Not Enough
New York, NY
Adjunct Professor in Psychology and Education, Teachers College

Columbia University
New York, NY

Gianluca Gini, PhD
Child and Adolescent Social Development and Well-Being Laboratory
Department of Developmental and Social Psychology
University of Padova
Padova, Italy

Karla J. Good, LSW
Program Manager of Community Outreach Initiatives
Center for Health Promotion and Disease Prevention—Windber Research
Institute
Windber, PA

Charvonne N. Holliday, MPH
Director, International Projects,
Research Associate, Bullying Prevention Initiatives,
Center for Health Promotion and Disease Prevention—Windber Research
Institute
Windber, PA

Susan P. Limber, PhD
Professor
Clemson University
Clemson, SC

Robert A. McGarry, EdD
Director of Education
Gay, Lesbian & Straight Education Network
New York, NY

Allison L. Messina, MHPE
Program Manager
Center for Health Promotion and Disease Prevention—Windber Research
Institute
Windber, PA

Stacie Molnar-Main, EdD
Strategic Initiatives Manager
Center for Schools and Communities/Center for Safe Schools
Camp Hill, PA

Janice E. Seigle, MPM
Strategic Corporate Initiatives Director (retired)
Highmark Inc.
Pittsburgh, PA

David Keller Trevaskis, JD
Pro Bono Coordinator of Legal Services
Pennsylvania Bar Association
Harrisburg, PA
Temple University School of Law
Philadelphia, PA

Carla Zema, PhD
Assistant Professor
Saint Vincent College
Latrobe, PA

Index